丛书主编：常俊跃

21世纪内容语言融合（CLI）系列英语教材

Language, Society and Culture

语言、社会与文化

孙鑫　黄洁芳　陈婧　王俊波　主编

北京大学出版社
PEKING UNIVERSITY PRESS

图书在版编目(CIP)数据

语言、社会与文化/孙鑫等主编.—北京：北京大学出版社,2022.3
21世纪内容语言融合（CLI）系列英语教材
ISBN 978-7-301-32770-8

Ⅰ.①语… Ⅱ.①孙… Ⅲ.①英语–高等学校–教材 Ⅳ.①H319.3

中国版本图书馆CIP数据核字（2021）第264056号

书　　名	语言、社会与文化 YUYAN、SHEHUI YU WENHUA
著作责任者	孙　鑫 等 主编
责任编辑	李　颖
标准书号	ISBN 978-7-301-32770-8
出版发行	北京大学出版社
地　　址	北京市海淀区成府路205号　100871
网　　址	http://www.pup.cn　新浪微博:@北京大学出版社
电子信箱	evalee1770@sina.com
电　　话	邮购部010-62752015　发行部010-62750672　编辑部010-62754382
印 刷 者	北京虎彩文化传播有限公司
经 销 者	新华书店
	787毫米1092毫米　16开本　13.75印张　424千字 2022年3月第1版　2023年2月第2次印刷
定　　价	69.00元

未经许可，不得以任何方式复制或抄袭本书之部分或全部内容。
版权所有，侵权必究
举报电话：010-62752024　电子信箱：fd@pup.pku.edu.cn
图书如有印装质量问题，请与出版部联系，电话：010-62756370

本专著为国家社会科学基金项目"内容教学法理论指导下英语专业整体课程体系的改革与实践研究"的研究成果之一(项目编号12BYY050);

本专著出版得到了大连外国语大学2020年学科建设专项经费资助。

前　言

随着我国英语教育的快速发展，英语专业长期贯彻的"以语言技能训练为导向"的课程建设理念及教学理念已经难以满足社会的需要。专家教师们密切关注的现行英语专业教育与中学英语教学脱节，语言与内容教学割裂，单纯语言技能训练过多，专业内容课程不足，学科内容课程系统性差，高低年级内容课程安排失衡及其导致的学生知识面偏窄、知识结构欠缺、思辨能力偏弱、综合素质发展不充分等问题日益突显。

针对上述问题，大连外国语大学英语专业在内容与语言融合教育理念的指导下确定了如下改革思路：

（一）遵循全新教学理念，改革英语专业教育的课程结构。改变传统单一的语言技能课程体系，实现内容课程与语言课程的融合，扩展学生的知识面，提高学生的语言技能。

（二）开发课程自身潜力，同步提升专业知识和语言技能。课程同时关注内容和语言，把内容教学和语言教学有机结合。以英语为媒介，系统教授专业内容；以专业内容为依托，在使用语言过程中提高语言技能，扩展学生的知识面，提高思辨能力。

（三）改革教学方法手段，全面提高语言技能和综合素质。依靠内容依托教学在方法上的灵活性，通过问题驱动、输出驱动等方法调动学生主动学习，把启发式、任务式、讨论式、结对子、小组活动、课堂展示、多媒体手段等行之有效的活动与学科内容教学有机结合，提高学生的语言技能，激发学生的兴趣，培养学生的自主性和创造性，提升思辨能力和综合素质。

本项改革突破了我国英语专业英语教学大纲规定的课程结构，改变了英语专业通过开设单纯的听、说、读、写、译语言技能课程提高学生语言技能的传统课程建设理念，对英语课程及教学方法进行了创新性的改革。首创了具有我国特色的英语专业内容与语言融合的课程体系；开发了适合英语专业的内容与语言融合的课程；提高学生综合运用语言的能力，扩展学生的知识面，提高学生的综合素质，以崭新的途径实现英语专业教育的总体培养目标。

经过十年的实验探索，改革取得了鼓舞人心的结果。

（一）构建了英语专业内容与语言融合教学的课程体系。课程包括美国历史文化、美国自然人文地理、美国社会文化、英国历史文化、英国自然人文地理、英国社会文化、澳新加社会文化、欧洲文化、中国文化、跨文化交际、《圣经》与文化、希腊罗马神话、综合英语（美国文学经典作品）、综合英语（英国文学经典作品）、综合英语（世界文学经典作品）、综合英语（西方思想经典）、英语视听说（美国经典电影）、英语视听说（英国经典电影）、英语视听说（环球资讯）、英语视听说（专题资讯）、英语短篇小说、英语长篇小说、英语散文、英语诗歌、英语戏剧、英语词汇学、英语语言学、语言与社会、语言与文化、语言与语用等。这些课程依托专业知识内容训练学生综合运用的语言能力，扩展学生的知识面，提高学生的多元文化意识，提升学生的综合素质。

（二）系统开发了相关国家的史、地、社会、文化、文学、语言学课程资源。在内容与语言融合教育理念的指导下，开发了上述课程所需要的教学课件及音频视频资源。开发的教材系统组织了教学内容，设计了新颖的栏目板块，设计的活动也丰富多样，在实际教学中受到了学生的广泛欢迎。在北京大学出版社、华中科技大学出版社、北京师范大学出版社、上海外语教育出版社的支持下，系列教材已经陆续出版。

（三）牵动了教学手段和教学方法的改革，取得了突出的教学效果。在内容与语言融合教育理念的指导下，教师的教学理念、教学方法、教学手段得到更新。通过问题驱动、输出驱动等活动调动学生主动学习，把启发式、任务式、讨论式、结对子、小组活动、课堂展示、多媒体手段等行之有效的活动与学科内容教学有机结合，激发学生的兴趣，培养学生自主性和创造性，提高学生的语言技能，提升思辨能力和综合素质。曾有专家教师担心取消、减少语言技能课程会对学生的语言技能发展产生消极影响。实验数据证明，内容与语言融合教学不仅没有对学生的语言技能发展和语言知识的学习产生消极影响，而且还产生了多方面的积极影响，对专业知识的学习也产生了巨大的积极影响。

（四）提高了教师的科研意识和科研水平，取得了丰硕的教研成果。开展改革以来，团队对内容与语言融合教学问题进行了系列研究，活跃了整个教学单位的科研气氛，教师的科研意识和科研水平也得到很大提高。课题组已经撰写研究论文70多篇，撰写博士论文3篇，在国内外学术期刊发表研究论文40多篇，撰写专著2部。

教学改革开展以来，每次成果发布都引起强烈反响。在中国外语教学法国际研讨会上，与会的知名外语教育专家戴炜栋教授等对这项改革给予关注，博士生导师蔡基刚教授认为本项研究"具有导向性作用"。在全国英语专业院系主任高级论坛上，研究成果得到知名专家博士生导师王守仁教授和与会专家教授的高度评价。在中国英语教学研究会年会及中国外语教育改革论坛上，本成果引起与会专家的强烈反响，教育部外指委石坚教授、仲伟合教授、蒋洪新教授等给予了高度评价。本项改革的系列成果两次获得大连外国语大学教学成果一等奖，两次获得辽宁省优秀教学成果奖一等奖，一次获得国家教学成果二等奖。目前，该项改革成果已经在全国英语专业教育领域引起广泛关注。它触及了英语专业的教学大纲，影响了课程建设的理念，引领了英语专业的教学改革，改善了教学实践，必将对未来英语专业教育的发展产生积极影响。

《语言、社会与文化》教材依照内容与语言融合的外语教育理念编写，即尽最大可能、以最合适的方式将目标语用于融合教授、学习内容和语言，以达到多种教育目标的教育理念。这一理念下的教学超出了单纯的语言教学，进行的是知识、能力、素质的全方位教育。

本教材共有12个单元，根据课文的长度和难度，每单元设置主要阅读课文1—2篇以及补充阅读课文1—2篇。教材的主要内容分为四大部分。第一部分是对课程的导入，包括语言与社会、语言与文化以及语言与性别的关系（第一单元至第三单元）。第二部分的课程内容涉及语言的不同层面在一定的社会文化环境下表现出来的特征，包括词语、习语、隐喻、委婉语和禁忌语及语篇（第四单元至第八单元）。第三部分的课程内容讨论到相关的理论及观点，如文化相对主义、语言相对论、语言帝国主义（第九单元至第十一单元）。第四部分把语言、社会与文化的关系放置于新的时代背景下，讨论语言在网络环境下的最新发展（第十二单元）。

教材摒弃对知识的直接呈现方式，对理论的引介深入浅出，设计多样化的教学活动，培养学生自主获取知识、发现问题和解决问题的能力。在每个单元的主课文后设有Knowledge Focus, Language Focus和Comprehensive Work三个板块的练习，分别从内容和语言两个方面对本单元的核心内容进行总结，并在相关内容的基础上进行拓展，既加深学生对于本单元内容的理解，也提高学生的综合语言水平。练习的设置有助于学生在使用教材的过程中，实现知识体系构建和语言技能训练的同步提高。

课程教学有两个目标：目标一是通过对相关语言现象的分析深入到理论学习。在这一目标下，我们既关注课文内容知识也强调对学生语言能力的培养。目标二是在达成目标一的基础之上培养学生批判性思维以及从事学术研究的基本素养。两个目标的关系是内容与语言有机的融合、知识体系由浅入深、从理论理解到实践产出这样一个循环上升的关系。

在内容与语言融合的教育理念指导下的《语言、社会与文化》教材不仅可以作为我国高校英语专业语言学方向的学生必修或选修课程教材，同时对于对语言学相关话题感兴趣的英语学习者和研究者也具有一定参考价值。

本教材是我国英语专业语言学课程改革的一项探索，凝聚了全体编写人员多年的辛勤付出。然而由于水平所限，难免存在疏漏和不足，希望使用本教材的师生能为我们提出宝贵的意见和建议。

编　者

于大连外国语大学

2021 年 5 月 1 日

Table of Contents

Unit 1   Language and Society ··· 1
   Text A   Sociolinguistic Phenomenon: An Imaginary World ······················· 2
   Text B   Sociolinguistic Phenomenon: A Real but Exotic World ···················· 4
   Text C   Relationships Between Language and Society ······························· 10

Unit 2   Language and Culture ··· 13
   Text A   Language and Culture ··· 14
   Text B   Language Driven by Culture, Not Biology, Study Shows ··············· 17
   Text C   Lost in Translation ·· 22

Unit 3   Language and Sex ··· 28
   Text A   Language and Sex (I) ·· 29
   Text B   Language and Sex (II) ··· 32
   Text C   Language and Women's Place ··· 40
   Text D   Gender Differences in Communication ······································· 43

Unit 4   Word Borrowing and Language Contact ·· 47
   Text A   Borrowing in the English Language ·· 49
   Text B   Loan Word ·· 51
   Text C   How Languages Influence Each Other ·· 57
   Text D   Contact Explanations and Internal Explanations of Change ········· 60

Unit 5   English Idioms ·· 64
   Text A   Understanding Idioms ··· 65
   Text B   English Idioms ·· 75
   Text C   Top Ten American Idioms and Their Origins ······························ 78

Unit 6   Metaphors and Thought ·· 80
   Text A   Metaphors We Live By ··· 82
   Text B   Teaching Metaphor Through Pop Culture ··································· 92

Text C	Thanksgiving Metaphors: "A Lot on My Plate"	94
Text D	Metaphor and Cultural Coherence	97

Unit 7 Euphemisms and Taboos in Different Cultures … 100

Text A	Taboo and Euphemism	101
Text B	Why Do We Use Euphemisms?	104
Text C	Taboo	110
Text D	Contamination and Camouflage in Euphemisms	113

Unit 8 Cultural Thought Patterns in Intercultural Education … 118

Text A	Cultural Thought Patterns in Inter-cultural Education (I)	120
Text B	Cultural Thought Patterns in Inter-cultural Education (II)	130
Text C	An American Writing Teacher in China	138

Unit 9 Cultural Relativism … 143

Text A	Understanding Cultural Relativism	144
Text B	This Forest Is Ours	150
Text C	Education Abroad—Going Native or Standing Firm	154
Text D	The Challenge of Cultural Relativism	156

Unit 10 Linguistic Relativism … 161

Text A	Language and Thought Processes	162
Text B	Language and Thought	169
Text C	Language May Shape Human Thought	173

Unit 11 Linguistic Imperialism … 175

Text A	What Is Linguistic Imperialism?	176
Text B	Global English	177
Text C	Quebec: A Case of Cultural and Linguistic Imperialism?	186
Text D	Lingua Franca Discourse	190

Unit 12 Language in an Online Global World … 194

Text A	Always on: New Literacy and Language in an Online Global World	195
Text B	Emojis, a New Writing System, a New Language, or Nothing New under the Sun?	204
Text C	The Age of Twitter	208

Unit 1   Language and Society

> Language is not an abstract construction of the learned, or of dictionary-makers, but is something arising out of the work, needs, ties, joys, affections, tastes, of long generations of humanity, and has its bases broad and low, close to the ground.
>
> —— Walt Whitman

Unit Goals

- To know the definitions of language and society
- To understand what sociolinguistics is about
- To know about the relationship between language and society

Before You Read

1. **One can communicate more or less the same idea in either of the following two ways:**
   - ✓ Bring it over here, would ja?
   - ✓ Could I ask you to bring that paintbrush over here?

   However, what are the different relationships people can assume between the speaker and listener? What social situations may cause the above difference in choice of linguistic expressions?

2. **Let us imagine that a small boy has been playing with the neighborhood children on a building site. His mother disapproves both of the locale and of the company he has been keeping, and views with particular horror the empty tin or other object he has acquired as a trophy. She wants both to express her disapproval and to prevent the same thing happening again. If you were the mother, which of the following sentences would you choose to utter and what other options do you have? Please explain your choices.**
   - ✓ That sort of place is not for playing in.

- ✓ I don't like you taking other people's things.
- ✓ They don't want children running about there.
- ✓ Just look at the state of your clothes.
- ✓ I'm afraid you'll hurt yourself.

Start to Read

Text A Sociolinguistic Phenomenon: An Imaginary World

What is there to say about language in relation to society?[1] It may be helpful to start by trying to imagine a society (and a language) about which there is very little to say. The little world described below is completely imaginary, and sociolinguists would agree that it is highly unlikely that any such world either does or even could exist, given what we know about both language and society.

In our imaginary world there is a society which is clearly defined by some natural boundary, impassable in either direction. The purpose of postulating this boundary is to guarantee, on the one hand, that no members of other communities join this one, bringing their own languages with them, and on the other, that members of this community never leave it and take their language to another, thereby complicating the perfect coincidence between language and community.

Everybody in this society has exactly the same language — they know the same constructions and the same words, with the same pronunciation and the same range of meanings of every single word in the language. (Any deviation from such an exact identity raises the possibility of statements such as "Person A knows pronunciation M, but Person B knows pronunciation N, for the same word," which would be a statement about language in relation to society.) An obvious problem is that very young members of the society, just learning to talk, must necessarily be different from everybody else. We might get round this problem by saying that child language is the domain of a branch of psychology rather than sociology, and that psychology can provide general principles of language acquisition which will allow us to predict every respect in which the language of children in this society deviates from the language of the adults. If psychology were able to provide the necessary principles, then there would be a good deal to say about language in relation to individual development, but nothing about language in relation to society. Needless to say, no psychologist would dream of claiming that this was possible, even in principle.

A consequence of the complete absence of any differences between members of this

---

1 Hudson defines Sociolinguistics as the study of language in relation to society.

community is that language change is thereby ruled out, since such change normally involves a difference between the oldest and youngest generations, so that when the former all die only the forms used by the latter survive. Since change seems to affect every language so far studied, this makes the language of our imaginary community unique. The only way to allow for change in a totally homogeneous community is to assume that every change affects every member of the community absolutely and simultaneously: one day, nobody has the new form, the next day, everybody has it. (It is very hard to see any mechanism which could explain such change, short of community-wide telepathy!)

Another characteristic of the community we are considering is that circumstances have no influence on what people say, either with respect to its content or its form. There are no "formal" and "informal" situations, requiring different vocabulary (such as *receive* versus *get*) or different pronunciations for words (like *not* versus -*n't*). Nor are there any "*discussions*" and "*arguments*," or "*requests*" and "*demands*," each requiring not only particular forms but also particular meanings. Nor are there any differences between beginnings, middles and ends of conversations, such as would require greetings and farewells. None of these differences due to circumstances exist because if they did they would require statements about society — in particular, about social interaction. Indeed, if we discount any influence of the social context, it is doubtful if speech is possible at all, since spoken messages are generally geared specifically to the needs of the audience.

Finally, we must assume that there is no connection between the culture of the postulated community and the meanings which its language (especially its vocabulary) allows it to express. The language must therefore contain no words such as cricket or priest, whose meanings could be stated only with reference to a partial description of the culture. To assume otherwise would be to allow rich and interesting statements about language in relation to society, since culture is one of the most important characteristics of society. Exactly what kinds of concepts the members of this community would be able to express is not clear — possibly they would only be able to assert logical truths such as "If p and q, then p," since any other kinds of word are likely to involve some reference to the community's culture.

All in all, our blue-print for a community is an unpromising one. All the restrictions imposed on it were necessary in order to guarantee that there should be nothing to say about its language in relation to society, beyond the simple statement "Such-and-such community speak language X." However, it will be noticed that this statement is precisely the kind which is generally made by linguists (or laypeople) about a language, and exhausts what they feel obliged to say about the language in relation to society. The purpose of this section has been to show that the only kind of community (or language) for which such a statement could be remotely adequate is a fictitious one.

(Excerpted from R. A. Hudson, *Sociolinguistics*, 2000)

Text B Sociolinguistic Phenomenon: A Real but Exotic World

We now turn to a real world, in which there is a great deal to be said about language in relation to society. It is the very exotic world of the north-west Amazon, described by A. P. Sorensen (1971) and J. Jackson (1974) (though we shall see that things are not so very different in the kind of society to which most of us are accustomed).

Geographically, the area in question is half in Brazil and half in Colombia, coinciding more or less with the area in which a language called Tukano can be relied on as a LINGUA FRANCA (i.e. a trade language widely spoken as a non-native language). It is a large area, but sparsely inhabited; around 10,000 people in an area the size of England. Most of the people are indigenous Indians, divided into over twenty tribes, which are in turn grouped into five "phratries" (groups of related tribes). There are two crucial facts to be remembered about this community. First, each tribe speaks a different language — sufficiently different to be mutually incomprehensible and, in some cases, genetically unrelated (i.e. not descended from a common "parent" language). Indeed, the only criterion by which tribes can be distinguished from each other is by their language. The second fact is that the five phratries (and thus all twenty-odd tribes) are exogamous (i.e. a man must not marry a woman from the same phratry or tribe). Putting these two facts together, it is easy to see the main linguistic consequence: a man's wife must speak a different language from him.

We now add a third fact, marriage is patrilocal (the husband and wife live where the husband was brought up), and there is a rule that the wife should not only live where the husband was brought up, but should also use his language in speaking to their children (a custom that might be called "patrilingual marriage"). The linguistic consequence of this rule is that a child's mother does not teach her own language to the child, but rather a language which she speaks only as a foreigner — as though everyone in Britain learned their English from a foreign au-pair girl. One can thus hardly call the children's first language their "mother-tongue" except by a stretch of the imagination. The reports of this community do not mention any widespread disruption in language learning or general "deterioration" of the languages concerned, so we can assume that a language can be transmitted efficiently and accurately even under these apparently adverse circumstances, through the influence of the father, the rest of the father's relatives and the older children. It is perhaps worth pointing out that the wife goes to live in a "long-house" in which the husband's brothers and parents also live, so there is no shortage of contacts with native speakers of the father's language.

What is there to say about language in relation to such a society? First, there is the question of relating languages as wholes to speakers, assuming for simplicity that it is possible to talk usefully about "languages about wholes." For any given language X, it will first be necessary to define who its native speakers are, but since this means referring to some tribe, and tribes are primarily defined with reference to language, there is clearly a problem. The solution is either to list all the long-houses belonging to the tribes concerned, or to specify the geographical area (or areas) where the tribe lives. (Most tribes do in fact have their own territory, which does not overlap with that of other tribes.) However, it will have to be borne in mind that about a quarter of the native speakers of language X will be made up of the married women who are dispersed among the other tribes, and similarly about a quarter of the people living in the area designated as "language X territory" will be non-native speakers of X, being wives from other tribes. Indeed, any given long-house is likely to contain native speakers of a variety of languages, on the assumption that brothers need not be attracted to girls of the same "other" tribe. In addition to the native speakers of language X, there will be people who speak it as non-natives, with every degree of fluency from almost native speaker to minimal. Thus anyone wishing to write a grammar for language X will need to say precisely from whom the grammar is claimed to be true — just for the native speakers left at home in the tribal area, or for all native speakers including those dispersed among the other tribes, or for all speakers, native or non-native, in the tribal area.

Secondly, there is the question of discourse: how is speech used in social interaction? There are questions which arise out of the number of languages available: for instance, how do people get by when they travel around within the area, as they very often do? Are they expected to use the language of the long-house which they are visiting? Apparently not — the choice of language is based solely on the convenience of the people concerned (except for the rule requiring wives to use their husbands' language when speaking to their children). If visitors do not know the long-house language, but someone there knows their language, they will use the visitors' language when speaking to them. What about language itself as a subject of conversation? Here too practical needs are put first, namely the need to know as many languages as possible in order to be able to travel and (for young people) to find a partner. It is quite normal to talk about a language, learning its vocabulary and phrases, and this continues into old age; yet people generally do not know how many languages they can speak, and do not think of language learning as a way of gaining prestige. Perhaps this is what we might expect in a society where everyone can be expected to speak at least (i) their father's language, (ii) their mother's language (which she will certainly have taught her children with a view to their seeking partners among her tribe) and (iii) the lingua franca, Tukano (which may be the father's or the mother's language). However, in addition to the aspects of discourse which are directly related to multilingualism, there are many other things to be said about the relations between speech and the social circumstances in this complex Amazonian society. For instance, there is a rule that if you are listening to someone whom you respect, at least for the first few minutes, you should repeat after them, word-for-word, everything they say.

Thirdly, there is the question of the relation of language to culture, on which we have little information in the reports on the north-west Amazon referred to above, but on which we can make some safe guesses. For instance, it would be surprising if any of the languages concerned lacked a word for "long-house" or "tribe," and we might reasonably expect a word for "phratry" (though such higher-level concepts often lack names). Similarly, we may predict that each language will have words to express most concepts relevant to the culture, and that most words in each language will express cultural concepts, definable only in terms of the culture concerned.

In the world of the north-west Amazon there is probably nothing that linguists could satisfactorily say about any language without at the same time making some fairly complicated statement about it in relation to society. In particular, they could not say which language they were describing by referring to some predefined community who use it (in the way in which one might feel entitled to talk about, say, "British English" or "Birmingham English"). The main source of this complexity is the rule of "linguistic exogamy," which might not be expected to be very widespread in the world. However, the other source is the amount of individual bilingualism (or, more accurately, multilingualism), which makes it hard to decide who is a speaker of a given language and who is not. This characteristic, widespread multilingualism, is anything but exceptional in the world as a whole, as an armchair sociolinguist can easily deduce from the fact that there are some six thousand languages in the world, but only about 160 nation states. As least some states must therefore contain a very large number of languages, and probably most contain a fair number, with an average around forty. In view of the need for communication with neighboring communities and government agencies, it is fair to assume that many members of most communities are multilingual. This means that the monolingual communities familiar to many of us may in fact be highly exceptional and even "exotic" from a global perspective.

(Excerpted from R. A. Hudson, *Sociolinguistics*, 2000)

After You Read

Knowledge Focus

1. Pair Work: Discuss the following questions with your partner.

1) What is the consequence of the complete absence of any differences between members in the imaginary world?
2) What makes it possible for change to occur in a totally homogeneous community as in the imaginary world?
3) Why is the blue-print for the imaginary world an unpromising one?
4) What is the main source of complexity when linguists try to refer to the languages used in the north-west Amazon case?

2. Solo Work: Tell whether the following statements are true or false according to the knowledge you learned and explain why.

1) Sociolinguists would agree that it is highly unlikely that any such world like the one in Text A either does or even could exist.
2) Psychology can provide general principles of language acquisition which will allow us to predict every respect in which the language of children deviates from the language of the adults.
3) A consequence of the complete absence of any differences between members of a community is that language change is thereby ruled out.
4) A patrilocal marriage is one that the husband lives where the wife was brought up.
5) Exogamy is the custom or an act of marrying a person belonging to another tribe, clan, or similar social unit.
6) Multi-lingual communities may in fact be highly exceptional and even "exotic" from a global perspective.

Language Focus

1. Fill in the blanks with the following words or expressions you have learned in Text A and Text B.

| postulate | homogeneous | exogamous | deviate |
| fictitious | exhaust | disruption | discourse |

1) Flexible exchange rates offer some cushioning against foreign shifts but tend to magnify the _____ from shifts of domestic origin.
2) The school building programme _____ an increase in educational investment.
3) She gave a _____ address on the application.
4) Despite the advantages of a _____ population, and those related to culture to be explored herein, there is no simple way to dismiss Japan's success.
5) I will not, however, _____ from the course laid down for me by the fundamental law of Venezuela and by my own conscience.
6) There is no such thing as a universal _____, and _____ exists only within a specific context.
7) The slightest doubt in the existence of _____ and endogamous "tribes" of absolute mutual exclusiveness was considered rank heresy.
8) We seem to have _____ this topic of conversation

Language, Society and Culture

2. Find the appropriate prepositions or adverbs that collocate with the words in bold letters.

1) We might **get** _____ this problem by saying that child language is the domain of a branch of psychology rather than sociology

2) A consequence of the complete absence of any differences between members of this community is that language change is thereby **ruled** _____.

3) Another characteristic of the community we are considering is that circumstances have no influence on what people say, either _____ **respect** _____ its content or its form.

4) _____ **view** _____ the need for communication with neighboring communities and government agencies, it is fair to assume that many members of most communities are multilingual.

5) If psychology were able to provide the necessary principles, then there would be a good deal to say about language _____ **relation** _____ individual development.

Comprehensive Work

1. Pair Work

Imagine you are sitting in a long-house in the north-west Amazon (and you are reasonably fluent in Tukano) and telling the residents there about your language. What kind of information will you cover? Try to make a list.

_____
_____
_____
_____

2. Group Work

➢ Form groups of 3 to 4, and decide on one popular topic in the group.
➢ Each member should give a short speech/talk about the topic.
➢ Record each member's talk and try to find out how one differs from others in pronunciation, word choice, word forms, use of grammatical structures, etc.
➢ Present the results/findings to the whole class.

3. Proofreading

The following passage contains TEN errors. Each line contains a maximum of ONE error. In each case, only ONE word is involved. You should proofread the passage and correct the errors in the following way.

For a wrong word, underline the wrong word and write the correct one in the blank provided at the end of the line.

For a missing word, mark the position of the missing word with a "∧" sign and write the word you believe to be missing in the blank provided at the end of the line.

For an unnecessary word, cross out the unnecessary word with a slash "/" and put the word in the blank provided at the end of the line.

There is inconsiderable variation in the speech of any one individual, but there are also definite bounds for that variation: no individual is free to do just exactly he or she pleases so far as language is concerned. You cannot produce words any way you please, inflect or not inflect words such as nouns and verbs arbitrarily, or make drastic alterations in word order in sentences when the mood suits you. If you do any or all of these things, the results will be unacceptable, even gibberish. The variation you are permitted has limits; what is surprising, as we will see, is these limits can be described with considerable accuracy, and that they also apparently apply to groups of speakers, not just individuals. That is, there are group norms so far as variation is concerned. Moreover, individuals have knowledge of the various limits (or norms), and that knowledge is both very precise and at the same time almost entirely conscious. It is also difficult to explain how individual speakers acquire knowledge of these norms of linguistic behavior, they appear to be much more subtle than the norms that apply to such matters as social behavior, dress, and table manners. As we will see, the task will be one of trying to specify the norms of linguistic behavior that exist in particular groups and then trying to account individual behavior in terms of these norms.	1. _____ 2. _____ 3. _____ 4. _____ 5. _____ 6. _____ 7. _____ 8. _____ 9. _____ 10. _____

4. Writing

You should spend about 40 minutes on this task.

Write about the following topic.

Some people believe government should spend money on saving languages of few speakers from dying out completely. Others think this is a waste of financial resources. Discuss both views and give your position.

Give reasons for your answer and include any relevant examples from your own knowledge or experience. Write at least 250 words.

5. Translation

1) Translate the following passage from English into Chinese.

Among the social scientists, the chief contributors to language study have been anthropologists and psychologists. The anthropologists have been concerned with languages as a cardinal aspect of culture, language origins and development, the analysis of primitive languages and the reciprocal relationships of these languages with primitive mental and social life. The general, social educational and abnormal psychologists have been concerned with the stages of speech development in human beings, especially the speech development of children, the relationships of speech and abnormal psychological states, the strategic significance of language in personality development and in the socialization of the individual, and its relationship to the processes of thought. (Hertzler 1965)

2) Translate the following passage into English.

在互联网搜索引擎 Google 中输入关键词"小姐妹",会出现 8970 条相关信息。不过这些信息中的"小姐妹"绝大部分是这个称谓的本意。诸如"一项专门针对福利院儿童的教育计划——小姐妹学前教育""动画片草原英雄小姐妹""孪生小姐妹双双中状元"等。

在关键词一栏继续输入"杭州"后,出现的 635 条信息中的"小姐妹"几乎都指女性朋友。一篇《在杭州邂逅美女》的文章中说,小姐妹本是女孩相互之间的称呼,因为她们所说的朋友已是男朋友的固定含义(所以用"小姐妹"来指代女性朋友)。如果你称一个陌生女人为小姐妹,就有可能让对方产生一种亲昵感,不过也有层次偏低之嫌。

Read More

Text C Relationships Between Language and Society

There are several possible relationships between language and society. One is that social structure may either influence or determine linguistic structure and/or behavior. Certain evidence may be adduced to support this view: the *age-grading* phenomenon whereby young children speak differently from older children and, in turn, children speak differently from mature adults; studies which show that the varieties of language that speakers use reflect such matters as their regional, social, or ethnic origin and possibly even their sex (or gender); and other studies which show that particular ways of speaking, choices of words, and even rules for conversing are in fact highly determined by certain social requirements.

A second possible relationship is directly opposed to the first: linguistic structure and/or behavior may either influence or determine social structure. This is the view that is behind the Whorfian hypothesis, the claims of Bernstein, and many of those who argue that languages rather than speakers of these languages can be "sexist." A third possible relationship is that the influence is bi-directional: language and society may influence each other. One variant of this approach is that this influence is dialectical in nature, a Marxist view put forward by Dittmar (1976), who argues (p. 238) that "speech behaviour and social behaviour are in a state of constant interaction" and that "material living conditions" are an important factor in the relationship.

A fourth possibility is to assume that there is no relationship at all between linguistic structure and social structure and that each is independent of the other. A variant of this possibility would be to say that, although there might be some such relationship, present attempts to characterize it are essentially premature, given what we know about both language and society. Actually, this variant view appears to be the one that Chomsky himself holds: he prefers to develop an asocial linguistics as a preliminary to any other kind of linguistics, such an asocial approach being, in his view, logically prior.

We must therefore be prepared to look into various aspects of the possible relationships between language and society. It will be quite obvious from doing so that correlational studies must form a significant part of sociolinguistic work. Gumperz (1971, p. 223) has observed that sociolinguistics is an attempt to find correlations between social structure and linguistic structure and to observe any changes that occur. Chambers (1995, p. xvii) echoes that view: "The correlation of dependent linguistic variables with independent social variables... has been the heart of sociolinguistics..." Social structure itself may be measured by reference to such factors as social class and educational background; we can then attempt to relate verbal behavior and performance to these factors. However, as Gumperz and others have been quick to indicate, such correlational studies do not exhaust sociolinguistic investigation, nor do they always prove to be as enlightening as one might hope. It is a well-known fact that a correlation shows only a relationship between two variables; it does not show ultimate causation. To find that X and Y are related is not necessarily to discover that X causes Y (or Y causes X), for it is also quite possible that some third factor, Z, may cause both X and Y (or even that some far more subtle combination of factors is involved). We will therefore always have to exercise caution when we attempt to draw conclusions from any such relationships that we observe.

A worthwhile sociolinguistics, however, must be something more than just a simple mixing of linguistics and sociology which takes concepts and findings from the two disciplines and attempts to relate them in simple ways. Hymes (1974, p. 76) has pointed out that a mechanical amalgamation of standard linguistics and standard sociology is not likely to suffice in that adding a speechless sociology to a sociology-free linguistics may miss entirely what is important in the relationship between language and society. Specific points of connection between language and society must be discovered, and these must be related within theories that throw light on how linguistic and social structures interact.

Holmes (1992. p. 16) says that "the sociolinguist's aim is to move towards a theory which provides a motivated account of the way language is used in a community, and of the choices people make when they use language." For example, when we observe how varied language use, is we must search for the causes. "Upon observing variability, we seek its social correlates. What is the purpose of this variation? What do its variants symbolize?" (Chambers, 1995, p. 207) For Chambers these two questions "are the central questions of sociolinguistics."

(Excerpted from R. Wardhaugh, *An Introduction to Sociolinguistics*, 2000)

Question for Discussion

To convince yourself that there are some real issues here with regard to the possible relationships between language and society, consider your responses to the following questions and compare them with those of others.

1) Does an Inuit "see" a snowscape differently from a native of Chad visiting the cold north for the first time because the Inuit has a well-developed vocabulary for types of snow and the native of Chad lacks this vocabulary?

2) If men and women speak differently, is it because the common language they share has a gender bias, because boys and girls are brought up differently, or because part of "gender marking" is the linguistic choices one can — indeed, must — make?

3) Is language just another cultural artifact, like property, possessions, or money, which is used for the expression of power and/or as a medium of exchange?

Unit 2 Language and Culture

> The limits of my language are the limits of my world.
> — Ludwig Wittgenstein
>
> Absolutely nothing is so important for a nation's culture as its language.
> — Wilhelm von Humboldt

Unit Goals

- To understand the relation of language and culture
- To understand the evolution of human language and culture
- To understand cultural difference as one of the differences between languages
- To know language as a culturally evolved system

Before You Read

1. Make a list of words that can be associated with a particular culture. As an example, think about words used at school that "outsiders" wouldn't understand. You may also consider jargon used by people in a particular profession or contemporary slang used among friends and/or online.

   _____
   _____
   _____
   _____

2. Please share your answers with your partner, and discuss some or all of the following questions.
   - Why do some groups create and use their own "languages"?
   - What are the effects of having shared a vocabulary and language?

语言、社会与文化
Language, Society and Culture

- How does language reflect culture? How does language shape culture?
- What exactly is culture? Is it static or fixed?
- How do new technologies and the Internet affect culture?

Start to Read

Text A Language and Culture

The connection between culture and language has been noted as far back as the classical period and probably long before. The ancient Greeks, for example, distinguished between civilized peoples and bárbaros "those who babble", i.e. those who speak unintelligible languages. The fact that different groups speak different, unintelligible languages is often considered more tangible evidence for cultural differences than other less obvious cultural traits.

The German romanticists of the 19th century such as Herder[1], Wundt[2] and Humbolt[3], often saw language not just as one cultural trait among many but rather as the direct expression of a people's national character, and as such as culture in a kind of condensed form. Herder for example suggests, "Denn jedes Volk ist Volk; es hat seine National Bildung wie seine Sprache" (Since every people is a People, it has its own national culture expressed through its own language).

Franz Boas[4], founder of American anthropology, like his German forerunners, maintained that the shared language of a community is the most essential carrier of their common culture. Boas was the first anthropologist who considered it unimaginable to study the culture of a foreign people without also becoming acquainted with their language. For Boas, the fact that the intellectual culture of a people was largely constructed, shared and maintained through the use of

---

1. Herder: Johann Gottfried von Herder (25 August 1744 — 18 December 1803) was a German philosopher, theologian, poet, and literary critic. He is associated with the periods of Enlightenment.

2. Wundt: Wilhelm Maximilian Wundt (16 August 1832 — 31 August 1920) was a German medical doctor, psychologist, physiologist, philosopher, and professor, known today as one of the founding figures of modern psychology. He is widely regarded as the "father of experimental psychology."

3. Humbolt: Friedrich Wilhelm Christian Karl Ferdinand, Freiherr von Humboldt (22 June 1767 — 8 April 1835), government functionary, diplomat, philosopher, founder of Humboldt Universität in Berlin, friend of Goethe and in particular of Schiller, is especially remembered as a linguist who made important contributions to the philosophy of language and to the theory and practice of education.

4. Franz Boas: Franz Boas (9 July 1858 — 21 December 1942) was a German American anthropologist, a pioneer of modern anthropology who has been called "the Father of American Anthropology" and "the Father of Modern Anthropology." Like many such pioneers, he trained in other disciplines; he received his doctorate in physics, and did post-doctoral work in geography. He applied the scientific method to the study of human cultures and societies; previously this discipline was based on the formulation of grand theories around anecdotal knowledge.

language, meant that understanding the language of a cultural group was the key to understanding its culture. At the same time, though, Boas and his students were aware that culture and language are not directly dependent on one another. That is, groups with widely different cultures may share a common language, and speakers of completely unrelated languages may share the same fundamental cultural traits. Numerous other scholars have suggested that the form of language determines specific cultural traits. This is similar to the notion of Linguistic Determinism, which states that the form of language determines individual thought. While Boas himself rejected a causal link between language and culture, some of his intellectual heirs entertained the idea that habitual patterns of speaking and thinking in a particular language may influence the culture of the linguistic group. Such belief is related to the theory of Linguistic Relativity. Boas, like most modern anthropologists, however, was more inclined to relate the interconnectedness between language and culture to the fact that, as B. L. Whorf[1] put it, "they have grown up together."

Indeed, the origin of language, understood as the human capacity of complex symbolic communication, and the origin of complex culture is often thought to stem from the same evolutionary process in early man. Linguists and evolutionary anthropologists suppose that language evolved as early humans began to live in large communities which required the use of complex communication to maintain social coherence. Language and culture then both emerged as a means of using symbols to construct social identity and maintain coherence within a social group too large to rely exclusively on pre-human ways of building community such as for example grooming. Since language and culture are both in essence symbolic systems, twentieth century cultural theorists have applied the methods of analyzing language developed in the science of linguistics to also analyze culture. Particularly the structural theory of Ferdinand de Saussure[2], which describes symbolic systems as consisting of signs (a pairing of a particular form with a particular meaning), has come to be applied widely in the study of culture. But also post-structuralist theories, that nonetheless still rely on the parallel between language and culture as systems of symbolic communication, have been applied in the field of semiotics. The parallel between language and culture can then be understood as analog to the parallel between a

---

1 B. L. Whorf: Benjamin Lee Whorf (24 April 1897 — 26 July 1941) was an American linguist. Whorf is widely known for his ideas about linguistic relativity. He has been credited as one of the fathers of this approach, often referred to as the "Sapir-Whorf hypothesis," named after him and his mentor Edward Sapir. Originally educated as a chemical engineer, he took up an interest in linguistics late in his life, studying with Sapir at Yale University. In the last ten years of his life he dedicated his spare time to linguistic studies, doing field work on Native American languages in the US and Mexico. He managed to become one of the most influential linguists of his time, even while still working as a fire inspector for the Hartford Fire Insurance Company.

2 Ferdinand de Saussure: Ferdinand de Saussure (26 November 1857 — 22 February 1913) was a Swiss linguist whose ideas laid a foundation for many significant developments in linguistics in the 20th century. Saussure is widely considered to be one of the fathers of 20th-century linguistics and of semiotics, and his ideas have had a monumental impact throughout the humanities and social sciences.

linguistic sign, consisting for example of the sound [kau] and the meaning "cow," and a cultural sign, consisting for example of the cultural form of "wearing a crown" and the cultural meaning of "being king." In this way it can be argued that culture is itself a kind of language. Another parallel between cultural and linguistic systems is that they are both systems of practice, that is, they are a set of special ways of doing things that is constructed and perpetuated through social interactions. Children, for example, acquire language in the same way as they acquire the basic cultural norms of the society they grow up in — through interaction with older members of their cultural group.

However, languages, now understood as the particular set of speech norms of a particular community, are also a part of the larger culture of the community that speaks them. Humans use language as a way of signaling identity with one cultural group and difference from others. Even among speakers of one language several different ways of using the language exist, and each is used to signal affiliation with particular subgroups within a larger culture. In linguistics such different ways of using the same language are called "varieties." For example, the English language is spoken differently in the USA, the UK and Australia, and even within English-speaking countries there are hundreds of dialects of English that each signals a belonging to a particular region and/or subculture. For example, in the UK the cockney dialect signals its speakers' belonging to the group of lower class workers of east London. Differences between varieties of the same language often consist in different pronunciations and vocabulary, but also sometimes of different grammatical systems and very often in using different styles (e.g. Cockney Rhyming slang or Lawyers' jargon). Linguists and anthropologists, particularly sociolinguists, ethnolinguists and linguistic anthropologists have specialized in studying how ways of speaking vary between speech communities.

A community's ways of speaking or signing are a part of the community's culture, just as other shared practices are. Language use is a way of establishing and displaying group identity. Ways of speaking function not only to facilitate communication, but also to identify the social position of the speaker. Linguists call different ways of speaking language varieties, a term that encompasses geographically or socioculturally defined dialects as well as the jargons or styles of subcultures. Linguistic anthropologists and sociologists of language define communicative style as the ways that language is used and understood within a particular culture.

The differences between languages do not consist only in differences in pronunciation, vocabulary or grammar, but also in different "cultures of speaking." Some cultures for example have elaborate systems of "social deixis," systems of signaling social distance through linguistic means. In English, social deixis is shown mostly through distinguishing between addressing some people by first name and others by surname, but also in titles such as "Mrs.," "boy," "Doctor" or "Your Honor," but in other languages such systems may be highly complex and codified in the entire grammar and vocabulary of the language. In several languages of east Asia, for example Thai, Burmese and Javanese, different words are used according to whether a speaker is addressing someone of higher or lower rank than oneself in a ranking system with animals and children ranking the lowest and gods and members of royalty as the highest. Other languages may use different forms of address when speaking to speakers of the opposite gender or in-law relatives and many languages have special ways of speaking to infants and children. Among other groups, the culture of speaking may entail not speaking to particular people; for example, many indigenous cultures of Australia have a taboo against talking to one's in-law relatives, and in some cultures, speech is not addressed directly to children. Some languages also require different ways of speaking for different social classes of speakers, and often such a system is based on gender differences, as in Japanese and Koasati[1].

Text B Language Driven by Culture, Not Biology, Study Shows

Language in humans has evolved culturally rather than genetically, according to a study by UCL (University College London) and US researchers. By modelling the ways in which genes for language might have evolved alongside language itself, the study showed that genetic adaptation to language would be highly unlikely, as cultural conventions change much more rapidly than genes. Thus, the biological machinery upon which human language is built appears to predate the emergence of language.

According to a phenomenon known as the Baldwin effect, characteristics that are learned or developed over a lifespan may become gradually encoded in the genome over many generations, because organisms with a stronger predisposition to acquire a trait have a selective advantage. Over generations, the amount of environmental exposure required to develop the trait decreases, and eventually no environmental exposure may be needed — the trait is genetically encoded.

An example of the Baldwin effect is the development of calluses on the keels and sterna of ostriches. The calluses may initially have developed in response to abrasion where the keel and sterna touch the ground during sitting. Natural selection then favored individuals that could develop calluses more rapidly, until callus development became triggered within the embryo and

---

1 Koasati: Koasati (also Coushatta) is a Native American language of Muskogean origin. The language is spoken by the Coushatta people, most of whom live in Allen Parish north of the town of Elton, Louisiana, though a smaller number share a reservation near Livingston, Texas, with the Alabama people.

could occur without environmental stimulation. The PNAS[1] paper explored circumstances under which a similar evolutionary mechanism could genetically assimilate properties of language — a theory that has been widely favoured by those arguing for the existence of "language genes."

The study modelled ways in which genes encoding language-specific properties could have coevolved with language itself. The key finding was that genes for language could have coevolved only in a highly stable linguistic environment; a rapidly changing linguistic environment would not provide a stable target for natural selection. Thus, a biological endowment could not coevolve with properties of language that began as learned cultural conventions, because cultural conventions change much more rapidly than genes.

The authors conclude that it is unlikely that humans possess a genetic "language module" which has evolved by natural selection. The genetic basis of human language appears to primarily predate the emergence of language.

The conclusion is reinforced by the observation that had such adaptation occurred in the human lineage, these processes would have operated independently on modern human populations as they spread throughout Africa and the rest of the world over the last 100,000 years. If this were so, genetic populations should have coevolved with their own language groups, leading to divergent and mutually incompatible language modules. Linguists have found no evidence of this, however; for example, native Australasian populations have been largely isolated for 50,000 years but learn European languages readily.

Professor Nick Chater, UCL Cognitive, Perceptual and Brain Sciences, says:

Language is uniquely human. But does this uniqueness stem from biology or culture? This question is central to our understanding of what it is to be human, and has fundamental implications for the relationship between genes and culture. Our paper uncovers a paradox at the heart of theories about the evolutionary origin and genetic basis of human language — although we have appeared to have a genetic predisposition towards language, human language has evolved far more quickly than our genes could keep up with, suggesting that language is shaped and driven by culture rather than biology.

The linguistic environment is continually changing; indeed, linguistic change is vastly more rapid than genetic change. For example, the entire Indo-European language group has diverged in less than 10,000 years. Our simulations show the evolutionary impact of such rapid linguistic change: genes cannot evolve fast enough to keep up with this "moving target."

Of course, co-evolution between genes and culture can occur. For example, lactose tolerance appears to have co-evolved with dairying. But dairying involves a stable change to the nutritional environment, positively selecting the gene for lactose tolerance, unlike the

---

1 PNAS: Proceedings of the National Academy of Sciences of the United States.

fast-changing linguistic environment. Our simulations show that this kind of co-evolution can only occur when language change is offset by very strong genetic pressure. Under these conditions of extreme pressure, language rapidly evolves to reflect pre-existing biases, whether the genes are subject to natural selection or not. Thus, co-evolution only occurs when the language is already almost entirely genetically encoded. We conclude that slow-changing genes can drive the structure of a fast-changing language, but not the reverse.

But if universal grammar did not evolve by natural selection, how could it have arisen? Our findings suggest that language must be a culturally evolved system, not a product of biological adaption. This is consistent with current theories that language arose from the unique human capacity for social intelligence.

After You Read

Knowledge Focus

1. Pair Work: Discuss the following questions with your partner.

1) How important is a language to a culture?
2) How do you understand that "culture is itself a language"?
3) What do varieties of language include?
4) What differences do languages have?

2. Solo Work: Decide whether the following statements are true or false.

1) Thus, the biological machinery of language could co-evolve with properties of it, as cultural conventions change much more rapidly than genes.
2) The authors claim that the genetic "language module" of humans has evolved by natural selection.
3) It is wrong to say that different genetic peoples have divergent language modules.
4) Slow-changing genes can drive the structure of a fast-changing language, but not the reverse.

Language Focus

1. Fill in the blanks with the proper form of the words in the brackets.

1) Then came changes in the computerized reservation systems, which made it necessary for smaller regional airlines to become _____ (affiliation) with major carriers in order to get their flights displayed prominently on travel agents' screens.
2) The Spanish-language television programs she watched _____ (perpetuate) stereotypes about gays, she said.

3) The board's bylaws should _____ (code) the size of the board and its membership.

4) The old building had a _____ (tangible) air of sadness about it.

5) To cultivate _____ (diverge) thinking is an important part of cultivating creativity.

6) Their gossips _____ (abrasion) her into restlessness.

7) The scheme is still in its _____ (embryo) stage.

8) Skepticism and trust are not necessarily _____ (compatible).

2. Fill in the blanks with the words or expressions you have learned in the texts.

endowment	offset	subject	incline	consist
lineage	trait	predisposition	entertain	in essence

1) Tom's generosity is one of his most pleasing _____.

2) To _____ these doubts about our science is to question the constitution of our society. It is no wonder that scientific knowledge is so difficult to hold up to scrutiny.

3) He didn't feel _____ to talk or move his muscles; he lay in this position for many hours.

4) The two things are the same in outward form but different _____.

5) Our deeds must _____ with our words.

6) Some studies show that women may be at greater risk for insomnia or have a _____ due to their sex. but explaining this from a purely scientific standpoint is not entirely possible at present.

7) His natural _____ are somewhat limited, and scarcely fit him for this post.

8) The women in this _____ subsequently married into powerful Roman families to protect their line.

9) Their wage increases would be _____ by higher prices.

10) _____ to your consent, I will try again.

3. Proofreading

The following passage contains TEN errors. Each line contains a maximum of ONE error. In each case, only ONE word is involved. You should proofread the passage and correct the errors in the following way:

For a wrong word, underline the wrong word and write the correct one in the blank provided at the end of the line.

For a missing word, mark the position of the missing word with a "∧" sign and write the word you believe to be missing in the blank provided at the end of the line.

For an unnecessary word cross out the unnecessary word with a slash "/" and put the word in the blank provided at the end of the line.

A new language opens up a whole new culture. A foreign language gives us an access to another culture, as our lives take on a new dimension. 　　The great German poet, Johann Wolfgang von Goethe, said in 1827: "Whoever is not acquainted to foreign languages knows anything of his own." Seeing like that, learning a language is almost comparative to a journey of discovery — and when we remember the great explorers and the 18th's century gentleman's grand tour, you might almost call a British invention. Therefore, to lose a language is to lose a whole culture.	1. _____ 2. _____ 3. _____ 4. _____ 5. _____ 6. _____ 7. _____ 8. _____ 9. _____ 10. _____

Comprehensive Work

1. Oral Discussion: The Extinguished Language—*Nushu*

　　An example is the Chinese spoken dialect and written form called *nushu*. It apparently was known and used only by women in the village of Jiang-yong in Hunan Province of South China. Women taught *nushu* only to their daughters and used it to write memoirs, create songs, and share their thoughts with each other. While women also knew and used the conventional Chinese dialect of their region, they used *nushu* to maintain female support networks in their male dominated society.

　　The last speaker and writer of *nushu* was a woman named Yang Huanyi. She died in 2004.

　　Discuss the following questions with your classmates with regard to the questions that follow.

1) What does it mean for languages to "die"?
2) How might you feel to learn years from now that our native tongue (or even our slang system) were facing extinction?
3) How integral is language to our sense of individual and group identity and culture?

2. Writing Practice

　　Make a summary of Text A in about 200 words. Please make sure to include the most important information.

3. Translation: Please translate the following passage into Chinese.

In the 1920s cultural anthropologists and linguists were making contact with languages strikingly different from their own. Edward Sapir expressed his conclusions as follows.

Human beings do not live in the objective world alone, nor alone in the world of social activity as ordinarily understood, but are very much at the mercy of the particular language which has become the medium of expression for their society. It is quite an illusion to imagine that one adjusts to reality essentially without the use of language and that language is merely an incidental means of solving specific problems of communication or reflection. The fact of the matter is that the "real world" is to a large extent unconsciously built up on the language habits of the group. No two languages are ever sufficiently similar to be considered as representing the same social reality. The worlds in which different societies live are distinct worlds, not merely the same world with different labels attached.

Read More

Text C Lost in Translation

Do the languages we speak shape the way we think? Do they merely express thoughts, or do the structures in languages (without our knowledge or consent) shape the very thoughts we wish to express?

Take "Humpty Dumpty sat on a..."[1] as an Example: even this snippet of a nursery rhyme reveals how much languages can differ from one another. In English, we have to mark the verb for tense; in this case, we say "sat" rather than "sit." In Indonesian you need not (in fact, you can't) change the verb to mark tense.

In Russian, you would have to mark tense and also gender, changing the verb if Mrs. Dumpty did the sitting. You would also have to decide if the sitting event was completed or not. If our ovoid hero sat on the wall for the entire time he was meant to, it would be a different form of the verb than if, say, he had a great fall.

---

1 Humpty Dumpty: Humpty Dumpty is a character in an English language nursery rhyme, probably originally a riddle and one of the best known in the English-speaking world. He is typically portrayed as an egg and has appeared or been referred to in a large number of works of literature and popular culture. The most common modern text is:

> Humpty Dumpty sat on a wall,
> Humpty Dumpty had a great fall.
> All the king's horses and all the king's men
> Couldn't put Humpty together again.

In Turkish, you would have to include in the verb how you acquired this information. For example, if you saw the chubby fellow on the wall with your own eyes, you'd use one form of the verb, but if you had simply read or heard about it, you'd use a different form.

Do English, Indonesian, Russian and Turkish speakers end up attending to, understanding, and remembering their experiences differently simply because they speak different languages?

These questions touch on all the major controversies in the study of mind, with important implications for politics, law and religion. Yet very little empirical work had been done on these questions until recently. The idea that language might shape thought was for a long time considered untestable at best and more often simply crazy and wrong. Now, a flurry of new cognitive science research is showing that in fact, language does profoundly influence how we see the world.

The question of whether languages shape the way we think goes back centuries; Charlemagne[1] proclaimed that "to have a second language is to have a second soul." But the idea went out of favor with scientists when Noam Chomsky's theories of language gained popularity in the 1960s and '70s. Dr. Chomsky[2] proposed that there is a universal grammar for all human languages—essentially, that languages don't really differ from one another in significant ways. And because languages didn't differ from one another, the theory went, it made no sense to ask whether linguistic differences led to differences in thinking.

The search for linguistic universals yielded interesting data on languages, but after decades of work, not a single proposed universal has withstood scrutiny. Instead, as linguists probed deeper into the world's languages (7,000 or so, only a fraction of them analyzed), innumerable unpredictable differences emerged.

Of course, just because people talk differently doesn't necessarily mean they think differently. In the past decade, cognitive scientists have begun to measure not just how people talk, but also how they think, asking whether our understanding of even such fundamental domains of experience as space, time and causality could be constructed by language.

For example, in Pormpuraaw, a remote Aboriginal community in Australia, the indigenous languages don't use terms like "left" and "right." Instead, everything is talked about in terms of absolute cardinal directions (north, south, east, west), which means you say things like, "There's

---

1 Charlemagne (possibly 742 — 28 January 814) was King of the Franks from 768 and Emperor of the Romans from 800 to his death. He expanded the Frankish kingdom into an empire that incorporated much of Western and Central Europe.

2 Avram Noam Chomsky (7 December 1928—) is an American linguist, philosopher, cognitive scientist, and political activist. He is an Institute Professor and professor emeritus of linguistics at the Massachusetts Institute of Technology. Chomsky is well known in the academic and scientific community as one of the fathers of modern linguistics, and a major figure of analytic philosophy.

an ant on your southwest leg." To say hello in Pormpuraaw, one asks, "Where are you going?" and an appropriate response might be, "A long way to the south-southwest. How about you?" If you don't know which way is which, you literally can't get past hello.

About a third of the world's languages (spoken in all kinds of physical environments) rely on absolute directions for space. As a result of this constant linguistic training, speakers of such languages are remarkably good at staying oriented and keeping track of where they are, even in unfamiliar landscapes. They perform navigational feats scientists once thought were beyond human capabilities. This is a big difference, a fundamentally different way of conceptualizing space, trained by language.

Differences in how people think about space don't end there. People rely on their spatial knowledge to build many other more complex or abstract representations including time, number, musical pitch, kinship relations, morality and emotions. So if Pormpuraawans think differently about space, do they also think differently about other things, like time?

To find out, my colleague Alice Gaby and I traveled to Australia and gave Pormpuraawans sets of pictures that showed temporal progressions (for example, pictures of a man at different ages, or a crocodile growing, or a banana being eaten). Their job was to arrange the shuffled photos on the ground to show the correct temporal order. We tested each person in two separate settings, each time facing in a different cardinal direction. When asked to do this, English speakers arrange time from left to right. Hebrew speakers do it from right to left (because Hebrew is written from right to left).

Pormpuraawans, we found, arranged time from east to west. That is, seated facing south, time went left to right. When facing north, right to left. When facing east, toward the body, and so on. Of course, we never told any of our participants which direction they faced. The Pormpuraawans not only knew that already, but they also spontaneously used this spatial orientation to construct their representations of time. And many other ways to organize time exist in the world's languages. In Mandarin, the future can be below and the past above. In Aymara, spoken in South America, the future is behind and the past in front.

In addition to space and time, languages also shape how we understand causality. For example, English likes to describe events in terms of agents doing things. English speakers tend to say things like "John broke the vase" even for accidents. Speakers of Spanish or Japanese would be more likely to say "the vase broke itself." Such differences between languages have profound consequences for how their speakers understand events, construct notions of causality and agency, what they remember as eyewitnesses and how much they blame and punish others.

In studies conducted by Caitlin Fausey at Stanford, speakers of English, Spanish and Japanese watched videos of two people popping balloons, breaking eggs and spilling drinks either intentionally or accidentally. Later everyone got a surprise memory test: For each event, can you remember who did it? She discovered a striking cross-linguistic difference in eyewitness memory. Spanish and Japanese speakers did not remember the agents of accidental events as well as did English speakers. Mind you, they remembered the agents of intentional events (for which their language would mention the agent) just fine. But for accidental events, when one wouldn't normally mention the agent in Spanish or Japanese, they didn't encode or remember the agent as well.

In another study, English speakers watched the video of Janet Jackson's[1] infamous "wardrobe malfunction"[2] (a wonderful nonagentive coinage introduced into the English language by Justin Timberlake[3]), accompanied by one of two written reports. The reports were identical except in the last sentence where one used the agentive phrase "ripped the costume" while the other said "the costume ripped." Even though everyone watched the same video and witnessed the ripping with their own eyes, language mattered. Not only did people who read "ripped the costume" blame Justin Timberlake more, they also levied a whopping 53% more in fines.

Beyond space, time and causality, patterns in language have been shown to shape many other domains of thought. Russian speakers, who make an extra distinction between light and dark blues in their language, are better able to visually discriminate shades of blue. The Piraha, a tribe in the Amazon in Brazil, whose language eschews number words in favor of terms like few and many, are not able to keep track of exact quantities. And Shakespeare, it turns out, was wrong about roses: Roses by many other names (as told to blindfolded subjects) do

---

1. Janet Damita Jo Jackson (16 May 1966—) is an American recording artist and actress. Born in Gary, Indiana, and raised in Encino, Los Angeles, she is the youngest child of the Jackson family of musicians. Having sold over 100 million records worldwide, Jackson is ranked as one of the best-selling artists in the history of contemporary music. Her longevity, records and achievements reflect her influence in shaping and redefining the scope of popular music. She has been cited as an inspiration among numerous performers.

2. A wardrobe malfunction is a euphemism for accidental indecent exposure of intimate parts. The term was used by singer Justin Timberlake on February 1, 2004 to explain the Super Bowl XXXVIII halftime show controversy, the incident during Super Bowl XXXVIII in which Janet Jackson's right breast was bared. Quoting Justin Timberlake, "I am sorry if anyone was offended by the wardrobe malfunction during the halftime of the Super Bowl. It was not intentional and is regrettable." The print version of the Urban Dictionary describes it as "an accidental or supposedly accidental failure of clothing to cover parts of the body intended to be covered, made famous by Justin Timberlake during a Super Bowl halftime when he tore off Janet Jackson's clothes."

3. Justin Randall Timberlake (31 January 1981—) is an American pop musician and actor. He has won six Grammy Awards as well as two Emmy Awards. Timberlake became famous in the late 1990s as the lead singer of the boy band 'N Sync.

not smell as sweet[1].

Patterns in language offer a window on a culture's dispositions and priorities. For example, English sentence structures focus on agents, and in our criminal-justice system, justice has been done when we've found the transgressor and punished him or her accordingly (rather than finding the victims and restituting appropriately, an alternative approach to justice). So does the language shape cultural values, or does the influence go the other way, or both?

Languages, of course, are human creations, tools we invent and hone to suit our needs. Simply showing that speakers of different languages think differently doesn't tell us whether it's language that shapes thought or the other way around. To demonstrate the causal role of language, what's needed are studies that directly manipulate language and look for effects in cognition.

One of the key advances in recent years has been the demonstration of precisely this causal link. It turns out that if you change how people talk, that changes how they think. If people learn another language, they inadvertently also learn a new way of looking at the world. When bilingual people switch from one language to another, they start thinking differently, too. And if you take away people's ability to use language in what should be a simple nonlinguistic task, their performance can change dramatically, sometimes making them look no smarter than rats or infants. (For example, in recent studies, MIT students were shown dots on a screen and asked to say how many there were. If they were allowed to count normally, they did great. If they simultaneously did a nonlinguistic task — like banging out rhythms — they still did great. But if they did a verbal task when shown the dots — like repeating the words spoken in a news report — their counting fell apart. In other words, they needed their language skills to count.)

---

1   From Shakespeare's *Romeo and Juliet*, 1600:
    Romeo and Juliet (II, ii, 1—2)
    Romeo Montague and Juliet Capulet meet and fall in love. They are doomed from the start as members of two warring families. Here Juliet tells Romeo that a name is an artificial and meaningless convention, and that she loves the person who is called "Montague," not the Montague name and not the Montague family. Romeo, out of his passion for Juliet, rejects his family name and vows, as Juliet asks, to "deny (his) father" and instead be "new baptized" as Juliet's lover. This one short line encapsulates the central struggle and tragedy of the play.
    JULIET:
    'Tis but thy name that is my enemy;
    Thou art thyself, though not a Montague.
    What's Montague? It is nor hand, nor foot,
    Nor arm, nor face, nor any other part
    Belonging to a man. O, be some other name!
    What's in a name? That which we call a rose
    By any other name would smell as sweet;
    So Romeo would, were he not Romeo call'd,
    Retain that dear perfection which he owes
    Without that title. Romeo, doff thy name,
    And for that name which is no part of thee
    Take all myself.

All this new research shows us that the languages we speak not only reflect or express our thoughts, but also shape the very thoughts we wish to express. The structures that exist in our languages profoundly shape how we construct reality, and help make us as smart and sophisticated as we are.

Language is a uniquely human gift. When we study language, we are uncovering in part what makes us human, getting a peek at the very nature of human nature. As we uncover how languages and their speakers differ from one another, we discover that human natures too can differ dramatically, depending on the languages we speak. The next steps are to understand the mechanisms through which languages help us construct the incredibly complex knowledge systems we have. Understanding how knowledge is built will allow us to create ideas that go beyond the currently thinkable. This research cuts right to the fundamental questions we all ask about ourselves. How do we come to be the way we are? Why do we think the way we do? An important part of the answer, it turns out, is in the languages we speak.

Corrections and Amplifications

Japanese and Spanish language speakers would likely say "the vase broke" or "the vase was broken" when talking about an accident. This article says that Japanese and Spanish speakers would be more likely to say "the vase broke itself."

Question for Discussion

1. What are the reasons that people get lost in translation?

2. How do you understand the author's opinion that the languages we speak shape the way we think?

3. Why does the author claim that Shakespeare's lines about roses was wrong?

4. As a bilingual, have you ever found that you sometimes think differently when you switch from one language to another?

Unit 3 Language and Sex

> Our use of language embodies attitudes as well as referential meanings. Women's language has as its foundation the attitude that women are marginal to the serious concerns of life, which are preempted by men.
>
> —— Robin Lakoff

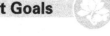

- To know about how men and women differ in their linguistic choices
- To know about theories explaining linguistic gender differentiation
- To understand the features of female language

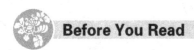

Think about the following questions and discuss together.

1. Is the idea of "differences" a popular one in your society?

2. Can you recall a recent occasion when the idea of "gender differences" was drawn on explicitly (for example, in the media or in a conversation: "Men are like this, women are like that")? Were tendencies (as opposed to absolutes) acknowledged?

3. Can you think of examples (in any language) of proverbs, plays, songs, or works of fiction (such as films) that focus explicitly on the way women and men do and should talk?

Start to Read

Text A Language and Sex (I)

It is known from linguistic research that in many societies the speech of men and women differs in all sorts of ways. In some cases, the differences may be quite large, overtly noted, and perhaps even actively taught to young children. In Gros Ventre, for example, an American Indian language from the north-eastern USA, palatalized dental stops in men's speech correspond to palatalized velar stops in the speech of women — men: /djatsa/; women: /kjatsa/ "bread". Again, in Yukaghir, a north-east Asian language, /tj/ and /dj/ in male speech correspond to /ts/ and /dz/ in the speech of women. We can be fairly sure in this last case that these differences are consciously made, since they also correlate with age differences: children also use the female /ts/ and /dz/ forms, while old people of both sexes use yet another set of variants, /cj/, /jj/. This means that a male speaker uses three different forms in the course of his lifetime, and is presumably therefore aware of the two changeovers that he makes.

Generally speaking, we cannot explain differences of this kind in terms of social distance. In most societies men and women communicate freely with one another, and there appear to be few social barriers likely to influence the density of communication between the sexes. We cannot, therefore, account for the development of gender differences in language in the same way as class, ethnic-group, or geographical dialects. How, then, do such differences arise? Why do men and women often speak differently? Let us take a few examples of the kind of differences that have been reported, and attempt to see what factors may have been important in their development.

The classic example of linguistic sex differentiation comes from the West Indies. It was often reported that when Europeans first arrived in the Lesser Antilles and made contact with the Carib Indians who lived there, they discovered that the men and women "spoke different languages." This would of course have been a very startling discovery, and one that does not appear to have been paralleled anywhere else in the world: nowhere else has sex differentiation been found to be so great that people have been led to propose that there were actually distinct men's and women's languages. However, it does seem that these reports were stretching things somewhat. A contemporary report (from the seventeenth century) says:

> The men have a great many expressions peculiar to them, which the women understand but never pronounce themselves. On the other hand, the women have words and phrases which the men never use, or they would be laughed to scorn. Thus it happens that in their

conversations it often seems as if the women had another language than the men.

From the evidence supplied by this seventeenth-century writer, as well as from the above quotation, it seems certain that, although there were clear differences between men's and women's speech, only a relatively small number of vocabulary items were involved. The men and women, that is, did not speak different languages. Rather, they spoke different varieties of the same language — the differences were lexical only. Even so, how can we explain these particular differences? The Indians themselves had an explanation which has also been quite widely accepted. The contemporary report quoted above continues:

The savage natives of Dominica say that the reason for this is that when the Caribs came to occupy the islands these were inhabited by an Arawak tribe which they exterminated completely, with the exception of the women, whom they married in order to populate the country. It is asserted that there is some similarity between the speech of the continental Arawaks and that of the Carib women.

The differences, that is, were believed to be the result of the mixing of the two language groups, Carib and Arawak, divided on sex lines, as the result of an invasion. This may or may not be true, and it is probably unlikely that we shall ever know what the origin of these differences was. One thing is clear, however: even if this explanation is true, we cannot apply it to the origin of linguistic gender differences in other parts of the world. We must also regard the "invasion" theory, even in this particular case, as rather suspect. First, the reported differences amongst the Carib Indians resemble to a considerable extent those found elsewhere in other American Indian languages. Secondly, the linguist Otto Jespersen has advanced another explanation which is, at least, equally plausible and which will perhaps apply to other cases as well. Jespersen suggests that sex differentiation, in some cases, may be the result of the phenomenon of *taboo*. He points out that it is known that when Carib men were on the war-path they would use a number of words which only adult males were allowed to employ. If women or uninitiated boys used these words, bad luck was considered likely to result. Taboo may perhaps therefore have a powerful influence on the growth of separate sex vocabularies generally. If taboos become associated with particular objects or activities such that, say, women are not permitted to use the original name, then new words or paraphrases are likely to be used instead, and sex differentiation of vocabulary items will result.

Taboo, however, is not a particularly good overall explanation of linguistic gender differentiation, either. First, it is not really clear how differences could become generalized to the whole community. And secondly, in many other non-lexical cases it is quite clear that we are not dealing with taboo. In research done in the 1930s, for example, quite notable sex differences were found in the American Indian language Koasati, a language of the Muskogean family, spoken in Louisiana. The differences, which seemed to be disappearing at the time the research was carried out, involved the phonological shapes of particular verb forms. Consider the following examples:

	male	female
"He is saying"	/ka:s/	/kā/
"Don't lift it!"	/lakauci:s/	/lakaucin/
"He is peeling it"	/mols/	/mol/
"You are building a fire"	/o:sc/	/o:st/

From this list the differences appear to be rather haphazard, but they are in fact entirely predictable according to a series of fairly complicated rules. There is also good reason to believe that the same kind of differentiation formerly existed in other Muskogean languages, but that in these languages the women's varieties have died out. This is partly confirmed by the fact that in Koasati itself it was only the older women who preserved the distinct forms: Younger women and girls used the male forms. Differences of this kind have been found in a number of other American languages. In addition to the Gros Ventre case mentioned above, sex differences of some kind have been found in the American Indian languages Yana and Sioux, and in the Inuit (Eskimo) spoken in Baffin Island.

Taboo does not appear to be involved in any of these cases. The two varieties of Koasati, for example, were learnt from parents who were equally familiar with both and would correct children when necessary. If a small boy said /kā/, for example, his mother would stop him and, herself using the male form, say, "No, you must say /ka:s/." No taboo prohibition prevented her from using this form. Similarly, when relating stories a man could quite properly use female forms when quoting a female character, and vice versa.

How can we explain differences of this type? In Koasati some of the female forms appeared to be older historically than the male forms. In other words, it seemed that linguistic changes had taken place in the male variety which had not been followed through (or were only just beginning to be followed) in the women's speech. The same sort of phenomenon occurs in other languages. Chukchi, for example, is a language spoken in eastern Siberia. In some dialects, the female variety has intervocalic consonants in some words, particularly /n/ and /t/, which are not present in male forms; for example, male: /nitvaqaat/; female: /nitvaqenat/. Loss of intervocalic consonants is a much more frequent and expected sound change than the unmotivated insertion of consonants, and very many examples of loss of consonants in this position have been attested in languages from all parts of the world. This kind of distinction would therefore appear to provide a clear indication that the female variety is older than the male dialect. In more than one language, therefore, women's speech is more conservative than that of men.

Another clue comes, again, from Koasati, and in particular from the attitudes which the

Koasati people themselves had to the two varieties. Older speakers, particularly the men, tended to say, when asked, that they thought the women's variety was better than that used by men. This is important, because it ties in in an interesting way with data we have from technologically more advanced speech communities. It also shows us that the gender varieties are not simply different: in at least two languages the male varieties are innovating and the female conservative, and in one case the female variety is evaluated as better as opposed to worse. Differences of this type should be easier to explain than linguistic differences, pure and simple.

(Excerpted from P. Trudgill, *Sociolinguistics*: *An Introduction to Language and Society*, 2000)

Text B   Language and Sex (II)

Sex differences in English are generally much smaller, less obvious and more subconscious. There are, it is true, a number of words and phrases which tend to be sex-bound. Most of these, incidentally, seem to be exclamations of some sort. This suggests that taboo may be involved in some way: it is certainly traditionally more acceptable in our society for men to swear and use taboo words than it is for women. Mostly, however, differences within English are phonetic and phonological, and taboo cannot be used as an explanation. The differences, moreover, are generally so small that most people are not at all consciously aware of them. It is also important to notice that these differences represent statistical tendencies and not absolute distinctions. Grammatical differences may also be involved, as we shall see below.

Much of the evidence we have for gender differences in English has come from some of the sociolinguistic research carried out in Britain and America that we have already mentioned, but we also have evidence from Australia, South Africa and New Zealand. The sets of data these surveys have provided have one extremely striking feature in common. In all the cases examined, it has been shown that, allowing for other factors such as social class, ethnic group and age, women on average use forms which more closely approach those of the standard variety or the prestige accent than those used by men, although we cannot predict which form a given man or woman is going to use on a given occasion. In other words, female speakers of English, like their Koasati counterparts, tend to use linguistic forms which are considered to be "better" than male forms.

We have examined some of the ways in which linguistic variables are correlated with social class. These same variables can also be used in a similar way to illustrate gender differentiation.

Consider the following figures. In Detroit, higher-class speakers use fewer instances of nonstandard multiple negation (e.g. *I don't want none*) than lower-class speakers. Allowing for social class, however, women on average use fewer such forms than men do:

Percentage of multiple negation used

	UMC	LMC	UWC	LWC
Male	6.3	32.4	40.0	90.1
Female	0.0	1.4	35.6	58.9

In the case of the LMC and the LWC these differences are very big indeed: men are much more likely to say *I don't want none* than women are. Women, this suggests, are far more sensitive to the stigmatized nature of this grammatical feature than men. This sensitivity, moreover, is not confined to grammatical features. In the speech of Detroit Blacks, for instance, women use a far higher percentage of non-prevocalic /r/ (a prestige feature here as in New York) than men, allowing for social class:

Percentage of non-prevocalic /r/ in Detroit Black speech

	UMC	LMC	UWC	LWC
Male	66.7	52.5	20.0	25.0
Female	90.0	70.0	44.2	31.7

Some writers have attempted to explain this sort of pattern in the black community by pointing out that the lower-class African American family is typically matriarchal and that it is the mother of a family who conducts business with the outside world and who has job contacts with speakers of prestige varieties. This explanation is not adequate, however, since exactly the same pattern is found in the white community and in British English. In Norwich English, for example, the same sort of pattern emerges with the (ng) variable (whether speakers say *walking* or *walkin'*). The table below gives the percentage of non-RP-in' forms used by speakers in different class and sex groups:

	MMC	LMC	UWC	MWC	LWC
Male	4	27	81	91	100
Female	0	3	68	81	97

Once again, women use a higher percentage of "better" forms than men do. In London English, too, men are more likely than women to use glottal stops in words like *butter* and *but*. And this phenomenon is not confined only to British and American English. In South Africa, for example, research has been carried out in the Transvaal, comparing the speech of English-speaking male and female high-school pupils of the same age in the same town. A study was made of the pronunciation of four vowels:

The vowel of *gate*, which in South Africa ranges from high-prestige RP [geɪt] to low-prestige South African [gɜt], with a lower and more central first element to the diphthong, as in RP *bird*.

The vowel of *can't*, which ranges from RP [kɑːnt], to South African [kɒːnt], with a vowel close in quality to that found in RP on — a low back rounded vowel.

The vowel of *out*, which ranges from RP [aʊt] to South African [æʊt], with a higher front first element resembling the vowel in RP *cat*. The vowel in *boy*, which ranges from RP [bɒi] to a variant with a high back rounded first element [buɪ] as in RP *school*. The results, giving the percentage of boys and girls using each variant in each case, are given below:

	RP		Non-RP	
gate	[geɪt]	[gɜit]		
boys	0	100		
girls	62	38		
can't	[kɑːnt]	[kɒːnt]		
boys	0	100		
girls	62	38		
out	[ɒut]	[aʊt]	[æʊt]	
boys	25	17	58	
girls	85	15	0	
boy	[bɔi]	[bɔ̧i]	[boi]	[buɪ]
boys	0	16	42	42
girls	15	38	47	0

The boys, we can see, are much more likely than the girls to use nonstandard local pronunciations.

In different parts of the English-speaking world, then, as well as in Koasati, female speakers have been found to use forms considered to be "better" or more "correct" than those used by men. This finding has also subsequently been replicated for large numbers of other languages in Europe and elsewhere. There is, however, an important qualification to be made at this point: in communities where the standard variety is acquired only through education and/or through contact with outside communities, women who are denied education and/or travel will obviously not use more standard forms than men — this has been reported for some Arabic-speaking communities, for example.

In fact, we can say that gender differentiation of this type is the single most consistent finding to emerge from sociolinguistic work around the world in the past thirty years. Why should this be? The correct answer is that we do not know exactly, but sociolinguists have come up with a number of different, necessarily speculative, suggestions.

Firstly, it has been pointed out that working-class speech, like certain other aspects of working-class culture in our society, seems to have connotations of or associations with masculinity, which may lead men to be more favorably disposed to nonstandard linguistic forms than women. This, in turn, may be because working-class speech is associated with the "toughness" traditionally supposed to be characteristic of working-class life and "toughness" is quite widely considered to be a desirable masculine characteristic.

Secondly, it has also been pointed out that many societies seem to expect a higher level of adherence to social norms from women than they do from men. If father comes home drunk on Saturday night and vomits over the living-room carpet, this is bad. But if mother does the same, many people would feel it is worse. A woman interviewed in a Norwegian dialect survey said, when asked why she used the prestige pronunciation [ɜg] "egg" while her brothers said [æg]: "It isn't *done* for a woman to say [æg]." As the New Zealand sociolinguist Elizabeth Gordon has pointed out, one area where "better" behavior has traditionally obviously been expected from women, because of double standards in our society, is in the area of sexual activity. She suggests that women may have a tendency to speak in a more prestigious way so as not to be thought sexually promiscuous.

Given that there are linguistic variables in a speech community which are involved in co-variation with social class (higher-class forms being more statusful or "correct" than lower-class forms), then there are social pressures on speakers to acquire prestige or to appear "correct" by employing the higher-class forms. Other things being equal, however, it is probably true to say that these pressures will tend to be stronger on women. On the other hand, there will also be pressure to continue using less prestigious nonstandard variants as a signal of group solidarity and personal identity. These pressures, however, will tend to be stronger on men than on women, because of concepts of masculinity current in our society.

As far as English is concerned, we have some interesting evidence about the way in which social values and sex roles affect speakers' attitudes towards linguistic variants, and hence their actual usage of these variants. We already have plenty of evidence to show that, in England, Standard English and the RP accent have high prestige. What, however, of the argument that working-class speech has favorable connotations for male speakers? Can we actually show that this is the case? The argument really hinges on the belief that lower-class, nonstandard linguistic varieties also have some kind of "prestige," and that this is particularly so in the case of men. Labov has called this kind of "prestige" *covert prestige* because attitudes of this type are not usually overtly expressed, and depart markedly from the mainstream societal values (of schools and other institutions) of which everyone is consciously aware. Favourable words like "good" and "nice," for instance, are usually reserved for standard prestige varieties.

(Excerpted from P. Trudgill, *Sociolinguistics: An Introduction to Language and Society*, 2000)

语言、社会与文化
Language, Society and Culture

After You Read

Knowledge Focus

1. Pair Work: Discuss the following questions with your partner.

1) How do the speeches of men and women differ in languages such as Gros Ventre and Yukaghir?
2) Can we explain the differences in the speeches of men and women in terms of social distance?
3) What are the major theories attempting to explain the differences between men's and women's speech? Can these theories offer good overall explanation of linguistic gender differentiation?
4) Why do women tend to use more standard linguistic forms than men?

2. Solo Work: Tell whether the following statements are true or false according to the knowledge you learned and explain why.

1) In Yukaghir, a north-east Asian language, different linguistic choices are made consciously between men and women.
2) Social distance can be used to explain the differences between men's and women's speech.
3) Taboo theory advanced by the linguist Otto Jespersen offers a powerful explanation for linguistic gender differentiation.
4) Sex differences in English are generally much smaller, less obvious and more subconscious.
5) In different parts of the English-speaking world, female speakers have been found to use forms considered to be more innovative than those used by men.
6) According to Robin Lakoff, nonstandard linguistic varieties enjoy a kind of overt prestige in mainstream societal values in England.

Language Focus

1. Fill in the blanks with the following words or expressions you have learned in Text A and Text B.

overtly	differentiation	counterpart	presumably
plausible	haphazard	subsequently	replicate

1) The exact number cannot be confirmed because of _____ between two datasets.
2) The little girl applied the cosmetic to her mouth in the adorably _____ way only a toddler can get away with.
3) Metal tools replaced their stone _____ many, many years ago.

4) It is now easier for French writers to write more _____ about the occupation because their country is now stressing forgiveness for whatever wrongs that were done then.

5) The drug prevents the virus from _____ itself.

6) That does not strike me as _____, even taking into consideration a failed sewer line.

7) If we go back in history, we come to artists who were fashionable and acclaimed in their time but who _____ went through periods of total oblivion.

8) High lifetime unemployment can lower life expectancy, _____ as a combined result of stress, depression, reduced health care and loss of social networks.

2. Fill in the blanks with the proper form of the words in the brackets.

1) A number of main entries have a second and sometimes a third spelling. These alternate spellings are called _____ (vary).

2) After the police stormed the JMI University and beat up students protesting the Citizenship Amendment Act (CAA) yesterday, several other campuses have risen in _____ (solid).

3) A nutritional study has been published by a _____ (prestige) medical journal.

4) The report is highly _____ (speculate) and should be ignored.

5) Their job is thankless, underappreciated, and _____ (stigma) by society.

6) It's a cliché to say that science is associated with _____ (masculine) and the arts with femininity.

7) She took his hand and made an _____ (exclaim) of shock.

8) Nurses in training should be given a guarantee of employment following _____ (quality).

Comprehensive Work

1. Group Work: Divide the class into groups of 3-4 and do the following reflection work.

Think of a language other than English (for example, Chinese).

➢ Do features exist in this language which can be seen as having the capacity to "define, degrade or stereotype" women, or to render them (relatively) invisible?

➢ If so, is there resistance to such features? Are language practices changing here?

➢ What would happen if men do produce "women's features," and vice versa?

➢ Are children, and adult learners, taught to use these features "appropriately"? If so, how?

2. Pair Work

Record and transcribe a short sample of spoken data (e.g. an interview from the television, a conversation between friends in a pub; a conversation from a play or soap opera) in which gender appears to be a salient feature. The sample(s) should be no more than five minutes in total. Try to analyze how gender identity is being constructed, represented, enacted and/or negotiated through discourse.

3. Pair Work

Select one or more media text(s) in which gender is a salient factor, such as advertisements in men's and women's lifestyle magazines, constructions of motherhood and fatherhood in parent craft magazines. Think about the following questions:

- What kinds of gendered "scripts" or existing discourses do speakers/writers draw upon?
- What kinds of "membership categories" are set up in the text? (e.g. wife/mother/lover/ single 30-something).

4. Proofreading

The following passage contains TEN errors. Each line contains a maximum of ONE error. In each case, only ONE word is involved. You should proofread the passage and correct the errors in the following way:

For a wrong word, underline the wrong word and write the correct one in the blank provided at the end of the line.

For a missing word, mark the position of the missing word with a "∧" sign and write the word you believe to be missing in the blank provided at the end of the line.

For an unnecessary word, cross out the unnecessary word with a slash "/" and put the word in the blank provided at the end of the line.

An obvious way that gender-differentiated language use reflects social hierarchies is through naming conventions, which are often simultaneous ways of referring to people and addressing them in interaction. Naming conventions have therefore been targeted by feminists for change. For example, there is only one form of address for men, *Mr.*, regardless marital status. Until recently, however, the marital status of women was distinguished by *Miss* and *Mrs.*, reflecting the notion that whether or not a woman in a heterosexual marriage is her defining characteristic. Feminists coined another address form, *Ms.*, for women who believed that their marital status should be irrelevant, as it is for men. Some women use *Ms.* with their own surname, and some use it along with their husband's surname, which they may have been taken after marriage.	1. _____ 2. _____ 3. _____ 4. _____

Surnaming practices also mark an area of conflict and change in how women are named. There is currently considerable variability as which surname American women choose after marriage: some retain their own surname, others adopt their husband's surname, some adopt a last name which is a hyphenated hybrid of their own surname and their husband's, and yet others use their own surname in professional settings and their husband in community, church, and leisure settings. Although some native English speakers object the whole issue is too confusing to straighten out, such speakers usually prefer a traditional naming practice, with the woman addressed as *Mrs.* plus husband's surname after marriage. The situation is more confusing, however, than being introduced to a man whom one has heard variably called *Richard*, *Dick*, *Richie*, and *Rich*; one must ask him what he prefers. To address a man as Richie when he will prefer *Richard* is to be deliberately insulting — just like ignoring a woman's preference about her form of address would also be insulting.	5. _____ 6. _____ 7. _____ 8. _____ 9. _____ 10. _____

5. Writing

You should spend about 40 minutes on this task.

Write about the following topic:

Recently there has been a popular belief that boys should be brought up in a poor and difficult environment and girls in a comfortable one. What is your opinion?

Give reasons for your answer and include any relevant examples from your own knowledge or experience. Write at least 250 words.

6. Translation

1) Translate the following passage from English into Chinese.

I was addressing a small gathering in a suburban Virginia living room — a women's group that had invited men to join them. Throughout the evening, one man had been particularly talkative, frequently offering ideas and anecdotes, while his wife sat silently beside him on the couch. Toward the end of the evening, I commented that women frequently complain that their husbands don't talk to them. This man quickly concurred. He gestured towards his wife and said, "She's the talker in our family." The room burst into laughter; the man looked puzzled and hurt. "It's true," he explained. "When I come home from work I have nothing to say. If she didn't keep the conversation going, we'd spend the whole evening in silence."

This episode crystallizes the irony that although American men tend to talk more than women in public situations, they often talk less at home. And this pattern is wreaking havoc with marriage. The pattern was observed by political scientist Andrew Hacker in the late '70s. sociologist Catherine Kohler Riessman reports in her book *Divorce Talk* that most of the women she interviewed — but only a few of the men — gave lack of communication as the reason for their divorces. Given the current divorce rate of nearly 50 percent, that amounts to millions of cases in the United States every year — a virtual epidemic of failed conversation.

2) Translate the following passage from Chinese into English.

语言学研究表明，在小学和初中阶段，男女生的语言能力的确存在一定的差别。一般来说，女孩子说话早，女生的语言能力的确优于男生。相关科学研究也告诉我们，男性和女性在兴趣爱好、思维方式以及语言表述等方面有很大不同。单就思维品质而言，男性更擅长抽象思维，女性更擅长形象思维。相比较而言，在对事物的理解上，男生更富有批判、创新精神。在对一个问题的理解上，这种差异是客观存在的，也是事物多样性的一种表现。

有鉴于此，如果我们的老师在上课的时候能够注意这个问题，更有意识地给男生、女生同样的机会，特别是在提问的时候加强引导，让男女生都对一个问题充分表达自己的看法，达到性别互补，可能更有利于问题的解决，对于培养学生学会全面思考问题、提高解决问题的能力都将大有裨益。

可以想见，如果能在课堂上让男生、女生充分展示各自的天性，对于活跃课堂气氛、促进思维向纵深发展，都将带来可喜的变化。这样，我们的课堂将更有深度，更富有教育意义，我们的老师将会在教书和育人两方面表现得更加优秀。

Read More

Text C Language and Women's Place

The first widely influential study of language-use features was presented by Robin Lakoff, first in a journal article and later in a book, both under the title "Language and Women's Place" (Lakoff 1973a, 1975). Lakoff's work led her to conclude that "woman's language" — by which she meant both language used to describe women and language typically used by women — had the overall effect of submerging a woman's personal identity (Lakoff 1973a: 48).

With respect to the use of language, women's identities are submerged because they are denied the means of expressing themselves strongly, encouraged to use expressions that suggest triviality, and to use forms that express uncertainty concerning what they are talking about. Lakoff described six categories of language use that are sharply differentiated by the sex of the speaker: lexical distinctions such as color terms, strong versus weak expletives, "women's" versus "neutral" adjectives, tag questions, question intonation with statement syntax, and strength of directive speech acts.

Color terminology

Lakoff claims that some fanciful and discriminating color words like "aquamarine," "mauve," "lavender," "beige," "ecru" are more likely to show up in women's active vocabulary, but absent from that of most men. In contrast, if a man should say something is mauve, one might well conclude he was imitating a woman sarcastically, or was a homosexual. Usually, men find such question as to whether something is "mauve" or "lavender" amusing but trivial.

Expletives

An experiment has been conducted by Lakoff: ask native speakers of standard English which of the following is spoken by a man, and which by a woman.

A: Oh dear, you've put the peanut butter in the refrigerator again.

B: Shit, you've put the peanut butter in the refrigerator again.

The result is that people would classify the first sentence as part of women's language, the second as men's language. In addition, many women are beginning to use sentences like B publicly. This shows that men's language is increasingly being used by women, but women's language is not being adopted by men. Yet, in any event, the "stronger" expletives are reserved for men, and the "weaker" ones for women.

Empty adjectives

Lakoff was perhaps the first to notice the difference between "women's" and "neutral" adjectives. There is a set of adjectives in English which express approval and admiration in addition to their strictly literal meanings. Some of these like "great" and "terrific," are neutral in the sense that they are readily and appropriately used either by men and women. Others of this set, such as "adorable," "charming" and "divine," are expected in women's speech, but not generally in men's. The difference between "a great idea," which either a man or a woman can appropriately say, and "a divine idea," which would be a cause for remark if a man said it, is that the second expression is a bit frivolous and expresses an idea that is important only for the speaker rather than the world at large.

Tag questions

A syntactic feature that Lakoff believes is more freely usable by women than by men is the tag questions form. Tag questions are appended to statements by taking the tense-bearing element of the verb phrase, reversing its negativity, selecting the pronoun appropriate to the subject of the statement and making a question out of these elements, as in "Howard wouldn't do such a thing, would he?" These constructions ask hearers to confirm explicitly that they agree with the statement. One reason speakers might use a tag question is to state a claim, when they are not fully confident that the person they are talking to will agree with that claim. Greater use of this form by women could mean that women, more often than not, are presenting themselves as unsure of their opinions and thereby as not really having opinions that count very much.

Question intonation

In answer to the question "When will dinner be ready?" women would tend to answer "Around six o'clock?" Women would feel inclined, or perhaps obliged, to adjust dinner time to suit the convenience of other members of the family. On the other hand, if asked "What time are we leaving for our trip tomorrow?" it would seem natural to expect a man to reply with something like "At 7.30 and I want everyone to be ready." In Lakoff's view, women would tend to avoid answering "At six o'clock, and everybody better be here," and few men would answer "At 7.30?"

Directives

Directives, things you can say to get someone else to do something for you, have a wide range of linguistic forms. The following range of possibilities is illustrated by Lakoff:

Close the door.

Please close the door.

Will you close the door?

Will you please close the door?

Won't you close the door?

These examples are listed in order of increasing politeness, in the sense that using the variants towards the end of the list leaves the addressee freer to refuse than using the ones at the beginning. Women seem to be taught to use the more polite, weaker, more self-effacing forms of directives.

The second part of Lakoff's analysis has to do with the meanings of words referring to sex in the language. Two major concerns here are general reference and overtones associated with sex-paired words.

General reference

It is common knowledge that lexical items which are semantically male are traditionally used for general reference, where the sex of the referent is no known and not relevant. This applies to the pronoun "he," which traditional grammars prescribe in contexts like "Each bicyclist must dismount and walk his bicycle across the intersection," where it is not known and it does not matter whether any particular bicyclist is female or male. It also applies to "man," either alone or in compounds, as in the following examples.

Man has learned to control his environment to an astonishing extent.

This discovery will benefit all *man*kind.

Overtones of sex-paired words

Sex-paired words, such as "wife" and "husband," are supposedly semantically equivalent, except that one refers to men and the other to women. Robin Lakoff (1973a, 1975) makes a strong case for the euphemistic use of "lady" as opposed to "gentleman," as if "woman" were an unpleasant term that ought to be avoided. Many other terms of this sort have worse connotations associated with the woman's term than the corresponding man's term. For instance, a "bachelor" and a "spinster" are both unmarried, and one is a man and the other a woman. A bachelor, however, is seen as probably being unmarried by choice and living a happy and perhaps somewhat libertine life, while a spinster conjures an image of an old and unappealing woman living a drab and unfulfilled life in consequence of her failure to marry.

In sum, Lakoff has found the overall effect of women's language — both language restricted in use to women and language descriptive or designating women — is this: it submerges a woman's personal identity, by denying her the means of expressing herself strongly, and, on the other hand, encouraging expressions that suggest triviality in subject matter and uncertainty about it; and, when a woman is being discussed, by treating her as an object — sexual or otherwise — but never a serious person with individual views.

Questions for Discussion

Almost 45 years ago Robin Lakoff concluded in her article "Language and Women's Place" that women's language had the overall effect of submerging a woman's personal identity. Are there any examples you can find in the use of Chinese language to prove or disprove Lakoff's opinion? What changes have you noticed or witnessed in the way men and women use Chinese language in the past 10 or 20 years?

Text D Gender Differences in Communication

Every race, culture, civilization, and society on this planet shares two things in common: the presence of both men and women, and the need to communicate between the two. The subject of gender differences appears to have engaged people's curiosity for as long as people have been writing down their thoughts, from as far back as the writing of the creation of Adam and Eve, to its current popular expression in books such as *Men Are from Mars, Women Are from Venus*. The assertion that men and women communicate in different ways, about different things, and for different reasons seems to go un-argued and is accepted as true by many.

A recent conversation between a young man, in his mid-twenties, and me, while at work, reaffirmed my belief that men and women communicate in different ways. Deborah Tannen, a leading scholar of communication, also shares this view of gender and communication. In her research, she finds that the basic uses of conversation by women are to establish and support intimacy; while for men it is to gain status. These styles and motives for communicating represent different cultural upbringings, and one is not necessarily better than the other. However, Tannen also notes in her findings that men tend to interrupt more and ask questions less. The most obvious differences in communication between men and women include listening, verbal communication, and non-verbal communication. When engaging in conversation with a young man (Michael) at my place of employment, I found listening was the most prevalent difference. When speaking with Michael, I realized that I had a tendency to listen to each and every word, while he listened to the main points. I am taught that when a guest enters the store that we are to be active listeners and to respond to everything that they have to say. I find that women react in a more positive way to this than men. Women show attentiveness through verbal and non-verbal cues. Many men avoid these cues to keep from appearing "one-down."

Most men do not listen to each and every word in a conversation. For example, when speaking with Michael, he seemed to be an active listener, but when the conversation came to an end he asked me what my name was. I had clearly stated my name at the beginning of the conversation. Michael even repeated my name, assuring me that he had heard and understood that my name was Allison. When Michael asked for my name again, I knew that he had been a selective listener and this caused him to forget my name. When engaging in this conversation I found myself judging and stereotyping quite a bit. Michael told me what he does for a living and how much he actually enjoys what he does. He is a military man. From previous experiences (schema), at my workplace, with military men, I couldn't help but wonder if he was the same way. With the exception of schema, judgment, and stereotyping, listening tends to be the most prevalent difference between men and women. Verbal communication is the second issue at hand. Tannen argues that men seek status in conversation while women seek acceptance.

When engaging in conversation with Michael, I find this previous statement to be true. Michael spoke of his career, his achievements, and his future. I spoke on issues that directly and indirectly related to his. We discussed the Army, his tour in Iraq, and our similar experiences. Men tell more stories and jokes than do women. Telling jokes is a masculine way to negotiate status. Men are almost always the heroes in their own stories. When women tell stories, they downplay themselves. I let Michael speak first because I did not want to say anything that made me sound less intelligent. When I spoke, I spoke in a non-assertive way, while he was very assertive and to the point. Men speak more monotonous and louder than most women. Critics of Tannen would argue from a very early age, males and females are taught different linguistic practices. For example, communicative behaviors that are considered acceptable for boys may be considered completely inappropriate for girls. Whereas a boy might be permitted to use rough language, a girl in the same situation might be reminded to use her manners and be lady-like.

The research on women and language shows that women experience linguistic discrimination in two ways: in the way they are taught to use language, and in the way general language usage treats them. So, for example, women reflect their role in the social order by using tag questions, qualifiers, and fillers to soften what they have to say. Women exhibit their subordinate status through avoiding direct and threatening communication. While in recent years this gap has narrowed, our society retains a tendency to imply that maleness is the standard for normalcy. Some would argue that. The most subtle of all differences are the non-verbal cues. Most men and women think they are capable of comprehending one another's body language. Since men and women tend to focus more on listening and verbal, non-verbal cues are often ignored. In conversation, women show more exaggerated emotions. Women smile more and nod their head while speaking and listening. Nodding the head is a sign of understanding and a way to gain acceptance. For example, when speaking with Michael I looked him straight in the eyes, smiled and, nodded my head when I agreed or could relate to what was being said. I noticed that Michael made more eye contact, possibly to show dominance. I on the other hand did not make nearly as much eye contact. I find it difficult to do so because I find that eye contact represents trust.

Until I trust a person I make minimal eye contact. Michael's perception of me may be that I am a very shy and timid person. My personal perception of Michael, based on the conversation is that he is a very independent person, he is very confident, and has a high self-esteem. I thought at first encounter that Michael would have an "allness attitude," however, to my surprise; he did not have this attitude at all. Although non-verbal cues are ignored, they are possibly the most important key in understanding the differences in communication between men and women. Ethics are very important in today's society. Ethical communication, or communication that facilitates the individual's freedom of choice by presenting that individual with accurate bases for choice, is important in interpersonal communication. Ethics set the stage for a fair and reasonable conversation. When I saw the three men walk through the front door with Michael, I thought to myself, "More military men coming into the store to harass our female employees." At that point I should have avoided personal conversation. I was unethical by engaging in conversation with Michael. The most logical response would have been to greet the men, ask if they need help, and then leave them alone to shop. I continued the conversation because I discovered that Michael was not just another soldier in the store with the intent to harass the female employees.

It is extremely difficult to distinguish what is ethical and what is unethical in communication. When engaging in conversation with Michael I noticed that our perceptions differed, the way we spoke was different, the non-verbal cues were different, and the words we used were different. Although the communication between Michael and I differed greatly, we were still able to understand one another and were able to carry on the conversation. It amazes me how different conversation between men and women can be, yet we are still able to make it work. Through recent research we have learned that gender differences in communication are not something that we are born with, they're not due to differences in brain matter, and they're definitely not due to the two sexes being from different planets. We are who we are and we communicate how we communicate because it is what society and culture demand of us. Although this sounds like a simple difference that can easily be resolved you might be surprised; disregarding everything you've ever learned about the difference between boys and girls is a mighty big task.

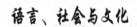

Language, Society and Culture

Questions for Discussion

What are your comments or reflections on the following sayings from China, Russia, and Japan, while thinking over the above article?

- "women's and children's opinion" (China)
- "A woman's tongue spreads gossip fast." (China)
- "Men talk like books, women lose themselves in details." (China)
- "The tongue is babbling, but the head knows nothing about it." (Russia)
- "Three inches of a woman's tongue can slay a man six feet tall." (Japan)

Unit 4 Word Borrowing and Language Contact

> Finding a name for something is a way of conjuring its existence.
> — Harold Rheingold
>
> Today only about five percent of our new words are taken from other languages. They are especially prevalent in the names of foods: focaccia, salsa, vindaloo, ramen.
> — Allan Metcalf

Unit Goals

- To know the definition of loan words and language contact
- To comprehend the causes behind the transfer of certain words and phrases from one language to another
- To investigate the social history of a language community

Before You Read

1. Match the following loan words with the language families they were "borrowed" from. In some cases cultural clues could make your job a little easier.

Loan Words	Languages and Language Families
1. Karma	A. Afrikaans
2. window	B. Bantu
3. poodle	C. Czech
4. ukulele	D. Dutch
5. gumbo	E. Finnish
6. mammoth	F. German
7. aardvark	G. Hawaiian Polynesian
8. robot	H. Icelandic
9. slogan	I. Russian
10. geyser	J. Sanskrit
11. sauna	K. Scandinavian
12. poppycock	L. Scottish Gaelic

Language, Society and Culture

2. **Fill in the table and try to detect the cultural contact reflected through loan-words both in English and Chinese.**

English	Chinese Source	Literal Meaning
1. Bok choy		
2. Bonsai		
3. Cheongsam		
4. China		
5. Chop suey		
6. Chow		
7. Chow mein		
8. Coolie		
9. Cumshaw		
10. Dimsum		
English Source	Chinese Transliteration	Alternate Chinese Variant
1. Baby		
2. Bar		
3. Bowling		
4. Brandy		
5. Buffet		
6. Bus		
7. Bye Bye		
8. Calorie		
9. Cartoon		
10. Cheese		

3. **List abbreviations that are so popular as to be often inserted into spoken Chinese.**

_____
_____
_____
_____

Start to Read

Text A Borrowing in the English Language

Where two different languages have contact over a certain period of time they will surely influence each other. Words might be taken over from one language and are adopted to the other. This process is called borrowing. Throughout its long history English had contact with many different languages such as Old Norse, French, and Latin, but also with the colonial languages.

The reasons for a language such as English to borrow words from other languages are manifold. Katamba remarks in this context that there is no purely linguistic reason for borrowing. According to him no limit exists to the number of words that can be generated in any language. But still, whenever the need for a new term arises, due to the contact between people from different cultures, the formation of a neologism, composed of elements of the own language, is only rarely done. One reason for borrowing a suitable word from another language is the need to find a term for an unfamiliar thing, animal, or cultural device. Then borrowing seems to be the easiest solution to this problem.

Another reason for just borrowing a term might also be the question of identity. This is especially the case with bilingual speakers who, by using a foreign element in their speech, make a statement about their own self-perception. In this context, code-switching also plays an important role. If a word is habitually used in code-switching, it perhaps might pass over from one language to the other and then eventually even become fully integrated. In such a way for example the Yiddish word *schmaltz* ("cloying, banal sentimentality") has been introduced to (American) English.

Moreover, a further, often underestimated reason for borrowing is prestige. Katamba notes here that people have "always liked to show off." Gibbon remarks in this discussion that the prestige question could even be one of the, if not the major reason for borrowing, because people would only take loanwords from other languages if they believed that either the device/object for which the denotation is taken over or the language, from which the term comes, itself is prestigious. Gramley holds that such terms mostly come from those languages he calls "languages of classical learning," i.e. Latin or Greek. Not only are whole words borrowed together with their meanings, but also new words, namely neologisms, are generated on the basis of morphemes borrowed from those languages. In English a product of such a process is *telephone* (from Greek *tēle-* meaning "afar, far off" and *phōnē* meaning "sound, voice").

Gramley goes on mentioning the controversial discussion which has been led about the words being taken over from those "classical languages" to English. On the one hand they serve to enrich the language, but on the other hand the words make certain stylistic registers more inaccessible to the masses. The meaning of some of these highly prestigious words is often not directly obvious to the average speaker of English, and thus, their meaning has to be learned. For example, the adjective *visible*, meaning "able to be seen" has no direct association to the verb to *see*, and therefore the link between these two has to be established by learning. Gramley therefore calls such words as *visible* "hard words." Those loans, especially some from Greek and Latin, which are felt to be pretentious or/and obscure by the average speaker of English are found to be denoted as "ink-horn terms."

Amongst the above mentioned reasons for borrowing from foreign languages, the most obvious and maybe also the most profound one is the introduction of new concepts for which there are no suitable words in the task language. Concerning this, Katamba writes that at various periods in world history different civilizations have been pre-eminent in one field or another (like for example sciences, trade, military, and medicine). According to him, the normal course of development was then that the language of this civilization became the lingua franca for that specific field during the period of their pre-eminence. This is also reflected by the concentration of borrowings in certain semantic fields from that language to others. In the middle Ages, the Arabic world was advanced in many sciences and thus, a lot of words have been passed on during this time to other languages and also to English. Some of the best known examples are *alchemy*, *alcohol*, and *algebra*. Many of those Arabic terms have not been borrowed directly into English, but were gradually passed on to English from other languages. Katamba mentions the typical way that many scientific Arabic words took. English often acquired them from French, which took them over from Spanish and Spanish finally had borrowed them directly from Arabic.

What gets obvious here is a very basic distinction that can be made between borrowings. Direct borrowing is when a language takes over a term directly from another language. The English word *omelette* is an example for direct borrowing because it has been taken over from French (French: *omelette*) directly, without any major phonological or orthographical changes. In contrast to that, indirect borrowing takes place when a certain word is passed on from the source language to another (as a direct borrowing), and then from that language is handed over to another and from this one maybe even to another. This process may go hand in hand with the development that the word, each time it is passed on from one language to another, is adjusted phonologically/orthographically to make it fit to the phonological/ orthographical system of the recipient language. The Turkish word *kahveh* has been passed on to Arabic as *kahva*, from there the Dutch borrowed it as *koffie* and finally it was taken over by the English in the form coffee. In this context, Katamba reminds us that there is danger of misunderstandings or alternations in the meaning, the more indirect a term is borrowed. In English there exists the term *howitzer* ("light gun"). It entered the language from Dutch and they had borrowed it from the Czech original *houfnice* which means "catapult."

To complicate matters even further, there is another distinction between the kinds of borrowings, i.e. the distinction between loan words and loanshifts. Most of the examples discussed above are loan words. That means, they have been imported/ adopted from another language, either directly or indirectly, and might have undergone phonological/ orthographical changes.

Loanshifts (loan translations/ calques) on the other side are formed in a quite different way. Here the borrowing is done by translating the vocabulary item or rather its meaning into the receiving language. Such a loanshift is the German word *Übermensch* which has been translated into English as Superman. Moreover, the term loan word itself is a loan translation from the German *Lehnwort*.

Generally, it has to be remarked, as Ball does, that the borrowing of a word into another language is always a gradual process which takes quite some time. This gradual might even lead to the result that foreign words which are borrowed become "nativised," in the case of English then "anglicised." Thus, they then become indistinguishable from indigenous English terms or as Jespersen has put it so nicely, with a quotation full of Norse loan words which a native speaker of English would not detect as foreign elements: "An Englishman cannot thrive or die or be ill without Scandinavian words; they are to the language what bread and eggs are to the daily fare."

Text B   Loan Word

At present there are around 6000 languages spoken in the world and every language has its own distinct vocabulary containing thousands of words. Speakers of each of these languages are in contact with others who speak different languages. It has been found that when languages come into contact, there is transfer of linguistic items from one language to another due to the borrowing of words. Expansion in vocabulary where new words enter a language is a natural consequence of language contact situations. Speakers learn words that are not in their native language, and very frequently, they tend to be fond of some of the words in other languages and "borrow" them for their own use.

According to Hock, "the term 'borrowing' refers to the adoption of individual words or even large sets of vocabulary items from another language or dialect." This process is called borrowing although the lending language does not lose its word, nor does the borrowing language return the word. A better term might be "copying" but "borrowing" has long been established in this sense and words that are borrowed are called loan words.

According to Kachru who is one of the experts in the area of contact linguistics, there are essentially two hypotheses about the motivations for the lexical borrowing in languages. One is termed the "deficit hypothesis" and the other one is the "dominance hypothesis." In the words of Kachru, "the deficit hypothesis presupposes that borrowing entails linguistic 'gaps' in a language and the prime motivation for borrowing is to remedy the linguistic 'deficit,' especially in the lexical resources of a language." This means that many words are borrowed from other languages because there are no equivalents in a particular borrowing language. For example, one will need to borrow words when s/he needs to refer to objects, people or creatures which are peculiar in certain places, which do not exist in his/her own environment and is not significant in the lives of his/her community, so no names have been given to refer to those things. Examples of such words are *kookaburra* (a kind of animal) that English has borrowed from a native Australian language—Wiradhuri, and *chipmunk*, from Alqonquian—an Amerindian language. Lexical borrowing also applies to cultural terms relating to food, dress, music, etc. peculiar to certain groups of people. English has borrowed musical terms from Italian such as soprano and tempo, culinary terms from French including casserole, fricassee, au gratin, puree and sauté. Conversely, some other languages have borrowed English words relating to entertainment, sports and words regarding Western culture. The Czech language has borrowed a lot of English sports terms such as "football," "hockey" and "tennis." Japanese has borrowed the words "baseball," "table tennis," and "gol" ... The women's magazines in Japan have borrowed English terms for cosmetics and modern fashion. Words are also borrowed for new concepts and ideas for which there are no local equivalents. This especially happens when a particular concept is introduced in a particular country. For example, some mathematical concepts such as algebra and algorithm were introduced by the Arabs. Glasnost was taken into English from Russian a few years ago to denote the new political and social climate initiated by President Gorbachov in the former USSR. This borrowing is seen in education and specialized areas also.

In Higa's view, the "dominance hypothesis" presupposes that when two cultures come into contact, the direction of culture learning and subsequent word-borrowing is not mutual, but from the dominant to the subordinate. The borrowing is not necessarily done to fill lexical gaps. Many words are borrowed and used even though there are native equivalents because they seem to have prestige. This is the case in a prolonged socio-cultural interaction between the ruling countries and the countries governed. An example of the dominance hypothesis is when in the past, the English used to borrow a lot of words from the languages of their colonizers, particularly from French. Later, when the English became very powerful, they colonized many other countries around the world. The people from these countries borrowed English words into their languages. At present, since the English speaking countries have become advanced, and the English language is one of the most influential languages of the world, English lends words to other languages more than it borrows. This contact between a language and English is termed "Englishization."

The number of loan words or the domains the loan words are from is determined by the degree of influence a language has on another language. For example, in the Philippines, there are more loan words from Spanish compared to English since the country was once colonized by Spain. The words from Spanish have influence in religion, social organization, law and government. In Malaysian history, Hinduism was the religious belief of Malays before Islamic spread to the Malay Empire. This explains the Indian influence where there are many loan words from Tamil and Sanskrit in Bahasa Melayu. After the arrival of Islam, a lot of Arabic words were borrowed for religious use. English is the third most important influence on Malay after Sanskrit and Arabic. English was imported to Malaysia through colonization, especially in the education system where the medium of instruction has been in English. Then, the early post-independence period focused on introducing and implementing Malay as the national language and medium of instruction in schools. The medium of instruction from primary up to tertiary level in the Malay language had to be fully established if the language was to be capable of functioning as a medium of teaching. Therefore, it needed to be modernized in order to create a scientific and technical discourse for the Malay language. Its vocabulary had to be widened so that new ideas in various specialized fields including science and technology could be expressed by borrowing or adjusting English phonemes, morphemes, phrases or sentences to be inserted within the Malay language. The policy of changing the medium of instruction from English to Malay has forced translation (mainly from English into Malay) to the forefront as it was crucial that science and technological information and information from other specialized areas be made available in Malay. This is when the borrowing of English words into Bahasa Melayu began. When there were no Malay equivalents for some of the English words, the words were left without being translated and instead, were borrowed for academic use. Examples of English loan words in Bahasa Melayu are petroleum, diesel, zink, elektronik, telekomunikasi, debit, kredit, invois, import, eksport, birokrasi, korporat, insentif, ego, kaunseling, etc. Such adaptation led to the expansion of the Malay vocabulary and this was given the most attention by the language planning committee. The Terminology Committee was set up to deal with the introduction of foreign words into Malay.

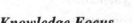

After You Read

Knowledge Focus

1. **Solo Work: Tell whether the following statements are true or false according to the knowledge you learned.**

    1) There are only few reasons for a language such as English to borrow words from other languages.

    2) Borrowing seems to be the easiest solution to finding a term for an unfamiliar thing, animal, or cultural device.

    3) Bilingual speakers use a foreign element in their speech to make a statement about their own identity.

    4) People would only borrow words from other languages when believing the prestige of either the device/object for which the denotation is taken over or the language, from which the term comes.

5) A lot of scientific words have been passed on during this time to English and also other languages due to the Roman advance in many sciences in the Middle Ages.

6) A loan word is done by translating the vocabulary item or rather its meaning into the receiving language.

7) The "deficit hypothesis" presupposes that when two cultures come into contact, the direction of culture learning and subsequent word-borrowing is not mutual, but from the dominant to the subordinate.

8) The degree of influence a language has on another language determines the number of loan words or the domains the loan words are from.

2. Pair Work: Do the following tasks with your partner.

1) List possible languages from which the English language has borrowed words.
2) Explain the reasons for word borrowing presented in Text A.
3) Define and illustrate direct and indirect borrowing in your own words.
4) Make a contrast between loan words and loanshifts.
5) Explain the two hypotheses about the motivations for the lexical borrowing in languages.
6) Compare and contrast the reasons for word borrowing stated in Text A and text B.
7) Make a statement about the influence on Philippines and Malaysia from other cultures in tenus of loan words.
8) Talk about the cultural contact between China and the UK through loan words.

Language Focus
1. Fill in the blanks with the words or expressions you have learned in the texts.

| manifold | neologism | denotation | pretentious |
| orthographical | culinary | implement | equivalent |

1) Import restraints are _____ to a sales tax and often apply to necessities.

2) He is a talented but _____ writer.

3) During the festival this year, a bigwig of the Singapore Tourism Board boldly declared its new mission — make Singapore a world _____ capital.

4) But the American phrase "grown man" leaves out the preposition and this _____ is now taking hold in Britain.

5) They must _____ reforms to reduce distortions, improve the allocation of resources, and increase domestic savings.

6) Hyponymy in semantics is related to _____ and connotation in logics.

7) The present paper suggested that developmental dyslexic children have no deficit in

representation of the whole character.

8) They are always quiet, always cheerful, comfortable, and appreciative of life and its _____ blessings.

2. Cloze: Choose the word that best completes each sentence.

Loan words are words 1) _____ by the speakers of one language from a different language (the source language). A loan word can also be called a borrowing. The abstract noun "borrowing" refers to the process of speakers adopting words from a source language into their native language. "Loan" and "borrowing" are of course 2) _____, because there is no literal lending process. There is no transfer from one language to another, and no 3) "_____" words to the source language. They simply 4) _____ to be used by a speech community that speaks a 5) _____ language from the one they originated in.

Borrowing is a 6) _____ of cultural contact between two language communities. Borrowing of words can go in both directions between the two languages in contact, but often there is an 7) _____, such that more words go from one side to the other. In this case the 8) _____ language community has some advantage of power, prestige and/or wealth that makes the objects and ideas it brings desirable and useful 9) _____ the borrowing language community. For example, the Germanic tribes in the first few centuries A.D. adopted 10) _____ loan words from Latin as they adopted new products via trading with the Romans. Few Germanic words, on the other hand, passed into Latin.

The actual process of borrowing is complex and involves many 11) _____ events (i.e. instances of use of the new word). Generally, some speakers of the borrowing language know the source language too, or at least enough of it to utilize the relevant words. They adopt them 12) _____ speaking the borrowing language. If they are 13) _____ in the source language, which is often the case, they might pronounce the words the same or similar to the way they are pronounced in the source language. For example, English speakers adopted the word garage from French, at first with a pronunciation 14) _____ to the French pronunciation than is now usually found. 15) _____ the very first speakers who used the word in English knew at least some French and heard the word used by French speakers.

1) A. adopted   B. adapted
    C. acclimatized   D. accommodated
2) A. similes   B. metaphors
    C. puns   D. hyperboles
3) A. lending   B. borrowing
    C. returning   D. loaning
4) A. come   B. begin
    C. start   D. arise

5) A. identical   B. same
   C. different   D. approximate
6) A. sequence   B. consequence
   C. symbol   D. sign
7) A. symmetry   B. asymmetry
   C. proportion   D. balance
8) A. resource   B. lending
   C. target   D. source
9) A. with   B. at
   C. to   D. in
10) A. numerous   B. few
    C. some   D. several
11) A. usable   B. utility
    C. usage   D. used
12) A. before   B. after
    C. when   D. as
13) A. monolingual   B. bilingual
    C. multilingual   D. nonliterate
14) A. nearer   B. further
    C. more adjacent   D. more remote
15) A. Assumedly   B. Consumedly
    C. Certainly   D. Presumably

Comprehensive Work

1. Research Work

A lot of English words or expressions have come into Chinese. Do a survey on what English expressions are used, who use them and when and where.

2. Writing Practice

Nobody can deny the existence of so many Chinese loan words in Japanese, Korean, and Vietnam. Search the information in the library or on the Internet and study the creation and development of these Chinese loan words. Write an article and explore the cultural contact behind China and other Asian countries.

3. Translation: Translate the following passage into Chinese.

Borrowing words from foreign languages through transliteration or semantic translation is an international norm. English has borrowed words from Chinese. Tea, coolie and kungfu are older examples, whilst guanxi (connection) and taikongnaut (astronaut) are more recent additions. In no situation have I ever seen, nor do I expect ever to see, Chinese characters jumbled into the English text of an official document or a serious publication in Britain or the United States. They are always spelled out in pinyin or using the Roman alphabet.

But some Chinese texts reproduce foreign words without translating them into Chinese, a worrisome trend, which, if it continues, will jeopardize the integrity of Chinese characters. It is understandable that in the early days of China's Reform and Opening Up some Chinese publications directly quoted a few English words so as to reflect readiness to learn from the outside world: given the circumstances then such a practice could indicate China's progress. It is also understandable if an editor is unable to find an appropriate translation before the press deadline and has to resort to inserting the original foreign word into the Chinese text. However, we cannot isolate our judgments from the context of a particular time. What is fashionable today looks the opposite tomorrow. U.S. President Truman posing with a pipe in his mouth and President Kennedy with a cigarette in his hand were seen as smart back in their time, but President Obama, also a smoker, is never seen smoking in public because to do so is thought unacceptable today.

Read More

Text C   How Languages Influence Each Other

Languages, like cultures, are rarely sufficient by themselves. The necessities of intercourse bring the speakers of one language into direct or indirect contact with those of neighboring or culturally dominant languages. The intercourse may be friendly or hostile. It may move on the humdrum plane of business and trade relations or it may consist of a borrowing or interchange of spiritual goods—art, science, religion. It would be difficult to point to a completely isolated language or dialect, least of all among the primitive peoples. The tribe is often so small that intermarriages with alien tribes that speak other dialects or even totally unrelated languages are not uncommon. It may even be doubted whether intermarriage, intertribal trade, and general cultural interchanges are not of greater relative significance on primitive levels than on our own. Whatever the degree or nature of contact between neighboring peoples, it is generally sufficient to lead to some kind of linguistic interinfluencing. Frequently the influence runs heavily in one direction. The language of a people that is looked upon as a center of culture is naturally far more likely to exert an appreciable influence on other languages spoken in its vicinity than to be influenced by them. Chinese has flooded the vocabularies of Korean, Japanese, and Annamite for centuries, but has received nothing in return. In the western Europe of medieval and modern times French has exercised a similar, though probably a less overwhelming, influence. English borrowed an immense number of words from the French of the Norman invaders, later also from the court French of Isle de France, appropriated a certain number of affixed elements of derivational value (e.g., -ess of princess, -ard of drunkard, -ty of royalty), may have been somewhat stimulated in its general analytic drift by contact with French, and even allowed French to modify its phonetic pattern slightly (e.g., initial v and j in words like veal and judge; in words of Anglo-Saxon origin v and j can only occur after vowels, e.g., over, hedge). But English has exerted practically no influence on French.

The simplest kind of influence that one language may exert on another is the "borrowing" of words. When there is cultural borrowing there is always the likelihood that the associated words may be borrowed too. When the early Germanic peoples of northern Europe first learned of wine-culture and of paved streets from their commercial or warlike contact with the Romans, it was only natural that they should adopt the Latin words for the strange beverage (vinum, English wine, German Wein) and the unfamiliar type of road (strata [via], English street, German Strasse). Later, when Christianity was introduced into England, a number of associated words, such as bishop and angel, found their way into English. And so the process has continued uninterruptedly down to the present day, each cultural wave bringing to the language a new deposit of loan words. The careful study of such loan words constitutes an interesting commentary on the history of culture. One can almost estimate the role which various peoples have played in the development and spread of cultural ideas by taking note of the extent to which their vocabularies have filtered into those of other peoples. When we realize that an educated Japanese can hardly frame a single literary sentence without the use of Chinese resources, that to this day Siamese and Burmese and Cambodian bear the unmistakable imprint of the Sanskrit and Pali that came in with Hindu Buddhism centuries ago, or that whether we argue for or against the teaching of Latin and Greek our argument is sure to be studded with words that have come to us from Rome and Athens, we get some inkling of what early Chinese culture and Buddhism and classical Mediterranean civilization have meant in the world's history. There are just five languages that have had an overwhelming significance as carriers of culture. They are classical Chinese, Sanskrit, Arabic, Greek, and Latin. In comparison with these even such culturally important languages as Hebrew and French sink into a secondary position. It is a little disappointing to learn that the general cultural influence of English has so far been all but negligible. The English language itself is spreading because the English have colonized immense territories. But there is nothing to show that it is anywhere entering into the lexical heart of other languages as French has colored the English complexion or as Arabic has permeated Persian and Turkish. This fact alone is significant of the power of nationalism, cultural as well as political, during the last century. There are now psychological resistances to borrowing, or rather to new sources of borrowing, that were not greatly alive in the Middle Ages or during the Renaissance.

Are there resistances of a more intimate nature to the borrowing of words? It is generally assumed that the nature and extent of borrowing depend entirely on the historical facts of culture relation; that if German, for instance, has borrowed less copiously than English from Latin and French it is only because Germany has had less intimate relations than England with the culture spheres of classical Rome and France. This is true to a considerable extent, but it is not the whole truth. We must not exaggerate the physical importance of the Norman invasion nor underrate the significance of the fact that Germany's central geographical position made it peculiarly sensitive to French influences all through the Middle Ages, to humanistic influences in the latter fifteenth and early sixteenth centuries, and again to the powerful French influences of the seventeenth and eighteenth centuries. It seems very probable that the psychological attitude of the borrowing language itself towards linguistic material has much to do with its receptivity to foreign words. English has long been striving for the completely unified, unanalyzed word, regardless of whether it is monosyllabic or polysyllabic. Such words as credible, certitude, intangible are entirely welcome in English because each represents a unitary, well-nuanced idea and because their formal analysis (cred-ible, cert-itude, in-tang-ible) is not a necessary act of the unconscious mind (cred-, cert-, and tang- have no real existence in English comparable to that of good- in goodness). A word like intangible, once it is acclimated, is nearly as simple a psychological entity as any radical monosyllable (say vague, thin, grasp). In German, however, polysyllabic words strive to analyze themselves into significant elements. Hence vast numbers of French and Latin words, borrowed at the height of certain cultural influences, could not maintain themselves in the language. Latin-German words like kredibel "credible" and French-German words like reussieren "to succeed" offered nothing that the unconscious mind could assimilate to its customary method of feeling and handling words. It is as though this unconscious mind said: "I am perfectly willing to accept kredibel if you will just tell me what you mean by kred-." Hence German has generally found it easier to create new words out of its own resources, as the necessity for them arose.

Questions for Discussion

1. What bring the speakers of one language into direct or indirect contact with those of neighboring or culturally dominant languages?
2. What is the simplest kind of influence that one language may exert on another?
3. How can we estimate the role which various peoples have played in the development and spread of cultural ideas?
4. Which five languages have had an overwhelming significance as carriers of culture?
5. What does the nature and extent of borrowing depend entirely on?

Text D Contact Explanations and Internal Explanations of Change

Let us turn now to a consideration of some major predictors of linguistic change — not predictors in an absolute sense of predicting that change will occur, but predictors in the sense of conditions under which certain kinds of change can take place. The major (general) social factors that are relevant for predicting the effects of contact-induced change are the presence versus the absence of imperfect learning, intensity of contact, and speakers' attitudes. Of these, the first will not be relevant for internal explanations of change, because the agents of internally motivated change are native speakers of the changing language, or nonnative speakers who have native-like fluency in the changing language, or incipient native speakers (if children produce innovations during the process of first-language acquisition). This is true both of the original innovator(s) of a novel linguistic feature and of those who participate in the spread of the innovation through a speech community.

The presence or absence of imperfect learning by a group of people is, however, a major predictor of the outcome of contact-induced change. Here is a brief characterization of the contrasting expectations. When the agents of change are fluent speakers of the receiving language, the first and predominant interference features are lexical items belonging to the nonbasic vocabulary; later, under increasingly intense contact conditions, structural features and basic vocabulary may also be transferred from one language to the other. The only major type of exception to this prediction is found in communities where lexical borrowing is avoided for cultural reasons; in such communities, structural interference may occur with little or no lexical transfer. The prediction for the outcome of contact situations in which one group of speakers shifts to another language, and fails to learn it fully, stands in sharp contrast to a situation in which imperfect learning plays no role: in shift-induced interference, the first and predominant interference features are phonological and syntactic; lexical interference lags behind, and in some cases few or no lexical items are transferred from the shifting group's original language to their version of the target language. Here too there is a class of potential exceptions. If the shifting group is a superstrate rather than a substrate population, then there may be a large number of transferred lexical items. (But it is doubtful that the famous case of the shift by Norman French speakers to English in England ca. 1200 CE, which is often cited as a prime example of superstrate shift, belongs in this category: by the time of the shift, the Norman French speakers in England were almost certainly fully bilingual, so that imperfect learning in fact played no role in the process of shift.)

The second social factor that affects contact-induced change, intensity of contact, is relevant to both of these general types of contact-induced change. Where imperfect learning plays no role, intensity of contact is typically derived from things like the duration of contact and the level of bilingualism in the receiving-language speech community. The longer the contact period and the greater the level of bilingualism, the more likely it is that structural features will be transferred along with lexical items. In shift-induced interference, intensity has to do with such factors as the relative sizes of the populations speaking the source and receiving languages, the degree of access to the target language by the shifting group, and the length of time over which the shift occurs: if there are many more shifting speakers than original target-language speakers, if the shifting group has only limited access to the target language, and if the shift occurs abruptly, a relatively large amount of shift-induced interference is likely. In the opposite situation, little or no shift-induced interference can be expected.

A typical example of the former type is the variety of English of a community of Yiddish speakers in the United States. In this community, Yiddish-speaking immigrants learned English, but Yiddish was their first language and remained their main language. Their contact with native English speakers was somewhat limited; within their community, they were certainly the majority; and they learned English as a second (or third, or ...) language rather abruptly. As a result, their English displayed moderate lexical interference but strong phonological and morphosyntactic interference from Yiddish, their first language. (These immigrants did not in fact shift from Yiddish to English; they remained Yiddish-dominant bilinguals throughout their lifetimes.) Ironically, given its reputation as an extreme case of (superstrate) shift-induced interference, the structural influence of Norman French on English illustrates the opposite set of conditions: between 1066 and ca. 1200, when the Normans finally shifted entirely to English in England, they were always vastly outnumbered by English speakers, and their access to English as spoken by native speakers was apparently unlimited. Nor was their shift to English abrupt; as noted above, by the time it occurred, the Norman population in England had apparently long been bilingual. Structural interference of French on English is quite modest, especially compared to the huge number of French loan words.

One complication here is that a significant amount of shift-induced interference is sometimes found in a long-term contact situation in which imperfect learning was important early on, but then bilingualism was established and maintained for a considerable period of time: the shifting group's version of the target language was fixed at a time when the level of bilingualism was low among members of the shifting group, and (possibly for attitudinal reasons: see below) it never converged toward the target language as spoken by the original target-language speech community. An example is the French spoken in the (originally) Breton community of Ile de Groix, France: as of 1970, only the oldest inhabitants were fluent speakers of Breton, but the French spoken in the community was heavily influenced by Breton in both structure and vocabulary.

Intensity of contact is a factor in internally motivated change if (and only if) we include under "contact" processes of person-to-person transmission of variants within a single speech community — that is, the spread of an innovation. The concept of social networks, as developed in e.g. Milroy 1987, is of obvious relevance here: the idea is that variants spread through networks, and close-knit social networks characterized by intense contact among the participants can facilitate the spread of innovations. Intensity of contact of course plays no role in the initial innovation of an internally motivated change; it can be relevant only for the spread of a change.

The third general social predictor, speakers' attitudes, is certainly relevant both in contact-induced change and in internally motivated change. This is admittedly a very vague notion, but it is difficult to make it precise — and equally difficult, unfortunately, to prove that it has affected the course of language history. Speakers may or may not be aware of the attitudinal factors that help to shape their linguistic choices, and historical linguists are (of course) unable to establish speakers' attitudes except in the tiny handful of instances in which metalinguistic comments on innovations are found in old documents. To take just one of many frustrating examples, a striking areal feature of at least some parts of the Pacific Northwest Sprachbund is an avoidance of loan words from French and English, the European languages with which the indigenous peoples first came into contact. In Montana Salish, for instance, there are hardly any English (or French) loan words, in spite of massive cultural assimilation to European-derived culture; a similar situation obtains in Nez Perce, an unrelated language whose speakers have long had close contact with Salishan tribes. The two tribes have instead constructed descriptive words from native morphemes to name items imported from Anglo culture, as in the Montana Salish word for "automobile," *p'ip'úyUn*, literally "it has wrinkled feet" (so named because of the appearance of tire tracks), and the Nez Perce word for "telephone," *cewcew'in'es*, literally "a thing for whispering." Modern elders, when asked by young tribal members how they would say (for example) "television set" in Salish, make up comparable words on the spot; but when asked why they don't just use the English word with a Salish pronunciation, they don't know — they merely shrug and say that's how it is. In other words, the reason for this culturally determined pattern of lexical innovation is unknown to current tribal members, and was possibly never a conscious avoidance pattern.

The clearest examples of speakers' attitudes as a cause of change therefore come from cases of deliberate change (though even here it is often impossible to prove that a change was made with full conscious intent). Some of these are internally motivated, at least in the sense that no direct language contact was involved; others are externally motivated, according to the definition of contact-induced change given above. Language planning is one prominent source of internally motivated deliberate changes. For instance, the twentieth-century Estonian language reformer Johannes Aavik introduced hundreds of new words and a sizable number of morphosyntactic features into Estonian, and many of these became permanently fixed in the language. Several striking examples of contact-induced changes that must be explained by speakers' attitudes come from situations in which a speech community wishes to distinguish its language, or more likely its dialect, more sharply from its neighbors' speech. Changes range from lexical substitution in certain languages of Papua New Guinea, to reversal of gender assignments, also in Papua

New Guinea, to phonological distortion of words in Lambayeque Quechua in Peru, and to a combination of the first and third of these types of change in Mokki, a language of Baluchistan that was created by lexical substitutions and distortions. Lexical substitutions are also found, of course, in teenage slang, which is usually (at least in the United States) a product of internally motivated lexical innovation.

A consideration of social predictors of externally and internally motivated language change could be extended to more fine-grained social factors, but the very general factors discussed here provide a good overall comparative picture of external and internal explanatory social factors. One of the three categories, speakers' attitudes, seems to be equally effective in internal and external causation. A second, intensity of contact, is very important to both innovation and spread of an innovation in contact-induced change, but it is relevant only to the spread of an innovation in internally motivated change. The third category, the differential effects of interference depending on whether or not imperfect learning played a role, is relevant only for contact-induced change.

Questions for Discussion

1. According to the author, what are the major predictors of linguistic change?
2. Make a contrast between contact situations in which one group of speakers shifts to another language, and fails to learn it fully and a contact situation in which imperfect learning plays no role.
3. Explain the role played by intensity of contact in language change.
4. Which point is stated through the example of Norman French influence on English?
5. State your understanding of social predictors of externally and internally motivated language change.

Unit 5   English Idioms

> I do not believe in pure idioms. I think there is naturally a desire, for whoever speaks or writes, to sign in an idiomatic, irreplaceable manner.
>
> ——Jacques Derrida

Unit Goals

- To understand the meaning and usage of English idioms
- To discuss the origins of English idioms
- To explore the relationship between idioms and culture

 **Before You Read**

1. The followings are some of the most common idioms in English.

   a. Please choose the correct meaning from the list on the right.

1) be par for the course	a. find compromises
2) give the game away	b. make people feel relaxed with each other
3) give and take	c. do something in a way that will give good results
4) have it in for sb.	d. choose what you want
5) know sth. inside out	e. be determined to hurt or criticize sb.
6) break the ice	f. spoil a secret surprise or joke
7) take your pick	g. know everything about a subject
8) be on the right track	h. happen as you would expect

   b. Fill the gaps in these sentences with the idioms in Exercise a.

   1) A: Which one can I have? B: _____.

   2) The train was half an hour late but I suppose that's _____, isn't it?

   3) They weren't very talkative at first, then someone told a joke and that really _____.

   4) You have to _____ in these situations. There's always an element of compromise.

   5) A: Peter's going to be there and there's going to be a band and you'll never guess ...

B: Oh don't say anything else. You'll _____.

6) You could ask Emma. She can recite most of the words in the film. She _____.

7) We've got all the answers right so far so it looks as though we _____.

8) My boss _____. She's constantly criticizing my work even when someone else has praised it.

2. **Religion is an important aspect of life. In Chinese and English there are idioms derived from Buddhism and Christianity/Greek myths respectively. Search in the dictionary or the library to fill up the following forms.**

Chinese idioms from Buddhism	English idioms from Christianity/Greek myths
借花献佛 佛眼相看 不看僧面看佛面 _____ _____ …	Judas' kiss a Pandora's box the lost lamb _____ _____ …

3. **Find five English idioms in your dictionary. Try to work out their origins by searching on the Internet or in the library. Share your findings with your classmates.**

English Idiom	Its Origins

Start to Read

Text A Understanding Idioms

Idioms are fixed expressions that are typically used in a figurative sense. For example, in the sentence *Exams are part of a carrot and stick method*, there are obviously no real carrots and sticks involved. The image is that of a donkey being encouraged to move forward by dangling a carrot in front of it or by hitting it with a stick. We can use this idiom to describe any event that involves more abstract rewards (the carrot) and threats (the stick). All languages are full of idioms, and native speakers use them spontaneously without even thinking about their figurative nature. Language learners generally find idioms hard to understand, and this is not surprising. For example, learners are often not sure what image the idiom is based on. If a native speaker proposes to *show you the ropes* and you are not familiar with this expression, you might not immediately understand that she is proposing to teach you how to do a certain job. It would help if you knew that the expression was originally used in the context of sailing, where an experienced sailor had to show a novice how to handle the ropes on a boat.

Are Idioms Arbitrary?

Linguists used to believe that idioms were completely arbitrary: that is, you could not guess their meaning from the words they consist of. Consequently, teachers used to tell their students that the only way to master idioms was to learn them by heart. Fortunately, we now know that many idioms can be explained after all, and so they can be learned in systematic ways. Research tells us that when idioms are presented as non-arbitrary features of language, students find them much easier to understand and remember. In the following sections we will demonstrate the non-arbitrary nature of idioms.

Why Idioms Mean What They Mean

Many idioms are derived from our general physical experiences. For example, the expressions *hot under the collar*, *breathe fire*, and *let off steam* all refer to being angry, and they do this through the image of anger as something hot inside us. This makes sense to us, because when people get angry they often get red in the face as a result of rising body temperature. Similarly, the figurative expressions *lend someone a hand*, *try your hand at something*, and *have your hands tied* all use the image of the hand to refer to performing an action. This also makes sense, because we know from everyday experience that most activities involve the use of our hands.

Other idioms are derived from more specific areas of experience (or domains), such as sport, war, or cooking. Some of these domains may no longer be common in present-day life, but if we learn the original context in which the idiom was used and if we understand the image it is based on, we will find it is easier to understand. A helpful way of remembering idioms is to group them according to the domain that they are derived from, as follows:

Idioms Derived from Sailing:

clear the decks	to first finish a job completely
a leading light	a good example to follow
be on an even keel	to make calm, steady progress

Idioms Derived from War:

stick to your guns	to refuse to change your opinion
fight a losing battle	to be unlikely to succeed
be in the front line	to have an important role

Idioms Derived from Entertainment (the Theatre, the Circus, etc.):

behind the scenes	in secret
waiting in the wings	ready to act when needed
a balancing act	a difficult compromise

If you recognize the origin of an idiom, you will often be able to work out its meaning on your own. For instance, the idiom *put something on the back burner* originates from the domain of cooking, and *take a back seat* comes from the domain of driving. Once you recognize these connections, it will be easier to understand sentences like these:

- *We put the project on the back burner.*
- *The students were working well together, so I decided to take a back seat.*

Idioms and Culture

In general, idioms that are derived from our physical experiences, such as those that associate anger with heat, show strong similarities across different cultures, and they tend to be fairly easy to understand. This is not surprising, because basic physical experiences (like being hot or cold, sick or well) are shared universally. This does not mean that these idioms can simply be translated word-for-word from one language to another: their precise form and wording will often differ across languages. Nevertheless, the general images are often the same.

On the other hand, idioms that are derived from more specific domains are likely to differ across cultures, even cultures that are closely related. That is because not all domains from which idioms are derived have been equally important in all cultures. For example, English is particularly rich in expressions that are derived from the domain of sailing, and this is hardly surprising when we consider England's long history as a seafaring nation. Another area where cultures differ is in the popularity of certain games and sports. English has a lot of idioms that are derived from the following domains:

Horse racing:

neck and neck	it is hard to say who will win
win hands down	to win easily
go off the rails	to go wrong, out of control

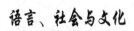

Gambling:

raise the ante	to increase the risk
hedge your bets	not to take any risks
pay over the odds	to pay too much

Card Games:

come up trumps	to perform unexpectedly well
follow suit	to do the same as others
not miss a trick	not to fail a single time

Running Contests:

jump the gun	to do something too soon
have the inside track	to have an advantage
quick off the mark	reaching quickly

Hunting:

don't beat about the bush	be direct, get to the point
it's open season on someone	it's a period to criticize someone
it's in the bag	success is certain

Using Idioms Effectively

An idiom derived from a "playful" domain like games or sports is more likely to be used in informal discourse than an idiom derived from a more serious domain, such as warfare. For example, *score an own goal* is likely to occur more often in informal discourse than *break ranks*.

An idiom typically evokes a scene that is part of a larger scenario. For example, a debate between two politicians can be described as if it were a boxing match, and — because English has many idioms derived from boxing — you can choose particular phrases to highlight a specific stage or aspect of the contest. So, before the actual debate starts, the two politicians may *flex their muscles* to frighten the opponent; during the debate one of them may carelessly *lower his guard* or bravely *stick his neck out* and perhaps *take it on the chin*; if the debate gets more intense the opponents will not *pull their punches*; if it seems that they really want to hurt each other, you can say that *the gloves are off*; and after a while one of them may be *on the ropes* (=close to defeat) and may finally admit defeat and *throw in the towel*.

Idioms and Sound Patterns

The above paragraphs help to explain the meaning and use of idioms, but they do not explain, for example, why we say *it takes two to tango* rather than "it takes two to waltz," nor why we say *go with the flow* rather than "go with the stream." Part of the answer lies in sound patterns. For example, up to 20% of English idioms are made up of words that alliterate (=use the same sound at the start of each word) or of words that rhyme. This is a useful fact to know, because alliteration (in idioms such as *through thick and thin*, *spick and span*, *below the belt*, *rule the roost*, *meet your match*) and rhyme (in idioms such as *an eager beaver*, *the name of the game*, *horses for courses*, *steer clear of*) can help you to remember expressions like these. Sound patterns are also at work in many common non-idiomatic expressions, such as compounds (e.g. *pickpocket*, *beer belly*); collocations (e.g. *tell the truth*, *wage war*); similes (e.g. *cool as a cucumber*, *fit as a fiddle*); proverbs (e.g. *curiosity killed the cat*, *where there's a will there's a way*); and many other phrases (e.g. *time will tell*, *from dawn till dusk*).

Word Order in Idioms

As we have seen, the meanings and the lexical makeup of idioms can often be explained in systematic ways. But what about **word order** in idioms of the form "X and Y"? For example, why do we say *give and take* rather than "take and give"? Here are some of the reasons why English idioms may choose one order of words rather than another:

1. The word order may be the most "logical," given the origin of the idiom. For example, in the expression *swallow something hook, line, and sinker*, the image is that of a fish that first swallows the bait on the hook of the fishing rod, and then swallows the line, and finally swallows even the sinker (=small heavy object that makes the line sink in the water). In short, the word order reflects the sequence of events in the literal scenario. So, recognition of the literal origin of the expression may help you to make sense of its word order. You may also want to try this with these idioms: *crash and burn*, *cut and dried*, and *signed and sealed*.

2. The word order may be the most "natural," because a flow of information tends to move from general to specific aspects. For example, the word order *alive and kicking* makes more sense than "kicking and alive," because kicking implies being alive. The first word creates a frame in which the second appears, as in *bread and butter* (you first need bread to put the butter on), *chapter and verse* (you first find the chapter and then the verse in that chapter), and *cloak and dagger* (you first only see the cloak and then — perhaps too late — the dagger).

3. The word order may sound best, because of its rhythm. English shows a preference for putting the longest word last (e.g. *part and parcel*, *belt and braces*, *rack and ruin*).

4. Finally, the word order may simply be the easiest to say. Compare which of the following pairs requires least movement of your tongue when you say them aloud: *it's raining cats and dogs* or "it's raining dogs and cats." You can also try this with *blood, sweat, and tears*; *home and dry*; *rough and tumble*; and, of course, *give and take*.

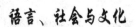

Conclusion

It should be clear that idioms are not as arbitrary as we used to think they were. We have shown here several aspects of idiomatic language — especially their source domains and the sound patterns they make — that can help us to tackle idioms in more systematic ways. And when we recognize the systems at work in a language, it becomes easier to understand, learn, and remember things.

After You Read

Knowledge Focus

1. **Solo Work:** Work out the meanings of the following idioms with the help of the dictionary, and then make a sentence with each of them. The first one is given as an example.

Idiom	Meaning	Sentence you make
carrot and stick	the use of both reward and punishment to induce cooperation	Exams are part of a carrot and stick method.
hot under the collar		
fight a losing battle		
win hands down		
flex one's muscles		
it takes two to tangle		
part and parcel		
bread and butter		
beat about the bush		
behind the scenes		

2. **Pair Work:** Discuss the following questions with your partner.

   1) What are idioms? Please give examples.
   2) What does the text mean by saying that idioms are arbitrary?
   3) Are idioms derived from our physical experiences? Beside the examples in the text, can you think of other idioms that are derived from our experiences?
   4) What are the major domains that many English idioms are derived from?
   5) Which of the three domains (sailing, entertainment, war) would you associate the following

idioms with? Please explain your reasons.

- take something on board
- close ranks
- steer clear of someone
- be centre stage
- a last-ditch effort
- the curtain comes down

6) Can idioms be translated word-for-word from one language to another? Why? Please give examples.

7) In what domains is English particularly rich in expressions and idioms? What about Chinese?

8) What sound pattern is frequently found in English idioms?

9) According to the text, why do English idioms choose one order of words rather than another?

10) What is a "logical" word order? Please give examples.

Language Focus

1. Fill in the blanks with the idioms/expressions you have learned in the text.

stick to one's guns	clear the decks
breathe the fire	neck and neck
cut and dried	hedge your bets
take a back seat	carrot and stick

1) I try to slow my heart down and _____ out of my lungs.

2) Sometimes I just have to resort to the _____ approach with my children.

3) If you feel that you're right, _____.

4) If we are going to dance, some of you can give me a hand to _____. Let's firstly shove the things out of the centre of the room.

5) Albert has decided to _____ now that his son is old enough to run the family business.

6) I don't know who is going to win this competition; I think we are running _____.

7) It is very important to _____ in any business, but investing in this enterprise is especially risky.

8) The plan is _____; nothing can stop it now.

2. Fill in the blanks with the proper form of the word in the brackets.

1) Most anarchist assassinations were bungled because of haste or _____ (spontaneous).
2) In criticism, it is essential to guard against subjectivism and _____ (arbitrary).
3) The final impression of her works is astonishing integrity and _____ (original).
4) The teacher laid emphasis on the _____ (precise) of the translation from the outset.
5) He wrote letters to his son with _____ (play) advice and the news of London.
6) The prosody of *Beowulf* is based on _____ (alliterate), not end rhymes.
7) You can't learn English well without watching out for _____ (idiom) ways of saying things.
8) The heart is a muscular organ that contracts _____ (rhythm).

3. Proofreading

The following passage contains TEN errors. Each line contains a maximum of ONE error. In each case, only ONE word is involved. You should proofread the passage and correct the errors in the following way:

For a wrong word, underline the wrong word and write the correct one in the blank provided at the end of the line.

For a missing word, mark the position of the missing word with a "∧" sign and write the word you believe to be missing in the blank provided at the end of the line.

For an unnecessary word, cross out the unnecessary word with a slash "/" and put the word in the blank provided at the end of the line.

Some years back I was invited to speak at a black-tie event for the French-American Chamber of Commerce at the Plaza Hotel in New York City. Because the audience would be primarily French nations, I was advised to avoid referring American idioms in my address. This is a fine kettle of fish, I thought while I sat down to purge my vocabulary of American idioms. What I was left at the end of the day was "Good evening," "Thank you" and a rented tuxedo.	1. _____ 2. _____ 3. _____ 4. _____ 5. _____
Imagine the audience's delight did I told them how I felt my butt was *fringed with noodles* (very lucky) to be there. These noodles, by the way, would be different from *hanging on my ears* — a Russian expression meaning, "I'm not pulling your leg."	6. _____ 7. _____

The French nationals gather at the Plaza clearly *had their butter, money for the butter and the woman who made it* (had it all). But, some of them also *had a glass up their noses* (one too many). No doubt I would have *had their posteriors banging on the ground* (laughing hysterically) if only I'd read Bhalla's guidebook.	8. _____
I'm Not Hanging Noodles on Your Ears does more than catalog humorous world idioms. It presents an often-confounding glimpse into the inner soul of foreign cultures. "Language most shows a man," the British playwright Ben Jonson once wrote. "Speak that I might see thee." But what I see when I hear that a Colombian who is hopeless in love has been *swallowed like a postman's sock*, or that *drowning the fish* in France is to lose by deliberate confusion? I have no idea when to use the phrase, but I can't wait to try it, even if I drown the fish in the attempt.	9. _____ 10. _____ 11. _____ 12. _____ 13. _____

Comprehensive Work

1. Discussions: Idioms and Culture

a. Idioms maintain close ties with people's life and the culture in which these idioms are created and used. Look at the following examples, and answer the questions that follow:

斩草除根	all at sea
揠苗助长	any port in a storm
顺藤摸瓜	half sea over
桃李满天下	in the same boat
雨后春笋	sink or swim
桃李满天下	to keep one's head above water
	...

Questions:

1) Examine the Chinese idioms above. Do they have anything in common? What domain of life are these idioms concerned with?

_____

2) Study the English idioms above. Do they also have something in common? What aspect of life are they concerned with?

_____

3) Compare Chinese idioms with English idioms. What message can you get from the comparison?

_____

4) Can you give more examples concerning the different cultural origins of Chinese and English idioms?

_____

2. Writing Practice

Do you think that idioms can be translated? What suggestions will you give for the translation of English idioms? Please write a composition in the following steps:

1) For the first part, write on your idea as to whether idioms are translatable or not. Give reasons or examples to illustrate your idea.

2) For the second part, give some suggestions for the translation of English idioms. You may also give examples in this part.

3) For the last part, give a natural conclusion to your composition.

3. Translation: Translate the following passage into Chinese.

When English speakers say someone "kicked the bucket," they don't literally mean a person put foot to pail. Instead, they're using an idiom, or an expression with a culturally specific meaning that's not contained in the words themselves.

Jag Bhalla's new book *I'm Not Hanging Noodles on Your Ears* provides a compendium of worldwide idioms. The book's title comes from a Russian expression meaning "I'm not pulling your leg," and though Bhalla hasn't found any Russians who know the source of this amusing image, he says that's not unusual when it comes to idioms.

Take, for instance, the English expression "let the cat out of the bag." The saying is actually left over from the 16th century, when unscrupulous salespeople sometimes tricked purchasers by putting a cat into a bag instead of a pig.

"If you didn't open the bag before you left the market, it would be too late to complain later," says Bhalla. "However, most modern English speakers have no idea that that is why we 'let the cat out of the bag.'"

Often, different cultures will come up with their own idioms to express the same idea. Where English speakers might accuse a hypocrite of being a "pot calling the kettle black," Arabic speakers would observe that "a camel cannot see its own hump."

And Bhalla adds that idioms can be a great indicator of what is important to a culture: "One of my favorite German ones, for example, attests to their great obsession with meat: 'To live the life of Riley' in German — to have a wonderful life, to live a life of luxury — is to 'live like a maggot in bacon.'"

Unit 5 English Idioms

Read More

Text B English Idioms

If you look up the word "idiom" in *Webster*, you will be given the following definition:

Idiom is an expression whose meaning is not predictable from the usual meanings of its constituent element as kick the bucket, hang one's head etc., or from the general grammatical rules of language, as the table round for the round table, and which is not a constituent of a larger expression of like characteristics.

This definition seems a bit dry and doesn't really tell anything about the function of idioms in English language.

English is a language particularly rich in idioms — those modes of expression peculiar to a language (or dialect) which frequently defy logical and grammatical rules. Without idioms English would lose much of its variety and humor both in speech and writing.

The background and etymological origins of most idioms is at best obscure. This is the reason why a study of differences between the idioms of American and British English is somewhat difficult. But it also makes the cases, where background, etymology and history are known, even more interesting. Some idioms of the "worldwide English" have first been seen in the works of writers like Shakespeare, Sir Walter Scott, Lewis Carroll or even in the paperbacks of contemporary novelists. An example of Shakespearian quotation can be found in the following sentence: "As a social worker, you certainly see the seamy side of life." Biblical references are also the source of many idioms. Sports terms, technical terms, legal terms, military slang and even nautical expressions have found their way to the everyday use of English language. Following are some examples of these, some used in either American or British English and some used in both:

"Having won the first two Tests, Australia is now almost certain to retain the Ashes." (Ashes is a British English idiom that is nowadays a well-established cricket term.)

"In his case the exception proves the rule." (A legal maxim — in full: "The exception proves the rule in cases not excepted." Widely used in both AmE and BrE.)

"To have the edge on/over someone." (This is originally American English idiom, now established in almost every other form of English, including BrE.)

"A happy hunting ground." (Place where one often goes to obtain something or to make money. Originally American English idiom from the *Red Indians' Paradise*.)

In the old days English idioms rarely originated from any other form of English than

British English. (French was also a popular source of idioms.) Nowadays American English is in this position. It is hard to find an AmE idiom that has not established itself in "worldwide English" (usually BrE). This is not the case with British English idioms which are not as widespread. It has to be remembered that it is hard to say which idioms are actively used in English and which are dying out or have already died. Idioms are constantly dying and new-ones are born.

Some idioms may have gone through radical changes in meaning. The phrase — There is no love lost between them — nowadays means that some people dislike one another. Originally, when there was only the British English form, it meant exactly the opposite. The shift in meaning is yet unexplained. All dialects of English have different sets of idioms and situations where a given idiom can be used. American English and British English may not, in this respect, be the best possible pair to compare because they both have been developing into the same direction, at least where written language is concerned, since the Second World War. The reason that there is so much American influence in British English is the result of the following:

- ◇ Magnitude of publishing industry in the U.S.
- ◇ Magnitude of mass media influence on a worldwide scale
- ◇ Appeal of American popular culture on language and habits worldwide
- ◇ International political and economic position of the U.S.

All these facts lead to the conclusion that new idioms usually originate in the U.S. and then become popular in so-called "worldwide English." This new situation is completely different from the birth of American English as a "variant" of British English. When America was still under the rule of the Crown, most idioms originated from British English sources. Of course there were American English expressions and idioms too, before American English could be defined as dialect of English. Some examples of these early American English idioms follow:

"To bark up the wrong tree." (Originally from raccoon-hunting in which dogs were used to locate raccoons up in trees.)

"Paddle one's own canoe." (This is an American English idiom of the late 18th Century and early 19th Century.)

Some of these early American idioms and expressions were derived from the speech of the American natives like the phrase that "someone speaks with a forked tongue" and the "happy hunting ground" above. These idioms have filtered to British English through centuries through books, newspapers and most recently through powerful mediums like radio, TV and movies.

Where was the turning point? When did American culture take the leading role and start shaping the English language and especially idiomatic expressions? There is a lot of argument on this subject. Most claim that the real turning point was the Second World War. This could be the case. During the War English-speaking nations were united against a common enemy and the U.S. took the leading role. In these few years and a decade after the War American popular culture first established itself in British English. Again new idioms were created and old ones faded away. The Second World War was the turning point in many areas in life. This may also be the case in the development of the English language.

In the old days the written language (novels, poems, plays and the *Bible*) was the source from which idioms were extracted. This was the case up until WWII. After the war new mediums had established themselves in English-speaking society, there was a channel for the American way of life and the popular culture of the U.S. TV, movies and nowadays the interactive medium have changed the English language more to the American English direction. Some people in the Europe speak the Mid-Atlantic English, halfway from the British English to American English.

The influence of American English can even be seen in other European languages. In Finland, we are adopting and translating AmE proverbs, idioms and expressions. It can be said that the spoken language has taken the leading role over the written and the only reason for this is TV and radio. Most proverbs and idioms that have been adopted to British English from American English are of spoken origin. This is a definite shift from the days before WWII. What will this development do to the English language? Will it decrease its value? This could be argued, but the answer would still be no. Languages develop and change. So is the case with English language and idioms.

How then does American English differ from British English in the use of idioms? There are no radical differences in actual use. The main differences are in the situations where idiomatic expressions are used. There have been many studies recently on this subject. American English adopts and creates new idioms at a much faster rate compared to British English. Also the idioms of AmE origin tend to spread faster and further. After it has first been established in the U.S., an American idiom may soon be found in other "variants" and dialects of English. Nowadays new British idioms tend to stay on the British Isles and are rarely encountered in the U.S. British idioms are actually more familiar to other Europeans or to the people of the British Commonwealth than to Americans, even though the language is same. The reason for all these facts is that Britain is not the world power it used to be and it must be said that the U.S. has taken the role of the leading nation in the development of language, media and popular culture. Britain just doesn't have the magnitude of media influence that the United States controls.

The future of idiomatic expressions in the English language seems certain. They are more and more based on American English. This development will continue through new mediums like the Internet and interactive mediums. It is hard to say what this will do to idioms and what kind of new idioms are created. This will be an interesting development to follow, and by no means does it lessen the humor, variety and color of English language.

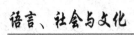

Language, Society and Culture

Questions for Discussion

1. Why is British English heavily influenced by American culture? Give examples.

2. When did American culture start to influence the English language and idiomatic expressions?

3. Are other European languages also influenced by American English?

4. What is the main difference between American English and British English in the use of idioms?

Text C Top Ten American Idioms and Their Origins

"And did we tell you the name of the game, boy; we call it riding the gravy train." Pink Floyd fans will undoubtedly recognize this like from the 1975 song "Have a Cigar." But what in the world does riding the gravy train mean? There are many idioms like this in use today that have interesting origins. Here's my top ten.

Riding the gravy train: "Gravy" has been slang for easy money since the early 1900s. In the 1920s railroad workers began using the phrase to describe a run with good pay and little work. Today the phrase also refers to living extravagantly while someone else foots the bill.

Dead ringer: Contrary to popular belief there isn't much evidence to prove that this phrase refers to bells with wires that went into graves, so that anyone mistakenly buried alive could ring the bell. A "dead ringer" was a look-alike horse that was substituted for a race horse in order to defraud bookies. Today the term is often used to identify an exact duplicate of something.

Scattered from here to breakfast: This phrase is sometimes heard as "scattered from hell to breakfast." The phrase may have originally been used in reference to cattle, suggesting they were spread out so far in the pastures that it would take all night to find them. Today the phrase often describes messes, meaning that a mess is so bad it would take all night to clean.

Straight from the horse's mouth: The best tips on horse races come from those closest to the horse — stable hands, trainers, etc. If one wanted the absolute best tip, one had to go a step better and get the tip directly from the horse.

Ace in the hole: In poker, when a card is dealt face down it is referred to as a hole. An ace is the most desirable card to have in this position, since it is hidden from other players. Today an "ace in the hole" is something akin to a secret weapon or a sure thing.

Lock, stock & barrel: The phrase means you have all of something. Originally the phrase referred to the parts of a musket — the barrel, the lock (firing mechanism), and the stock (wooden butt-end).

Can't hold a candle to...: Today the phrase means someone or something is lacking in comparison to another. Apprentices used to be expected to hold candles so that the craftsmen could see their work. If someone is unfit to do even this, they are not at all comparable to "the master."

Fast and loose: Originally this was a term in a card game designed to cheat customers. A customer was led to believe a certain card was stuck fast to the table, but the operator could easily free the card at the opportune time. Today the phrase means inconstant and unreliable.

Mad as a Hatter: It is possible that the mercury originally used in hat making caused some kind of madness in hatters (hat makers) but there isn't solid proof of this. In New Zealand, a hatter was a miner who worked alone. Since complete solitude can make some go mad, the phrase "mad as a hatter" came about. Today the phrase generally refers to any crazy person.

No dice: In the early 1900s gambling with dice was illegal in some states. There are documented cases of gamblers swallowing dice to get a case thrown out of court. No dice = no proof or conviction.

Fill in the blanks with the idioms that you've learned from the text.
1) I've been _____ all my life; it's about time I paid my dues.
2) I asked if we could go to the party, but Mom said _____.
3) She played _____ with the company's good name.
4) In speed and efficiency of delivery they cannot _____ their European competitors.
5) "Are you sure she's leaving?"
    "Definitely, I heard it _____."
6) Anyone who thinks the moon is made of green cheese must be _____.
7) His remarkable ability to always score the last point in the match is his team's _____
8) Has anyone ever told you are a _____ for Bill Clinton?

Unit 6   Metaphors and Thought

> The greatest thing by far is to be a master of metaphor.
> —Aristotle
>
> All slang is metaphor, and all metaphor is poetry.
> —Gilbert K. Chesterton

Unit Goals

- To understand the meaning and usage of English metaphors
- To discuss the relationship between metaphors and human thought
- To understand how our use of metaphors reflect the way we think and act

Before You Read

1. Understanding Metaphors

a. Metaphor is a figure of speech in which one object is compared to a similar other. Identify the two things being compared in each sentence and tell in what way they are alike.

1) The lake was a huge mirror in the moonlight.

_____

2) The playground became a lake after the thunderous rain.

_____

3) I am the glue that holds us together.

_____

b. Underline the sentences in the following list that are metaphors, and explain how the two items in each sentence are alike. Circle the two items being compared.

- *Jenny sings like a bird.*
- *Mary is a pack rat.*
- *We always go to the beach for vacation.*
- *The dancer moved around the stage like a spinning top.*

- As my sister ran to the room, my brother said, "Let's hide from her!"
- We could not persuade her to go with us.
- My friend is a stubborn mule.
- Our lawn is a green carpet from the fence to the street.

2. Creating Metaphors

The following table lists some of the things that the brain has been compared to and describes why they are similar to the brain. Create your own metaphors and fill in the blanks in the form.

The Brain is a...	Because it...
spider web	is delicate, hypersensitive, and connects many things. It responds instantly and simultaneously to outside events.
lamp	allows you to see things better.
mirror	can see things as others see it and see other things and oneself from all angles.
camera	
map	

3. Study the following sentences, especially the underlined words/expressions. What metaphorical images are used in these sentences?

Sentences with Metaphors	Metaphorical Image
1) Your claims are <u>indefensible</u>. 2) He <u>attacked</u> every weak point in my argument. 3) His criticisms were right on <u>target</u>. 4) I've never <u>won</u> an argument with him. 5) You disagree? Okay, <u>shoot</u>! 6) He <u>shot</u> down all of my arguments.	Argument is compared to _____.
1) You are wasting your time. 2) You need to budget your time. 3) Is that worth your while? 4) He's living on borrowed time. 5) I lost a lot of time when I got sick. 6) You don't use your time, profitably.	Time is compared to _____.

✧ For further discussion: What do these metaphors say about our culture's attitude towards argument (or time)?

Start to Read

Text A Metaphors We Live By

Is it true that all of us, not just poets, speak in metaphors, whether we realize it or not? Is it perhaps even true that we live by metaphors? In <u>Metaphors We Live By</u> *George Lakoff, a linguist, and Mark Johnson, a philosopher, suggest that metaphors not only make our thoughts more vivid and interesting but they actually structure our perceptions and understanding. Thinking of marriage as a "contract agreement," for example, leads to one set of expectations, while thinking of it as "team play," "a negotiated settlement," "Russian roulette," "an indissoluble merger," or "a religious sacrament" will carry different sets of expectations.* <u>Metaphors We Live By</u> *has led many readers to a new recognition of how profoundly metaphors not only shape our view of life in the present but set up the expectations that determine what life will be for us in the future.*

Metaphor is for most people device of the poetic imagination and the rhetorical flourish—a matter of extraordinary rather than ordinary language. Moreover, metaphor is typically viewed as characteristic of language alone, a matter of words rather than thought or action. For this reason, most people think they can get along perfectly well without metaphor. We have found, on the contrary, that metaphor is pervasive in everyday life, not just in language but in thought and action. Our ordinary conceptual system, in terms of which we both think and act, is fundamentally metaphorical in nature.

The concepts that govern our thought are not just matters of the intellect. They also govern our everyday functioning, down to the most mundane details. Our concepts structure what we perceive, how we get around in the world, and how we relate to other people. Our conceptual system thus plays a central role in defining our everyday realities. If we are right in

suggesting that our conceptual system is largely metaphorical, then the way we think what we experience, and what we do every day is very much a matter of metaphor.

But our conceptual system is not something we are normally aware of. In most of the little things we do every day, we simply think and act more or less automatically along certain lines. Just what these lines are is by no means obvious.

One way to find out is by looking at language. Since communication is based on the same conceptual system that we use in thinking and acting, language is an important source of evidence for what that system is like.

To give some idea of what it could mean for a concept to be metaphorical and for such a concept to structure an everyday activity, let us start with the concept ARGUMENT and the conceptual metaphor ARGUMENT IS WAR. This metaphor is reflected in our everyday language by a wide variety of expressions.

It is important to see that we don't just talk about arguments in terms of war. We can actually win or lose arguments. We see the person we are arguing with as an opponent. We attack his positions and we defend our own. We gain and lose ground. We plan and use strategies. If we find a position indefensible, we can abandon it and take a new line of attack. Many of the things we do in arguing are partially structured by the concept of war. Though there is no physical battle, there is a verbal battle, and the structure of an argument—attack, defense, counter-attack, etc.—reflects this. It is in this sense that the ARGUMENT IS WAR metaphor is one that we live by in this culture; it structures the actions we perform in arguing. Try to imagine a culture where arguments are not viewed in terms of war, where no one wins or loses, where there is no sense of attacking or defending, gaining or losing ground. Imagine a culture where an argument is viewed as a dance, the participants are seen as performers, and the goal is to perform in a balanced and aesthetically pleasing way. In such a culture, people would view arguments differently, experience them differently, carry them out differently, and talk about them differently. But we would probably not view them as arguing at all: they would simply be doing something different. It would seem strange even to call what they were doing "arguing". Perhaps the most neutral way of describing this difference between their culture and ours would be to say that we have a discourse form structured in terms of battle and they have one structured in terms of dance. This is an example of what it means for a metaphorical concept, namely, ARGUMENT IS WAR, to structure (at least in part) what we do and how we understand what we are doing when we argue. The essence of metaphor is understanding and experiencing one kind of thing in terms of another. It is not that arguments are a subspecies of war. Arguments and wars are different kinds of things—verbal discourse and armed conflict—and the actions performed are different kinds of actions. But ARGUMENT is partially structured, understood, performed, and talked about in terms of WAR. The concept is metaphorically structured, the activity is metaphorically structured, and, consequently, the language is metaphorically structured.

Moreover, this is the ordinary way of having an argument and talking about one. The normal way for us to talk about attacking a position is to use the words "attack a position." Our conventional ways of talking about arguments presuppose a metaphor we are hardly ever conscious of. The metaphor is not merely in the words we use — it is in our very concept of an argument. The language of argument is not poetic, fanciful, or rhetorical; it is literal. We talk about arguments that way because we conceive of them that way — and we act according to the way we conceive of things.

The most important claim we have made so far is that metaphor is not just a matter of language, that is, of mere words. We shall argue that, on the contrary, human thought processes are largely metaphorical. This is what we mean when we say that the human conceptual system is metaphorically structured and defined. Metaphors as linguistic expressions are possible precisely because there are metaphors in a person's conceptual system. Therefore, whenever in this book we speak of metaphors, such as ARGUMENT IS WAR, it should be understood that metaphor means metaphorical concept.

Arguments usually follow patterns, that is, there are certain things we typically do and do not do in arguing. The fact that we in part conceptualize arguments in terms of battle systematically influences the shape arguments take and the way we talk about what we do in arguing. Because the metaphorical concept is systematic, the language we use to talk about that aspect of the concept is systematic.

We saw in the ARGUMENT IS WAR metaphor that expressions from the vocabulary of war, e.g., attack a position, indefensible, strategy, new line of attack, win, gain ground, etc., form a systematic way of talking about the battling aspects of arguing. It is no accident that these expressions mean what they mean when we use them to talk about arguments. A portion of the conceptual network of battle partially characterizes the concept of an argument, and the language follows suit. Since metaphorical expressions in our language are tied to metaphorical concepts in a systematic way, we can use metaphorical linguistic expressions to study the nature of metaphorical concepts and to gain an understanding of the metaphorical nature of our activities.

To get an idea of how metaphorical expressions in everyday language icon give us insight into the metaphorical nature of the concepts that structure our everyday activities, let us consider the metaphorical concept TIME IS MONEY as it is reflected in contemporary English.

Time in our culture is a valuable commodity. It is a limited resource that we use to accomplish our goals. Because of the way that the concept of work has developed in modern Western culture, where work is typically associated with the time it takes and time is precisely quantified, it has become customary to pay people by the hour, week, or year. In our culture TIME IS MONEY in many ways: telephone message units, hourly wages, hotel room rates, yearly budgets, interest on loans, and paying your debt to society by "serving time." These practices are relatively new in the history of the human race, and by no means do they exist in all cultures. They have arisen in modern industrialized societies and structure our basic everyday activities in a very profound way. Corresponding to the fact that we act as if time is a valuable commodity — a limited resource, even money — we conceive of time that way. Thus we understand and experience time as the kind of thing that can be spent, wasted, budgeted, invested wisely or poorly, saved, or squandered.

TIME IS MONEY, TIME IS A LIMITED RESOURCE, and TIME IS A VALUABLE COMMODITY are all metaphorical concepts. They are metaphorical since we are using our everyday experiences with money, limited resources, and valuable commodities to conceptualize time. This isn't a necessary way for human beings to conceptualize time; it is tied to our culture. There are cultures where time is none of these things.

The metaphorical concepts TIME IS MONEY, TIME IS A LIMITIED RESOURCE, and TIME IS A VALUABLE COMMODITY form a single system based on sub-categorization, since in our society money is a limited resource and limited resources are valuable commodities. These sub categorization relationships characterize entailment relationships between the metaphors: TIME IS MONEY entails that TIME IS A LIMITED RESOURCE, which entails that TIME IS A VALUABLE COMMODITY.

We are adopting the practice of using the most specific metaphorical concept, in this case TIME IS MONEY to characterize the entire system. Of the expressions listed under the TIME IS MONEY metaphor, some refer specifically to money (spend, invest, budget, probably cost), others to limited resources (use, use up, have enough of, run out of), and still others to valuable commodities (have, give, lose, thank you for). This is an example of the way in which metaphorical entailments can characterize a coherent system of metaphorical concepts and a corresponding coherent system of metaphorical expressions for those concepts.

The very systematicity that allows us to comprehend one aspect of a concept in terms of another (e.g., comprehending an aspect of arguing in terms of battle) will necessarily hide other aspects of the concept. In allowing us to focus on one aspect of a concept (e.g., the battling aspects of arguing), metaphorical concept can keep us from focusing on other aspects of the concept that are inconsistent with that metaphor. For example, in the midst of a heated argument, when we are intent on attacking our opponent's position and defending our own, we may lose sight of the cooperative aspects of arguing. Someone who is arguing with you can be viewed as giving you his time, a valuable commodity, in an effort at mutual understanding. But when we are preoccupied with the battle aspects, we often lose sight of the cooperative aspects.

(Excerpted from G. Lakoff & M. Johnson, *Metaphors We Live By*, 2003)

Language, Society and Culture

After You Read

Knowledge Focus

1. Solo work: Tell whether the following statements are true or false according to the knowledge you learned.

1) For most people, metaphor is simply viewed as a language phenomenon, which is something we can do without in our daily life.

2) Metaphor is mostly pervasive in language, but not in thought and action.

3) Language is the only way to find out what our conceptual system is.

4) ARGUMENT IS WAR metaphor is one that we live by in this culture because we conceptualize argument as a verbal battle.

5) In a culture where an argument is viewed as a dance, people would carry the argument in a way very different from ours.

6) Metaphorical linguistic expressions can be used to study the nature of metaphorical concepts and the metaphorical nature of our activities.

7) The metaphor TIME IS MONEY can be applied to all cultures in the world.

8) In focusing on the battling aspects of arguing, the metaphorical concept of ARGUMENT IS WAR also stresses the cooperative aspect.

2. Pair Work: Discuss the following questions with your partner.

1) Why is language an important source of evidence for what our conceptual system is like?

2) In the metaphor "Argument is war," what message of our culture is conveyed in terms of our conceptual system?

3) How does the metaphorical concept influence language?

4) In the metaphor "Time is money," what can we know about our culture's attitude towards time?

5) Why do the authors say that metaphorical entailments can characterize a coherent system of metaphorical concepts?

6) While comprehending one aspect of a concept in terms of another and focusing on one aspect of a concept, what do metaphors fail to do? Give examples to clarify.

Language Focus

1. Fill in the blanks with the idioms/expressions you have learned in the text.

| mundane | conceptualize | structure (v.) | lose ground |
| subspecies | icon | quantify | correspond to |

1) Marilyn Monroe and James Dean are still _____ for many young people.
2) Do you think it's true that men and women _____ in different ways?
3) The sophisticated Kunqu began to _____ in the course of the Qing dynasty and virtually disappeared in the middle of the 19th century.
4) A grasp of _____ affairs is genuine knowledge; understanding of worldly wisdom is true learning.
5) The salaries of teachers should _____ these of people in comparable professions.
6) If you work at home, you need to be able to _____ your days.
7) The cost of the flood damage is impossible to _____.
8) In their original description these types are morphologically distinct enough to classify them as _____.

2. Fill in the blanks with the proper form of the word in the brackets.

1) The phrase "born again" is used _____ (metaphor) to mean that someone has suddenly become very religious.
2) A pyramid provides a useful _____ (concept) model for organizing scientific knowledge.
3) As a consequence, such a reorientation of art will lead to the reorientation of _____ (aesthetical).
4) Now that the civil war is over, relative _____ (normal) has returned to the south of the country.
5) The law is morally _____ (defend) and in need of reform.
6) The Queen has maintained political _____ (neutral) throughout her reign.
7) A banquet is a large formal luncheon or dinner that is _____ (custom) followed by speeches and/or a ceremony.
8) Many township in the coastal area have begun to _____ (industrial).
9) There was a great _____ (inconsistent) between what he said and what he did.
10) His voice slowly fell, he was conscious that in this room his accents and manner wore a roughness not _____ (observe) in the street.

3. Cloze: Choose the word that best completes each sentence.

A metaphor's only cause of death is the acceptance of its poetic meaning into the normal vocabulary of the host language.

It is difficult to clearly 1)_____ the living metaphor from the dead because a language is dynamic, and individualistic — and therefore never a 2)_____. If one has never heard a given word in a specific metaphorical context, they will more likely see it 3)_____ a living metaphor. But 4)_____ who has accepted the use of this word in this same context as normal will not likely identify it as a metaphor 5)_____.

All 6)_____ often I would find myself learning a new field, and with it, the metaphors that were new and 7)_____ to me, but so long dead to people already in the field, 8)_____ I would find humor among the words that was totally baffling to them. This was 9)_____ the metaphors that were new (and punishable) to me, were not at all treated as metaphors by them. This 10)_____ contrast between each of our respective treatments of this same metaphor — one clearly as living, 11)_____ clearly as dead — led me to recognize that our perspectives had set the value, and not the definition of the word itself.

This, in turn, led to the following criteria 12)_____ distinguishing living from dead metaphors: 13)_____ when one can no longer see evidence of life, can a metaphor be officially 14)_____ dead: but a metaphor — living or dead — is always new and alive to someone hearing it for the first time. Thus this distinction seems 15)_____ more scholastic than practical.

1) A. different B. distinguish C. differ D. distinct
2) A. singular B. plural C. singularity D. plurality
3) A. as B. with C. being D. to be
4) A. one B. those C. he D. some
5) A. above all B. for all C. all in all D. at all
6) A. very B. too C. much D. the
7) A. living B. lively C. alive D. dead
8) A. which B. in which C. and D. that
9) A. because B. why C. when D. how
10) A. wide B. weak C. vast D. strong
11) A. other B. others C. the other D. the others
12) A. of B. for C. in D. by
13) A. Even B. Only C. Until D. Till
14) A. claimed B. proclaimed C. announced D. declared
15) A. many B. less C. far D. the

Comprehensive Work
1. Discussions: Metaphors

Read and analyze the poem "The Writer" by Richard Wilbur. Try to find out and discuss the use of metaphors in this poem.

Please then reflect on your own writing habits. Compare yourself as a writer to the writer in the poem, and brainstorm possible metaphors for yourself as a writer. You may use the following questions as a help to brainstorm your ideas.

The Writer
By Richard Wilbur

In her room at the prow of the house
Where light breaks, and the windows are tossed with linden,
My daughter is writing a story.

I pause in the stairwell, hearing
From her shut door a commotion of typewriter-keys
Like a chain hauled over a gunwale.

Young as she is, the stuff
Of her life is a great cargo, and some of it heavy:
I wish her a lucky passage.

But now it is she who pauses,
As if to reject my thought and its easy figure.
A stillness greatens, in which

The whole house seems to be thinking,
And then she is at it again with a bunched clamor
Of strokes, and again is silent.

I remember the dazed starling
Which was trapped in that very room, two years ago;
How we stole in, lifted a sash

And retreated, not to affright it;
And how for a helpless hour, through the crack of the door,
We watched the sleek, wild, dark

And iridescent creature
Batter against the brilliance, drop like a glove
To the hard floor, or the desk-top,

And wait then, humped and bloody,
For the wits to try it again; and how our spirits
Rose when, suddenly sure,

It lifted off from a chair-back,
Beating a smooth course for the right window
And clearing the sill of the world.

It is always a matter, my darling,
Of life or death, as I had forgotten. I wish
What I wished you before, but harder.

2. Writing Habits Questions (for brainstorming)

1) What are your best memories about writing?
2) What is the easiest thing about writing for you, and why?
3) What is the most difficult thing about writing for you, and why?
4) What different kinds of writing do you do? Who reads your writing? Where is your writing published or shared with others?
5) What materials and/or equipment do you like to have on hand when you write? What are these items for? Why do you have them?
6) What steps do you follow when you write? Outline your writing process, using a simple, informal outline format.
7) Are you a procrastinator when it comes to writing? What do you try to avoid? What do you typically do instead?
8) What's the biggest influence on the way you write? Why does it make a difference?
9) If someone else were observing you as a writer, what would they notice? What would they see or hear?
10) Overall, how would you describe yourself as a writer? What kind of writer are you, and why do you say so?

3. Writing Practice: Writing Metaphor Assignment

After reading and analyzing Richard Wilbur's poem "The Writer," consider your experiences as a writer—the frustrations and the satisfactions you felt as you shaped words into meaning.

For this assignment, choose a metaphor that will tell others about you as a writer. You will build an extended metaphor, just as Wilbur has in his poem. Your goal is to show others what you are like as a writer.

Tips:

◇ The metaphor you choose can take the form of an animal (e.g., an elephant, a fox, an ostrich), a machine (e.g., a bulldozer, a tank, a computer), or something else. Any metaphor you choose will be correct if you support your assertion.

◇ Remember to provide detailed support for your metaphor. Think about specific characteristics of yourself as a writer that compare to the item you have chosen for your metaphor.

◇ Choose the format that works best for your explanation. You might choose comparison/contrast to work through the ways that you compare to the object you've chosen. You could choose to write a persuasive paper that explains why the metaphor you've chosen is best. Other formats will work as well. Don't feel limited to these two.

4. Translation: Translate the following paragraph into Chinese.

Metaphor has traditionally been construed as a linguistic phenomenon: as something produced and understood by speakers of natural language. So understood, metaphors are naturally viewed as linguistic expressions of a particular type, or as linguistic expressions used in a particular type of way. We adopt this linguistic conception of metaphor in what follows. In doing so, we do not intend to rule out the possibility of non-linguistic forms of metaphor. Many theorists think that non-linguistic objects (such as paintings or dance performances) or conceptual structures (like love as a journey or argument as war) should also be treated as metaphors. Indeed, the idea that metaphors are in the first instance conceptual phenomena, and linguistic devices only derivatively, is the dominant view in what is now the dominant area of metaphor research: cognitive science. In construing metaphor as linguistic, we merely intend to impose appropriate constraints on a discussion whose focus is the understanding and analysis of metaphor within contemporary philosophy of language.

Read More

Text B   Teaching Metaphor Through Pop Culture

If there's one thing an English teacher loves, it's a metaphor, and the music of just about any artist out there is full of them.

Take Bon Jovi as an example. They sing of roses, cowboys on steel horses, some bad medicine, and highways, just to name a few. Another image Bon Jovi uses over and over is the train; some of their song titles are "Homebound Train," "Mystery Train," and "Last Chance Train," and several of their other lyrics speak of trains as well.

Bon Jovi's use of the train metaphor is not an original one. In fact, it is potentially one of the most often-used metaphors in American musical history. Wikipedia lists more than 800 train songs (although some are the same songs recorded by different artists, and the list is a world-wide list).

What makes the train metaphor so appealing?

Here in Arkansas and other parts of the South, the train is a cultural and historical symbol. The railroad had profound impact on Arkansas' development and population patterns. Towns bypassed by the railroads suffered economically, and many failed to thrive or survive.

Beyond culture and history, though, trains also represent long journeys, those things everyone is on. And in their journeys, trains (and people) have many stops, releasing people and bringing new people aboard. And if one isn't on a train himself, he needs only to be at the station and the train will bring people to him and take people away as they are on their own journeys.

Trains can also be a metaphor for love, or more specifically, for an act of love that two people do together. In Bon Jovi's "Homebound Train," the train represents both a journey and the act of love. Consider:

It's been a million years
That I been gone
I been everywhere, now I'm heading home
Been a lot of girls, but
There's a woman I know
Said don't take no plane
Better take a train

Cause I like it real slow . . .

I'm on my way
I'm heading home
To be with my baby
Where I belong
Coming down the tracks now
See, I done my time
I'm going back
To that home of mine
Well, here I come baby

Here I come baby
Here I come baby

All the way back home
On that homebound train
I'm going down, down, down, down, down
On that homebound train

Of course, as with any journey, the very thing that brings so much happiness can also bring much misery and pain. Bon Jovi's "The Distance" illustrates this:

There's a train out in the distance, destination still unknown
Far away where no one's waiting, so far from home, so far from home . . .
Like that lonesome whistle blowing
I keep on going, keep on going . . .

I'll never give up the fight
I'll go the distance

In Bon Jovi's "Last Chance Train," the train is both literal and figurative:

You gotta meet me tonight
I'm on a last chance train
Leave a flower at the station, I know my destination
Love bring me home again

Let the scarecrows laugh coming down the tracks
At the broken hearts that don't come back
'Cause the train has left the station with my pain ...

And in their "Love Ain't Nothin' But a Four-Letter Word," the train is the main character's hope:

She was waiting alone at the station praying for her train to arrive
Thinking 'bout her destination, a tattered bag was all she had in life ...

Of all the train metaphors in Bon Jovi's music, though, perhaps the most intriguing is the one in which a woman is compared to the "Mystery Train":

She's a ride on a mystery train
To a place you've never been before
Better hold on tight to that mystery train
You're not in Kansas anymore
She's a ride
Mystery train

And if you want to explore the train metaphor more, perhaps start by visiting some of the area's historic depots: Choctaw Route Station, 1010 East Third Street, Little Rock; Mo-Pac Station (Union Station), Markham and Victory Streets, Little Rock; or Rock Island Argenta Depot, Fourth and Hazel Streets, North Little Rock.

Questions for Discussion

1. Who is Bon Jovi? What metaphorical images are found in their songs and music?
2. Why is the train metaphor frequently used by many artists?
3. In Bon Jovi's "Homebound Train," what does the train represent?

Text C Thanksgiving Metaphors: "A Lot on My Plate"

The phrase "a lot on my plate" is used almost interchangeably with "a lot on my mind." Does this suggest that the mind is a separable platter that the conscious feeds from? What are the subtle differences between these two that may offer insight into how we think? To answer these questions, we first need to examine the meaning of the metaphor "plate" in this context.

At times we may find ourselves burdened by the course of life's events. We recognize that no single event is unbearable, but that the sum of the events is far more than we are able to take in. We overload.

What is quite interesting is how we phrase this undesirable state as "a lot on my plate": the metaphor "plate" serving up the suggestion that our life is a meal. Our experience with life becomes an experience with food. Since our earliest life experiences were quite centered on feeding, it is only natural that metaphors associating our experiences with feeding would work on an intuitive level with us.

In our menu of entertainment choices, we may "take in a show" that is dubbed a "smorgasbord of stunning visuals" or a "feast for your eyes." A scene within may be "of poor taste" or the "icing on the cake." This is as true in real life experiences as it is in virtual events.

A plate of food is an arrangement of flavors, be they bite size and mixed, such as in a salad or stew, or collected in piles, such as on a Thanksgiving plate, a dim sum, sushi or curry platter. A typical plate, then, is a selection of different foodstuffs within a singular territory. More so, a plate represents a snapshot of our diet.

The classic Thanksgiving plate consists of the essentials: turkey, stuffing, potatoes, corn, salad, cranberry sauce, a bun and of course — the gravy. So powerful is the drive to feast that we put "as much on our plate as possible," then consciously force ourselves to remember to "save room for dessert" in our feast. The drive to feast is so strong, so zealous that it could be equated to a *bloodlust*. How often do we depict such human meals as "a feeding frenzy," finding easy similarity to the behavior of hungry sharks.

The turkey is the kill, made fresh by being served warm and stuffed with new innards. Gravy is the blood of the human carnivore, salty, thick and warm — oozing life from the mashed potatoes that bathe in the warm animal fat of melted butter. This would simply be a kill, if not for the potatoes themselves, the corn and the cranberry sauce. But we are not carnivores, we are omnivores.

Trapped in cans, bottles, bags, wrappers and boxes are the foods that will find their way to the plate. Packaging is as natural to humans as it is to all life, whether as the plastic-wrap skin of a grape or the not-quite-tin can of a pecan. The packages are arranged into types — sections — that if intuitive are easy to find and remember. Meats, fruit, vegetables, breads, dairy, personal hygiene and so on.

As natural as packing, so is the arrangement of food in the wild. An ecosystem is a supermarket, allowing each member of its society to feed, and have its preference. The fields yield grains, such as the corn or, ultimately buns. Some soils support the growth of roots, such as potatoes, while other soils make way for fruit-bearing plants. Leafy greens prefer their own type of soil, and like the others, find themselves in groups. And with that roving centerpiece of flesh, the parts of the human feed-lot are complete.

A dinner plate is a single-serving feed lot. We graze from food to food, tiring of one, then wandering to the next. We have the comfort of knowing that if we turn our backs on the corn for one moment, the crows won't clean us out (though bigger brother/brat Billy just may). What we put on our plate, and what has landed there by other hands, has become ours.

As we assume new tasks or responsibilities, take up hobbies or lifestyles, we fill our plates, according to metaphor. The things of our life are our diet, and become a must whether eagerly feasted on, or *procrastinatingly* pushed around the plate. Even mere information finds its way to our plate, and may become a lot to digest, or too much to take in.

Somehow, this metaphor concludes that "doing" is "eating." That to "take a bite out of life" is to feed by living. What exactly is being fed?

The mind hungers for knowledge and experience. We feed our children's growing minds by teaching them. And we don't feed them a single staple subject. Instead, we wander around an educational dinner plate feeding them 45 minute servings of the three staples "Readin', Ritin' and 'Rithmatic," ending eagerly and in overzealous self-servings with the dessert of recess. With the word "dessert" deriving from "clear the table," and "recess" from "go back," one can see a tone of resetting, as if an original point of reference is somehow desirable.

Salt, sour, bitter and sweet — the four classic taste senses. (Note: *"Umami,"* the fifth sense, is a taste for decayed protein, such as found in aged steak or old cheese.) Between turkey (salty) and cranberry sauce (sour, bitter and sweet), the four sensations are pretty much spent. Spuds and bread are pretty timid flavours on their own and we are urged not to "fill up on them." Dessert would appear to balance out the taste buds of a normal meal, but as you may notice, the few who have a remaining appetite are destined for pumpkin pie. Pumpkin pie is not sweet. Instead, it fringes on sweetness and with the pie's spices, it nearly straddles the four tastes, smoothed into homogeny by the taste bud sealant *whipped cream*.

The Thanksgiving plate, like the ecosystem, supermarket or classroom, offers the necessities in balance. The plate of mind's eye seeks similar balance, but can only hold so much. The overloaded Thanksgiving dinner plate, the crowded ecosystem, the overstocked supermarket or the packed curriculum result in the same consequences — food falling off, half-eaten carcasses, products being discounted and students daydreaming or dropping out. Whether ignored or ousted, the excessive load will fall to the floor as being "too much to take."

Procrastination, neglect and fatigue — the very signs of having more on one's plate than they can handle — are seen on the faces of schoolchildren, office workers and tired ecosystems alike. They're all fed up, and they can't take any more — they've just had too many *things* on their plate.

Questions for Discussion

1. What does the metaphor "a lot in my plate" mean? What is the origin of this metaphor?

2. What aspect of life is this metaphor concerned with? Can you give more similar examples?

3. What metaphorical image does this metaphor "a lot in my plate" present? Explain it with details.

Text D Metaphor and Cultural Coherence

The most fundamental values in a culture will be coherent with the metaphorical structure of the most fundamental concepts in the culture. As an example, let us consider some cultural values in our society that are coherent with our UP-DOWN spatialization metaphors and whose opposites would not be.

"More is better" is coherent with MORE IS UP and GOOD IS UP. "Less is better" is not coherent with them.

"Bigger is better" is coherent with MORE IS UP and GOOD IS UP. "Smaller is better" is not coherent with them.

"The future will be better" is coherent with THE FUTURE IS UP and GOOD IS UP. "The future will be worse" is not.

"There will be more in the future" is coherent with MORE IS UP and THE FUTURE IS UP.

"Your status should be higher in the future" is coherent with HIGH STATUS IS UP and THE FUTURE IS UP.

These are values deeply embedded in our culture. "The future will be better" is a statement of the concept of progress. "There will be more in the future" has as special cases the accumulation of goods and wage inflation. "Your status should be higher in the future" is a statement of careerism. These are coherent with our present spatialization metaphors; their opposites would not be. So it seems that our values are not independent but must form a coherent system with the metaphorical concepts we live by. We are not claiming that all cultural values coherent with a metaphorical system actually exist, only that those that do exist and are deeply entrenched are consistent with the metaphorical system.

The values listed above hold in our culture generally—all things being equal. But because things are usually not equal, there are often conflicts among these values and hence conflicts among the metaphors associated with them. To explain such conflicts among values (and their metaphors), we must find the different priorities given to these values and metaphors by the subculture that uses them. For instance, MORE IS UP seems always to have the highest priority since it has the clearest physical basis. The priority of MORE IS UP over GOOD IS UP can be seen in examples like "Inflation is rising" and "The crime rate is going up." Assuming that inflation and the crime rate are bad, these sentences mean what they do because MORE IS UP always has top priority.

In general, which values are given priority is partly a matter of the subculture one lives in and partly a matter of personal values. The various subcultures of a mainstream culture share basic values but give them different priorities. For example, BIGGER IS BETTER may be in conflict with THERE WILL BE MORE IN THE FUTURE when it comes to the question of whether to buy a big car now, with large time payments that will eat up future salary, or whether to buy a smaller, cheaper car. There are American subcultures where you buy the big car and don't worry about the future, and there are others where the future comes first and you buy the small car. There was a time (before inflation and the energy crisis) when owning a small car had a high status within the subculture where VIRTUE IS UP and SAVING RESOURCES IS VIRTUOUS took priority over BIGGER IS BETTER.

Nowadays the number of small-car owners has gone up drastically because there is a large subculture where SAVING MONEY IS BETTER has priority over BIGGER IS BETTER.

In addition to subcultures, there are groups whose defining characteristic is that they share certain important values that conflict with those of the mainstream culture. But in less obvious ways they preserve other mainstream values. Take monastic orders like the Trappists. There LESS IS BETTER and SMALLER IS BETTER are true with respect to material possessions, which are viewed as hindering what is important, namely, serving God. The Trappists share the

mainstream value VIRTUE IS UP, though they give it the highest priority and a very different definition. MORE is still BETTER, though it applies to virtue; and status is still UP, though it is not of this world but of a higher one, the Kingdom of God. Moreover, THE FUTURE WILL BE BETTER is true in terms of spiritual growth (UP) and, ultimately, salvation (really UP). This is typical of groups that are out of the mainstream culture. Virtue, goodness, and status may be radically redefined, but they are still UP. It is still better to have more of what is important, THE FUTURE WILL BE BETTER with respect to what is important, and so on. Relative to what is important for a monastic group, the value system is both internally coherent and, with respect to what is important for the group, coherent with the major orientational metaphors of the mainstream culture.

Individuals, like groups, vary in their priorities and in the ways they define what is good or virtuous to them. In this sense, they are subgroups of one. Relative to what is important for them, their individual value systems are coherent with the major orientational metaphors of the mainstream culture.

Not all cultures give the priorities we do to up-down orientation. There are cultures where balance or centrality plays a much more important role than it does in our culture. Or consider the non-spatial orientation active-passive. For us ACTIVE IS UP and PASSIVE IS DOWN in most matters. But there are cultures where passivity is valued more than activity. In general the major orientations up-down, in-out, central-peripheral, active-passive, etc., seem to cut across all cultures, but which concepts are oriented which way and which orientations are most important vary from culture to culture.

(Excerpted from G. Lakoff & M. Johnson, *Metaphors We Live By*, 2003)

Questions for Discussion

1. What is the main idea of this article? What relationship exists between metaphors and culture?

2. What elements of culture, according to the authors, will influence the way metaphors relate to culture?

3. Which example in the text best illustrates the influence of subculture? Can you find a different example in our life and language?

Unit 7 Euphemisms and Taboos in Different Cultures

> Any euphemism ceases to be euphemistic after a time and the true meaning begins to show through. It's a losing game, but we keep on trying.
>
> — Fred W. Friendly
>
> Life is livable because we know that wherever we go most of the people we meet will be restrained in their actions towards us by an almost instinctive network of taboos.
>
> — Havelock Ellis

Unit Goals

- To understand the relationship between names and things
- To comprehend the nature of euphemism and taboo
- To learn to tell the motives for euphemizing
- To know the definitions of euphemism and taboo

 Before You Read

1. To test your knowledge of the English language, have a look at the following euphemisms and try to explain them.

1) senior citizen	2) law-enforcement officer	3) undertaker
4) collateral damage	5) pro-choice	6) white meat
7) adult video	8) economical with the truth	9) tired and emotional
10) person with a visual impairment	11) substance abuser	12) downsizing

2. **Find out euphemism for birth both in Chinese and English and then detect the cultural belief behind it.**

Start to Read

Text A Taboo and Euphemism

The word "taboo" comes from the Tongan word tabu, which the English initially started using in the late eighteenth century. The Tongan culture of Polynesia, as well as many other cultures, believed that certain objects, actions, and words could expel harmful power onto people. According to Keith Allan and Kate Burridge in *Forbidden Words: Taboo and the Censoring of Language*, taboo is a "proscription of behavior that affects everyday life." These taboos surround many different things ranging from names of ancestors to certain natural processes of the body.

Taboos generally come from social constrictions on behavior that may cause discomfort, harm or injury to the speaker or the listener. What is considered a taboo and how each taboo is handled depends greatly on the cultural norms of a given society. These norms determine what is acceptable and what must be avoided. Because of this, we are constantly censoring our everyday language for all situations.

It should be noted that there are cultural taboos and linguistic taboos within every culture. Sometimes the linguistic taboos don't align with a cultural taboo on a certain behavior; however, cultural taboos generally have corresponding linguistic taboos. In other words, it is possible to have a linguistic taboo on speaking about a certain behavior or process while the behavior itself is not taboo (i.e. menstruating as a natural process of the body is not a tabooed act but to speak about it candidly and directly is considered taboo in many cultures). Certain behaviors and practices are frowned upon in many different societies and the usage of particular words and phrases elicit the same or similar disapproval.

Taboos surround topics such as: bodies and their effluvia (sweat, snot, feces, menstrual fluid, etc.); the organs and acts of sex, micturition and defecation; diseases, death and killing (including hunting and fishing); naming, addressing, touching and viewing persons and sacred beings, objects and places; food gathering, preparation and consumption. Across many different societies and cultures, people believe that these tabooed things have the ability to cause metaphysical, moral or physical harm and may lead to the contamination of others. Societies that recognize supernatural powers and show concern for offending nonhuman powers treat words very carefully due to the power that they associate with them and the possible supernatural consequences. To violate a taboo is to potentially suffer illness, death, corporal punishment, incarceration, social ostracism or simple disapproval.

Taboo and censoring of language motivate language change by "promoting the creation of highly inventive and often playful new expressions, or new meanings for old expressions, causing existing vocabulary to be forgone." Allan and Burridge examine politeness and impoliteness as they pertain to what is referred to as x-phemisms. X-phemisms are orthophemism (straight talk), euphemism (sweet talk), and dysphemism (offensive speech). For example, for the topic of defecation, an orthophemism would be "feces"; a possible euphemism would be "poop"; and a dysphemism would be "shit."

A dysphemism is a word or phrase with "connotations that are offensive either about the denotatum and/or to the people that are being addressed or have overheard the word or phrase." In other words, it is a phrase that employs the use of metaphor to speak indirectly about a subject but can result in discomfort for the speaker or the listener. Dysphemisms are considered to be the dispreferred language expressions and sometimes aim to insult or damage face. As alternatives to these less preferred language expressions, we use orthophemisms and euphemisms. Orthophemism refers to a word or phrase that is more formal and more direct than the euphemism, while euphemisms are typically more colloquial and figurative.

In general, the use of alternative expressions such as those classified as euphemisms and sometimes orthophemisms are tied to the idea of linguistic politeness in their attempt to maintain what is referred to as face. One of the approaches to linguistic politeness involves "general conditions on the conventions of social activity types and their interaction orders." More precisely, there are unspoken "rules" of discourse within a given society. Watts addresses linguistic politeness, basing this theory on a combination of Robin Lakoff's rules of pragmatic competence and Paul Grice's conversational maxims. Lakoff breaks down the "rules of politeness" into two categories: "be clear" and "be polite." Under Lakoff's rule of "be polite", Watts adds the maxims "don't impose," "give options," and "be friendly." Under the rule of "be clear", Watts incorporates Grice's maxims "quantity," "quality," "relevance," and "manner." The combination of the two sets of rules can be applied to face theory.

The face theory basically describes the nature of these conditions as saving/maintaining face. Face maintenance can be described as a balancing of trying to show "mutually shared forms of consideration" for others while not seeming to be uncooperative and losing respect that may be gained or desired in the eyes of others. In the simplest definition, face refers to one's public image. Face is closely tied to feelings of embarrassment or humiliation, which are connected to vulnerability. This vulnerability is evidence for the emotional investment that is assigned to our face. Due to this general vulnerability, people maintain one another's face under the assumption that others will cooperate in this collective maintenance as a general rule of politeness.

To clarify, our use of euphemisms or "sweet talk" is not only to save our own face but also to save the face of others. Two aspects of face are reported by Brown and Levinson. The first is the desire of a person to have their attributes, achievements, ideas, possessions and goals regarded well or highly by others in their community. The second aspect involves the want of a person not to be imposed upon or offended by others. By using a word, phrase or expression that is considered to be a dysphemism a person is not only risking being regarded less highly but they are also imposing upon their listener during the discourse. The Gricean maxim, "don't impose," can be applied here and there is a clear connection between the use of euphemisms and linguistic politeness.

An interesting thing to think about with regards to the use of orthophemisms, euphemisms and dysphemisms is that certain words or phrases can switch between these three categories based on the context of their usage. For example, during moments of intimacy, a couple may refer to tabooed body parts in a way that would be considered dysphemistic in another situation such as a doctor's surgery. Or if an adult were to refer to the toilet as the "potty" with another adult, they may lose face. While the word "potty" is a euphemism commonly used to refer to the toilet by and to small children, it would not be acceptable for an adult to use the term in any other context, making it a dysphemism in that specific situation.

Not only do euphemisms, orthophemisms and dysphemisms have an interchangeable nature within different contexts, but there are also dysphemistic euphemisms and euphemistic dysphemisms. This suggests that x-phemisms are on a spectrum.

Text B Why Do We Use Euphemisms?

As defined in our glossary, a euphemism is an inoffensive expression (such as "Thanks for coming in") used in place of one that's considered offensively blunt ("You suck"). That definition may sound fairly straightforward, but in practice euphemisms can be as complicated as the people who use them.

Most style guides treat euphemism as a dishonest type of wordiness—something to be avoided in formal essays and reports. Consider these cautionary notes:

> *In academic writing, ... you should avoid euphemisms and instead express yourself as directly and honestly as you can.*
>
> *Euphemisms ... should usually be avoided in essay writing. In expository writing, and in life, excessive politeness suggests insincerity and evasiveness.*
>
> *Euphemisms can make your writing sound wordy and pretentious. Whenever possible, avoid this kind of indirect language.*

> "Euphemisms are unpleasant truths wearing diplomatic cologne."
> — Quentin Crisp

Most of us would agree that certain euphemisms are, at best, shady and misleading. For example, "revenue enhancement" can be a sneaky way of saying "tax increase," and "downsizing" is usually bureaucratese for "firing employees."

But does that mean all euphemisms are inherently dishonest? Decide whether our communication would be improved if in all instances we avoided the expression "passed away" or spelled out the meaning of "the 'N' word."

Simply put, euphemisms come in various disguises, and our motives for employing them are complex. As with other words, the value of a euphemism resides in how, when, and why it's used.

After reading the following passages, identify some of the euphemisms that you're most familiar with. Then decide which of these euphemisms (if any) might be used appropriately in formal writing, and be prepared to explain why.

A Definition of *Euphemism*

In selecting euphemistic words and phrases I have accepted [Henry] Fowler's definition: "Euphemism means the use of a mild or vague or periphrastic expression as a substitute for blunt precision or disagreeable use." In speech or writing, we use euphemism for dealing with taboo or sensitive subjects. It is therefore the language of evasion, hypocrisy, prudery, and deceit.

Euphemisms as Comfort Words

Euphemisms represent a flight to comfort, a way to reduce tension when conversing. They are comfort words. Euphemistic discourse softens the harsh, smooths the rough, makes what's negative sound positive. It is akin to diplomatic language in which "We had a frank exchange of views" might mean, "We hurled insults at each other for a full hour."

Euphemisms add nuance and vagueness to conversation that's often welcome. Could anyone get through a day without heeding a call of nature or speculating about whether Jason and Amy may be sleeping together? Civilized discourse would be impossible without recourse to indirection. Euphemisms give us tools to discuss touchy subjects without having to spell out what it is we're discussing.

Euphemisms as Dangerous Disguises

"Poor" is not a bad word. Replacing it with euphemisms such as "underprivileged" and "under-served" (as I do elsewhere in this book) are well intentioned and sometimes helpful, but euphemisms are also dangerous. They can assist us in not seeing. They can form a scrim through which ugly truth is dimmed to our eyes. There are a lot of poor people in America, and their voices are largely silenced.

Euphemisms as Shields

To speak euphemistically is to use language like a shield against the feared, the disliked, and the unpleasant. Euphemisms are motivated by the desire not to be offensive, and so they have polite connotations; in the least euphemisms seek to avoid too many negative connotations. They are used to upgrade the denotatum (as a shield against scorn); they are used deceptively to conceal the unpleasant aspects of the denotatum (as a shield against anger); and they are used to display in-group identity (as a shield against the intrusion of out-groupers).

Euphemisms as Secret Agents

Euphemisms are not, as many young people think, useless verbiage which can and should be said bluntly; they are like secret agents on a delicate mission; they must airily pass by a stinking mess with barely so much as a nod of the head, make their point of constructive criticism and continue on in calm forbearance. Euphemisms are "unpleasant truths wearing diplomatic cologne."

Euphemism as Spin

While in contemporary parlance the use of euphemism is often about sugar-coating, in practice this is not always the case: euphemism can also be used to neutralize politics or negativity, to confuse, to conceal meaning, and to outright deceive. Euphemism is often considered a form of spin, used notably by politicians, bureaucrats, and advertisers to package something—an idea, a policy, a product—as attractive through disingenuous or manipulative means. Such linguistic trickery is, of course, nothing new; its systematic and highly politicized use is thought to have its origins in George Orwell's novel *Nineteen Eighty-Four* (1949), where "newspeak" was the new language imposed by the state to restrict the lexicon, eliminate gradations of meaning, and, ultimately, control thought.

The Moral Problem of Grotesque Euphemisms

George Orwell rightly detested double-talk, cheap euphemism, and deliberate obscurity—the language of "strategic hamlets" and "enhanced interrogation," and all the other phrases that are used to muddy up meaning. But euphemism is a moral problem, not a cognitive one. When Dick Cheney calls torture "enhanced interrogation," it doesn't make us understand torture in a different way; it's just a means for those who know they're doing something wrong to find a phrase that doesn't immediately acknowledge the wrongdoing.

Whatever name Cheney's men gave torture, they knew what it was. A grotesque euphemism is offensive exactly because we recognize perfectly well the mismatch between the word and its referent. It's an instrument of evasion, like a speeding getaway car, not an instrument of unconsciousness, like a blackjack.

After You Read

Knowledge Focus

1. Solo Work: Tell whether the following statements are true or false according to the knowledge you learned.

1) Taboos cover many different topics ranging from names of ancestors to certain natural processes of the body.
2) The cultural norms of a given society determine what is acceptable and what must be avoided and we are constantly censoring our everyday language for all situations.
3) Cultural taboos align with linguistic taboos within every culture.
4) "Poop" would be an orthophemism for the topic of defecation.
5) A dysphemism is a phrase that employs the use of metaphor to speak directly about a subject, which causes comfort for the speaker or the listener.
6) In general, the use of euphemisms, orthophemisms and dysphemisms is related to the idea of linguistic politeness.
7) Lakoff breaks down the "rules of politeness" into two categories: "be clear" and "be polite."
8) The use of euphemisms or "sweet talk" is to save our own face, namely, our public image.
9) The first aspect of face is the desire of a person to have his attributes, achievements, ideas, possessions and goals regarded well or highly by others in his community.
10) The boundaries of euphemisms, orthophemisms and dysphemism stay constant in spite of context.

2. Pair Work: Discuss the following questions with your partner.

1) Which categories of society tend to produce taboo words?
2) What are the social conditions producing taboos?
3) Explain the relation between cultural and linguistic taboos with an example beyond the textbook.
4) Define and illustrate euphemisms, orthophemisms and dysphemisms.
5) What is the relation between taboos and X-phemisms?
6) What is the primary reason under the use of euphemisms, orthophemisms and dysphemisms?
7) Present your understanding of the face theory.
8) Summarize the reasons why people use euphemism.

Language Focus

1. Fill in the blanks with the words or expressions you have learned in the texts.

| proscription | censor | align | elicit |
| metaphysical | contamination | forgone | connotation |

1) It's just one of those words that's got so many negative _____.
2) However, _____ can occur at any point along the food chain, from field to table.
3) Many police departments attempt to impose ethical standards and effective policing through policy, _____, and punishment.
4) The _____ world outlook sees things as isolated, static and one-sided.
5) For the fact of the matter is that it is technically impossible to _____ the Internet and a waste of time and money to attempt to do so.
6) How can I _____ these bricks with the rest of the wall?
7) Tens of thousands of workers are being idled and profits _____ to temporarily clear the air and ensure a breathable contest for the world's top athletes.
8) It operates a monetary reward scheme to _____ information on textile origin fraud.

2. Cloze: Choose the word that best completes each sentence.

Culture can have a large impact on what language is used to describe serious illness. People from a Greek background can be extremely 1) _____ to issues relating to death, dying and cancer. There can be a desire to protect the sick person from receiving bad news. This is 2) _____ the notion that the bad news itself would exacerbate the suffering. There is also concern 3) _____ the patient may lose hope. In this context, in the Greek culture, many people 4) _____ use euphemisms such as "that terrible sickness" or "the situation". The role of the Greek Orthodox church is also very important within the Greek culture in determining the behaviour of people 5) _____ they grieve. Another example includes Aboriginal Australians, who may use the term "finish up" as a euphemism 6) _____ dying.

Best practice generally suggests that euphemisms should be avoided in palliative care. It is suggested that 7) _____ words may impair the patient's ability to think clearly about their illness. Vague terms and medical jargon need to be 8) _____. If technical language does need to be used, a Health Care person should be careful to explain such terms fully to the family in 9) _____ language. The use of a euphemism may also suggest to the patient that the health professional considers the issue 10) _____ a taboo topic themselves. Certainly, Health Care persons need to be clear, open and 11) _____ in their communication. Caution must especially be 12) _____ when using euphemisms with children. Children are more likely to be concrete thinkers, and less likely to 13) _____ on the nuances of a euphemism. For example, if a Health Care person or parent tells a sibling of a child who has died 14) _____ they are sleeping, the child may expect them to wake up. Further, when they experience that their sibling did not wake from "sleep" after dying, they may themselves become 15) _____ of going to sleep.

1) A. indifferent   B. sensitive   C. fragile   D. excited
2) A. thanks to   B. in spite of   C. related to   D. regardless of
3) A. that   B. which   C. on   D. about
4) A. refuse to   B. prefer to   C. insist to   D. likely to
5) A. if   B. unless   C. as   D. that
6) A. on   B. of   C. about   D. for
7) A. vague   B. unclear   C. uncertain   D. dim
8) A. decreased   B. maximized   C. minimized   D. increased
9) A. accessible   B. obtainable   C. understandable   D. affordable
10) A. discussed   B. being discussed
    C. discussing   D. having discussed
11) A. simple   B. direct   C. vague   D. considerate
12) A. exercised   B. made   C. conducted   D. carried
13) A. pick out   B. take up   C. take to   D. pick up
14) A. when   B. that   C. if   D. as
15) A. expressive   B. cheerful   C. fearful   D. doubtful

Comprehensive Work

1. Research Work

Find out euphemism for the following words and phrases.

1) beggar	2) cheap	3) die	4) drugs	5) fat
6) fire (v.)	7) kill	8) lazy	9) old	10) old age
11) old person	12) poor nation	13) poor student	14) poor	15) problem
16) sales	17) sales woman	18) say	19) school	20) secretary
21) selfish	22) sick	23) steal	24) stupid	25) suicide (to commit)
26) toilet	27) ugly	28) unemployed	29) used	30) wrong

2. Writing Practice

Dysphemism, the opposite of euphemism, is the substitution of a more offensive or disparaging word or phrase for one considered less offensive. Though often meant to shock or offend, dysphemisms may also serve as in-group markers to signal closeness. Write an article and explore the use of dysphemism in both English and Chinese.

3. Translation: Translate the following passage into Chinese.

When propagandists use glittering generalities and name-calling symbols, they are attempting to arouse their audience's interest with vivid, emotionally suggestive words. In certain situations, however, the propagandist attempts to pacify the audience in order to make an unpleasant reality more palatable. This is accomplished by using words that are bland and euphemistic.

Since war is particularly unpleasant, military discourse is full of euphemisms. In the 1940's, America changed the name of the War Department to the Department of Defense. Under the Reagan Administration, the MX-Missile was renamed "The Peacekeeper." During war-time, civilian casualties are referred to as "collateral damage," and the word "liquidation" is used as a synonym for "murder."

The comedian George Carlin notes that, in the wake of the First World War, traumatized veterans were said to be suffering from "shell shock." The short, vivid phrase conveys the horrors of battle — one can practically hear the shells exploding overhead. After the Second World War, people began to use the term "combat fatigue" to characterize the same condition. The phrase is a bit more pleasant, but it still acknowledges combat as the source of discomfort. In the wake of the Vietnam War, people referred to "post-traumatic stress disorder": a phrase that is completely disconnected from the reality of war altogether.

Read More

Text C Taboo

A taboo is a prohibition on human activity declared as sacred and forbidden or dangerous or unclean either physically or spiritually. Breaking a taboo may cause serious consequences,

ranging from imprisonment to social ostracism. The idea of a universal taboo is questionable, but some taboos, such as cannibalism, incest, and genocide, occur in the majority of societies. Taboos often remain in effect after the original reason behind them has expired. Study of taboos by anthropologists has led to deeper understanding of the development of different societies, and the similarities among cultures spread throughout the world. Even if the actual taboos are not universal, the concept of prohibiting particular acts is, indicating that humankind as a whole aspires to goodness.

Definition of Taboo

A taboo is a strong social prohibition or ban relating to any area of human activity or social custom declared as sacred and forbidden; breaking of the taboo is usually considered objectionable or abhorrent by society. The term was borrowed from the Tongan language and appears in many Polynesian cultures. In those cultures, a tabu (or tapu or kapu) often has specific religious associations. It was a word brought back and introduced into the English language by Captain James Cook in 1777, after his long sea voyage to the South Seas.

Some taboo activities or customs are prohibited under law and transgressions may lead to severe penalties. Breaking of other taboos may have social implications, such as embarrassment, shame, and rudeness.

Nature of Taboos

The idea of a universal taboo is questionable, but some (such as the cannibalism, incest taboos, and genocide) occur in the majority of societies. Taboos can include dietary restrictions, restrictions on sexual activities and relationships, restrictions of bodily functions, restrictions on the state of genitalia such as circumcision, exposure of body parts, nudity, and restrictions on the use of offensive language. Taboos often extend to cover discussion of taboo topics. This can result in taboo deformation (euphemism) or replacement of taboo words.

Taboos may serve many functions, and often remain in effect after the original reason behind them has expired. Some have argued that taboos therefore reveal the history of societies when other records are lacking. Researchers such as James Frazer, who compiled the comprehensive documentation of cultural beliefs and practices around the world in his 1890 publication *The Golden Bough*, and Marvin Harris, a leading figure in cultural materialism, proposed explanations of taboos as a consequence of the ecologic and economic conditions of their societies.

Sigmund Freud provided an analysis of taboo behaviors, highlighting strong unconscious motivations driving such prohibitions. In this system, described in his collection of essays *Totem and Taboo*, Freud postulated a link between forbidden behaviors and the sanctification of objects to certain kinship groups. Freud also stated that the only two "universal" taboos are that of incest and patricide, which formed the eventual basis of modern society.

Taboo Consumption

1. Meat

Various religions forbid the consumption of certain types of meat. For example, Judaism prescribes a strict set of rules, called Kashrut, regarding what can and cannot be eaten. Certain sects of Christianity also hold to these or similar rules. In Islamic practice, the laws of Haram and Halal dictate, among other things, certain foods which may not be eaten. Hindus, Jains and Buddhists often follow religious directives to observe vegetarianism and avoid eating meat. Since Hinduism lacks a central dogma, however, many Hindus do eat meat, while among many modern Indian Hindus, all meat is considered a taboo except mutton (usually in India the goat's flesh, or sometimes sheep's flesh), chicken and fish.

Cultural taboos against the consumption of some animals may be due to their species' standing as a pet or animal companion. For example, dog meat is taboo in the United States and Europe, but is common in Southeast Asia. Similarly, horse meat is rarely eaten in the US and the UK, but is common in some parts of continental Europe and is considered a delicacy in Japan (basashi). Within a given society, some meats will be considered taboo simply because they are outside the range of the generally accepted definition of a foodstuff, not necessarily because the meat is considered repulsive in flavor, aroma, texture, or appearance.

Some authorities impose cultural food taboos in the form of law. In some cases, this has been alleged to constitute dietary persecution and possibly human rights abuse.

Health reasons may also contribute to a taboo. For example, eating undercooked pork has a risk of trichinosis, while many forms of seafood can cause extreme cases of food poisoning.

Scavengers and carnivores are frowned upon in many taboo systems, perhaps from their potential to pick up disease and parasites from other creatures.

2. Human Meat

Of all the taboo meat, human flesh ranks as the most proscribed. Historically, man has consumed the flesh of fellow humans in rituals, and out of insanity, hatred, or when facing starvation — never as a common part of one's diet.

3. Taboo Vegetables

In certain versions of Buddhism, onions and chives are taboo. Specifically, Kashmiri Brahmans forbid "strong flavored" foods. This encompasses garlic, onion, and spices such as black pepper and chili pepper. Brahmans believe that pungent flavors on the tongue inflame the baser emotions.

In Yazidism, the eating of lettuce and butter beans is taboo. The Muslim religious teacher and scholar, Falah Hassan Juma, links the sect's belief of evil found in lettuce to its long history of persecution by Muslims and Christians. The Caliphs of the Ottoman Empire carried out massacres against the Yazidis in the eighteenth and nineteenth centuries, with the faithful slain in the lettuce fields then dotting northeastern Iraq. Another historical theory claims one ruthless potentate who controlled the city of Mosul in the thirteenth century ordered an early Yazidi saint executed. The enthusiastic crowd then pelted the corpse with heads of lettuce.

Taboo Drinks

1. Coffee and Tea

In addition to alcohol, coffee and tea are also taboo drinks for members of the Church of Jesus Christ of Latter-day Saints and some other Mormon groups. For some Mormons this taboo extends to other caffeinated beverages, but usually not to chocolate.

2. Alcohol

Some religions—most notably Islam, Sikhism, the Baháí Faith, Latter-day Saints, the Nikaya and most Mahayana schools of Buddhism and some Protestant denominations of Christianity—forbid or discourage the consumption of alcoholic beverages.

3. Blood

Drinking blood is a strong social taboo in most countries, often with a vague emotive association with vampirism (the consumption of human blood). Followers of Judaism, Islam, and Jehovah's Witnesses are forbidden to drink blood, or eat food made with blood.

On the other hand, the Maasai and Batemi people of Tanzania drink cow's blood mixed with milk as a major part of their diet. In Kenya, camel blood is drunk. In many areas such as Brazil, the Philippines, and Mexico, blood is a main ingredient in favorite dishes.

Interpersonal Taboos

Taboos that apply to human interactions include sex, nudity, and bodily functions. Many of these taboos focus on human sexuality, and in fact sexuality itself balances on the edge of taboo. Sexual practices such as intermarriage, miscegenation, homosexuality, incest, bestiality, pedophilia, and necrophilia are all taboo in many cultures. The exposing of certain body parts such as ankles in the Victorian British Empire and women's faces in Saudi Arabia and Afghanistan are also a form of taboo in those areas. The United States holds public nudity as a taboo where in other areas (such as Europe) nudity is much more accepted.

Taboos against bodily functions also exist in many cultures. Burping and flatulence are looked down upon and seen as vulgar.

The use of profanity is taboo in many circles. Seen as improper, swearing or cursing is frowned on as being uncivilized. This again, as many taboos, is not agreed upon and exercised in degrees in different groups of people.

Some taboos originated partly in response to uncleanliness, as well as religious belief. Thus, physical contact with a menstruating woman has been taboo in many cultures, thought to be defiling. Those who had been in contact with dead bodies may also be restricted in their physical contact with food or others.

Conclusion

Taboos are widely agreed upon negative entities that are shunned and avoided. As peoples' morals and values are different, so vary the taboos they believe in. Thus, it is hard to agree on any universal taboos. Genocide, cannibalism, and incest taboos are considered the only taboos that might reach the level of universal.

There are taboos in every subject and they vary from culture to culture. What unites these different ideas is the quest for the knowledge of right and wrong. This mission links people of all ideologies in an attempt to better themselves and create a morally just human race.

Questions for Discussion

1. What is your definition of taboos?
2. Which categories fall within taboo consumption?
3. What is your conclusion of taboos?

Text D Contamination and Camouflage in Euphemisms

We often use euphemisms to tell it like it isn't. People excuse themselves to use the restroom when they have no intention of resting there, talk of ill acquaintances who ultimately bought the farm without funds or agricultural acumen, and slyly recommend an adult entertainment on late-night cable that is hardly mature and even less amusing. Linguists have traditionally characterized euphemism as a lexical substitution strategy for representationally displacing topics that evoke negative affect (e.g., substitution of "use the restroom" for "urinate"). This strategy may serve the ostensibly noble motive of sparing an addressee from communicative discomfort, but it may also serve the communicator's self-presentational concerns as well. When source identity cues are eliminated from an interaction (e.g., one corresponds anonymously with an addressee in an Internet chat room), communicators' use of euphemism has been shown to fall off sharply. Thus people may be less inclined to use euphemisms to minimize the threat to an addressee's face than to protect their own.

With frequent use, a euphemism can become an easily recognizable, conventional label for the unpleasant topic it was coined to veil. Yet conventionality would seem, prima facie, to work against a euphemism's effectiveness in mitigating face threat. After all, if the literal label for a distasteful topic (e.g., urinate) has such strong associations as to elicit negative affect upon its mere mention, might a euphemism that has itself become a conventional label for the topic (e.g., use the restroom) have strong negative associations as well? Verbal tropes such as euphemisms and metaphors can be thought as having "careers" in the vernacular. Over the course of a trope's career, the discourse processes it educes and referential goals it serves may change dramatically. Lexicographer Hugh Rawson suggested that the career of a euphemism is limited by a linguistic incarnation of the economic principle known as Gresham's Law, whereby debased currency eventually drives full-value tokens out of circulation. Just as "bad money drives out the good" in a monetary system, Rawson argued that through frequent usage, euphemisms become tainted by their associations with distasteful topics. This process eventually drives them out of conversational circulation and leads to the creation of new euphemisms to replace them. Other language scholars have made similar claims about the role of "associative contamination" (i.e., chronic semantic linkage with an unpleasant topic) in a euphemism's demise. Etymologist Otto Jespersen lamented the "usual destiny of euphemisms," in which an "innocent word" used to replace an indecent one becomes "just as objectionable as the word it has ousted and now is rejected in its turn." In various critiques of political correctness in English, psycholinguist Steven Pinker has characterized the career of a euphemism as a "treadmill" that ultimately wears out the term when it becomes ubiquitous in text and discourse.

Common to all accounts of associative contamination in euphemism are two implicit empirical claims. First, they imply that the "face value" of a euphemism depreciates as it becomes conventional in discourse, and thus communicators' perceptions of a euphemism's politeness and its familiarity in the vernacular are negatively correlated. Familiarity is, on this view, the principal source of contamination that precipitates a euphemism's fall into disfavor. Unfamiliar euphemisms should appear less contaminated than their familiar counterparts and thereby enjoy an advantage in politeness. Second, the associative contamination hypothesis implies that the attributional consequences of using a familiar euphemism are decidedly negative for a speaker.

Specifically, a speaker who refers to a distasteful topic using a familiar (and hence contaminated) euphemism hazards being perceived as impolite and/or indifferent to the addressee's sensibilities. When the euphemism is highly conventional (e.g., use the bathroom), it should not, according to this view, afford the speaker a discernible advantage in face value over the literal term (urinate).

There have been several incarnations of the "associative contamination" hypothesis in linguistic scholarship, but its empirical claims have never been validated. Moreover, despite its intuitive appeal, the hypothesis is at odds with other generalizations regarding pragmatic phenomena in communication. In particular, consider Searle's observation that interlocutors abide by a maxim advising that they "speak idiomatically unless there is some special reason not to." Searle offered this amendment to Grice's cooperative principle to explain how conventional expressions acquire communicative uses distinct from their literal meanings. For example, the utterances "Can you tell me what time it is?" and "Are you capable of telling me what time it is?" might be semantically equivalent, but only the former, idiomatic expression will likely be taken as solely a request (albeit indirect) for information. Violating the idiomaticity maxim leads addressees to infer that the speaker must have a special reason for using an unfamiliar utterance form. In the example above, an addressee might infer that the purpose of the unconventional form is not to acquire information, but rather to insult her intelligence! In the case of an unconventional euphemism (e.g., make room for tea), addressees may, upon reflection, interpret it as a polite speech act (e.g., a phrasal substitution for urinate); however, its conspicuousness as a breach of the idiomaticity maxim nonetheless seems to work against its mission in mitigating face threat.

If a euphemism is to succeed in reducing the communicative discomfort associated with a distasteful topic, it is imperative that it not call undue attention to itself. In this regard, euphemism succeeds as a discourse strategy in the same manner camouflage succeeds in its military mission — by rendering its subject as inconspicuous as possible in the surrounding context. There are several ways euphemisms can achieve a linguistic low profile. One common strategy is to describe the offensive topic using terms similar in frequency, generality, and sociolinguistic register to the other vocabulary in the discourse context. Although military euphemisms such as collateral damage and neutralization seem aloof and impersonal ways to refer to death, it is these very qualities that enabled them to blend so well into Pentagon press briefing boilerplate before they were "outed" by critics of doublespeak. Another time-honored tactic is to refer to the offending topic at a superordinate level of conceptual abstraction. For example, there are numerous bland uses for a bathroom (washing, shaving, brushing teeth, etc.), and so referring to urination and defecation as other instances of the event category using the bathroom casts them in a less offensive light than basic-level descriptors. Similarly, the subject of sexual intercourse seems far less spicy when abstractly alluded to as doing it, an expression so general that it borders on semantic vacuity.

A third strategy for introducing a valenced topic in a low-key manner is to take Searle's idiomaticity maxim to an extreme—that is, to describe the topic in the most stale, soporific terms available. The use of expressions has typically been identified (and bemoaned) as evidence of an inattentive communicator. In the domain of media discourse, Wanta and Leggett observed that sports announcers use of cliché (e.g., hit paydirt) increased under dramatic game circumstances (e.g., a close score), presumably because their attention was bound up in the ongoing action. Communication scholars have identified clichés as not only a symptom of inattentiveness in social interaction, but also a contributor. Burgoon and Langer review evidence indicating that the presence of cliché expressions in discourse can trigger a rigid, "mindless" mode of information processing that favors stimulus generalization over discrimination and heuristic reasoning over deliberation. If a speaker's goal is to promote mindfulness and concentration among audience members, such expressions should be avoided. On the other hand, if her goal is to allude to an unpleasant topic in an innocuous manner, she may well wish to assuage her audience's attentional vigilance by way of cliché. The mindless processing of a conventional euphemism counteracts the contamination it may have acquired from chronic association with its conceptual referent.

The "camouflage" hypothesis we have outlined above makes predictions that directly contradict the associative contamination hypothesis. First, it predicts that conventionality enhances the perceived politeness of euphemisms, rather than depleting it. This increase is predicated on the fluency with which clichés are comprehended and their capacity to encourage mindless, non-reflective discourse processing. For example, the euphemistic cliché use the bathroom is easily identified by fluent English speakers as a polite, perfunctory way of referring to urination and/or defecation. From a communicative pragmatics perspective, it constitutes the simplest way to refer to the topic within the constraints imposed by sociocultural norms of polite talk. Any other communication strategy short of omission or deception holds greater face threat risks. Dysphemisms (piss, shit, etc.) and ostensibly literal references to the subject (urinate, defecate, etc.) hazard the greatest risk, which is why polite speakers seek out alternative encodings. Unfamiliar euphemisms (make room for tea, tend the night soil, etc.) violate the idiomaticity maxim and hence invite deliberation about the expression's meaning, as well as consideration of the reasons why the maxim might have been flouted. Conventional euphemisms afford the speaker comparative safety by being easy to both understand and overlook.

Second, the camouflage hypothesis predicts that there are, relatively speaking, and positive attributional consequences for using a conventional euphemism. Speakers of course run the risk of incurring negative attributions (impolite, inappropriate, immature, etc.) by choosing to broach a taboo topic in the first place, regardless of how they encode it. To minimize the attributional penalty addressees may impose for this choice, it is in speakers' interest to avoid putting the evidence against them on prominent display. As discussed earlier, the presence of literal or unfamiliar descriptors of a taboo topic is more salient in discourse than cliché. The lower profile of euphemistic holds the benefit of making them less noticeable and less memorable as evidence supporting negative attributions toward the speaker.

Questions for Discussion

1. How have linguists traditionally characterized euphemism?
2. According to lexicographer Hugh Rawson, what limit the career of a euphemism?
3. What are the two implicit empirical claims common to all accounts of associative contamination in euphemism?
4. What are the ways through which euphemisms can achieve a linguistic low profile?
5. What are the contradictions between predictions made by the "camouflage" hypothesis and the "associative contamination" hypothesis?

Unit 8 Cultural Thought Patterns in Intercultural Education

> Conversation should be pleasant without scurrility, witty without affectation, free without indecency, learned without conceitedness, novel without falsehood.
> —William Shakespeare
>
> Rhetoric in Chinese society thus came to be very much akin to sheer propriety. The utility which rhetoric was to serve was the maintenance of harmony. The way to this goal was through ceremony, etiquette, and methodology.
> —Robert Oliver

Unit Goals

- To understand cultural differences reflected in daily conversation and written language
- To understand the definitions of rhetoric and contrastive rhetoric
- To be aware of the cultural roots of the Chinese and Western rhetorical systems

 Before You Read

Group Work:

Many misunderstandings or miscommunication between Chinese and North Americans are rooted in their different customs and social values.

1. **Analyze the following 4 cases of miscommunication and then try to explain from the Chinese and North American perspectives.**

   Case 1
   Kathy and David, a couple from the US, signed a one-year contract to work in China. Both were extroverted and soon made some Chinese friends.

Before long, people started calling them at home. David was sometimes away on business trips for a few days, and if someone looked for him, Kathy often would find the conversation awkward.

"Where did he go?" The caller typically would ask.

"Can I pass on any message?" Kathy asked politely, trying to avoid the question.

"Is he out of town?" The caller was usually very persistent.

"Yes, can I help you in any way?" Kathy tried to be polite, but she could not help feeling uncomfortable.

Case 2

As a visiting professor in an American university, Zhang Chonghua was invited to give a lecture to a group of American students. He talked about university students in China. During the question-and-answer section after the lecture, one female student asked a question that surprised Prof. Zhang.

"When you talked about female students, you referred to them as girls. Why?"

"It is because they are girls. That's what they are called."

Zhang tried to answer, but he did not really understand the intent of the question.

"I don't quite understand your question, I'm afraid."

"In the States, we call ourselves 'woman' if we're old enough to go to the university. Calling us 'girls' is insulting."

Case 3

Kim and Yang liked each other a lot. Soon they had their first date and went to dinner together. They both ordered a couple of small dishes. When the first course came, Yang felt the portion was not as big as he had expected, and started to worry whether there would be enough food.

"Do you think we have enough food?" he asked.

"I think so, unless you want to order more," Kim responded.

"Well, I think you are hungry. Let's get one more dish."

"I'm fine. You can order more if you like," Kim said.

Yang ordered one more dish.

As the rest of the courses came, Yang realized that there was more food than he had thought.

"It looks like we have more than enough food," he said.

"I told you so, but you said there was not enough."

"I thought you wanted more."

"No, I didn't. I told you it was enough for me. You wanted to order more."

"I did it for you."

"I told you it would be enough for ME. You didn't seem to be listening." Kim raised her voice.

"I did listen to you. But you said I could order more if I wanted."

Kim's face turned very red. "That's because you kept saying there wasn't enough food. I thought you ordered for yourself!"

"No, I ordered for you!"

"So you didn't listen to me!"

"I did!"

Case 4

A (American): What a splendid garden you have here — the lawn is so nice and big. It's certainly wonderful, isn't it?

B (Chinese): Oh no, I don't think so at all. We don't take care of it all, so it simply doesn't always look as nice as we would like it so.

A (American): Oh no, I don't think so at all. But since it's such a big garden, of course, it must be quite a tremendous task to take care of it all by yourself. But even so, you certainly do manage to make it look nice all the time. It certainly is nice and pretty anytime one sees it.

B (Chinese): No, I'm afraid not, not at all.

2. Discuss with your group members on the following questions.

1) Are the greetings conducted in the same way in English culture and Chinese culture? Why or why not?
2) What are the differences in making introductions between English and Chinese people?
3) What causes the difference in exchanging compliments between English and Chinese people?
4) How do English and Chinese people express thanks and reply differently? Which way do you prefer?

Start to Read

Text A Cultural Thought Patterns in Inter-cultural Education (I)

The teaching of reading and composition to foreign students does differ from the teaching of reading and composition to American students, and cultural differences in the nature of rhetoric supply the key to the difference in teaching approach.

> ... Rhetoric is a mode of thinking or a mode of "finding all available means" for the achievement of a designated end. Accordingly, rhetoric concerns itself basically with what goes on in the mind rather than with what comes out of the mouth... Rhetoric is concerned with factors of analysis, data gathering, interpretation, and synthesis... What we notice in the environment and how we notice it are both predetermined to a significant degree by how we are prepared to notice this particular type of object... Cultural anthropologists point out that given acts and objects appear vastly different in different cultures, depending on the values attached to them. Psychologists investigating perception are increasingly insistent that what is perceived depends upon the observer's perceptual frame of reference.[1]

Language teachers, particularly teachers of English as a second language, are late-comers in the area of international education. For years, and until quite recently, most languages were taught in what might be called a mechanistic way, stressing the prescriptive function of such teaching. In recent years the swing has been in the other direction, and the prescriptive has practically disappeared from language teaching. Descriptive approaches have seemed to provide the answer. At the present moment, there seems to be some question about the purely descriptive technique, and a new compromise between description and prescription seems to be emerging. Such a compromise appears necessary to the adequate achievement of results in second-language teaching. Unfortunately, although both the prescriptivists and the descriptivists have recognized the existence of cultural variation as a factor in second-language teaching, the recognition has so far been limited to the level of the sentence — that is, to the level of grammar, vocabulary, and sentence structure. On the other hand, it has long been known among sociologists and anthropologists that logic *per se* is a cultural phenomenon as well.

> Even if we take into account the lexical and grammatical similarities that exist between languages proceeding from a common hypothetical ancestor, the fact remains that the verbal universe is divided into multiple sectors. Sapir, Whorf, and many others, comparing the Indian languages with the Occidental languages, have underlined this diversity very forcefully. It seems, indeed, as if the arbitrary character of language, having been shown to be of comparatively little significance at the level of the elements of a language, reasserts itself quite definitely at the level of the language taken as a whole. And if one admits that a language represents a kind of destiny, so far as human thought is concerned, this diversity

---

[1] Robert T. Oliver, "Foreword," *Philosophy, Rhetoric and Argumentation*, ed. Maurice Nathanson and Henry W. Johnstone, Jr. (University Park, Pennsylvania, 1965), pp. x—xi.

of languages leads to a radical realitivism. As Peirce said, if Aristotle had been Mexican, his logic would have been different; and perhaps, by the same token, the whole of our philosophy and our science would have been different.

The fact is that this diversity affects not only the languages, but also the cultures, that is to say the whole system of institutions that are tied to the language. . .[and] language in its turn is the effect and the expression of a certain world view that is manifested in the culture. If there is causality, it is a reciprocal causality...

The types of structures characteristic of a given culture would then, in each case, be particular modes of universal laws. They would define the Volksgeist...[1]

Logic (in the popular, rather than the logician's sense of the word) which is the basis of rhetoric, is evolved out of a culture; it is not universal. Rhetoric, then, is not universal either, but varies from culture to culture and even from time to time within a given culture. It is affected by canons of taste within a given culture at a given time.

Every language offers to its speakers a ready-made interpretation of the world, truly a Weltanschauung, a metaphysical word-picture which, after having originated in the thinking of our ancestors, tends to impose itself ever anew on posterity. Take for instance a simple sentence such as "I see him..." This means that English and, I might say, Indo-European, presents the impressions made on our senses predominantly as human activities, brought about by our will. But the Eskimos in Greenland say not "I see him" but "he appears to me...." Thus the Indo-European speaker conceives as workings of his activities what the fatalistic Eskimo sees as events that happen to him.[2]

The English language and its related thought patterns have evolved out of the Anglo-European cultural pattern. The expected sequence of thought in English is essentially a Platonic-Artistotelian sequence, descended from the philosophers of ancient Greece and shaped subsequently by Roman, Medieval European, and later Western thinkers. It is not a better nor a worse system than any other, but it is different.

---

1 Mikel Dufrenne, *Language and Philosophy*, trans. Henry B. Veatch (Bloomington, 1963), pp. 35—37.

2 Leo Spitzer, "Language — The Basis of Science, Philosophy and Poetry," *Studies in Intellectual History*, ed. George Boas et al. (Baltimore, 1953), pp. 83—84.

> ...As human beings, we must inevitably see the universe from a centre lying within ourselves and speak about it in terms of a human language by the exigencies of human intercourse. Any attempt rigorously to eliminate our human perspective from our picture of the world must lead to absurdity.[1]

A fallacy of some repute and some duration is the one which assumes that because a student can write an adequate essay in his native language, he can necessarily write an adequate essay in a second language. That this assumption is fallacious has become more and more apparent as English-as-a-second-language courses have proliferated at American colleges and universities in recent years. Foreign students who have mastered syntactic structures have still demonstrated inability to compose adequate themes, term papers, theses, and dissertations. Instructors have written, on foreign-student papers, such comments as: "The material is all here, but it seems somehow out of focus," or "Lacks organization," or "Lacks cohesion." And these comments are essentially accurate. The foreign-student paper is out of focus because the foreign student is employing a rhetoric and a sequence of thought which violate the expectations of the native reader.

> A personality is carved out by the whole subtle interaction of these systems of ideas which are characteristic of the culture as a whole, as well as of those systems of ideas which get established for the individual through more special types of participation.[2]

The fact that sequence of thought and grammar are related in a given language has already been demonstrated adequately by Paul Lorenzen. His brief paper proposes that certain linguistic structures are best comprehended as embodiments of logical structures.[3] Beyond that, every rhetorician from Cicero to Brooks and Warren has indicated the relationship between thought sequence and rhetoric.

> A paragraph, mechanically considered, is a division of the composition, set off by an indentation of its first sentence or by some other conventional device, such as extra space between paragraphs... Paragraph divisions signal to the reader that the material so set off constitutes a unit of thought.
>
> For the reader this marking off of the whole composition into segments is a convenience,

---

1 Michael Polanyi, *Personal Knowledge: Towards a Post-critical Philosophy* (Chicago, 1958), p.9.
2 Sapir, "Anthropology and Psychiatry," *Culture, Language and Personality* (Los Angeles, 1964), p. 157.
3 *Logik und Grannatik* (Mannheim, Germany, 1965).

though not a strict necessity... Since communication of one's thought is at best a difficult business, it is the part of common sense (not to mention good manners) to mark for the reader the divisions of one's thought and thus make the thought structure visible upon the page...

Paragraphing, obviously, can be of help to the reader only if the indicated paragraphs are genuine units of thought... For a paragraph undertakes to discuss one topic or one aspect of a topic.[1]

The thought patterns which speakers and readers of English appear to expect as an integral part of their communication is a sequence that is dominantly linear in its development. An English expository paragraph usually begins with a topic statement, and then, by a series of subdivisions of that topic statement, each supported by example and illustrations, proceeds to develop that central idea and relate that idea to all the other ideas in the whole essay, and to employ that idea in its proper relationship with the other ideas, to prove something, or perhaps to argue something.

A piece of writing may be considered unified when it contains nothing superfluous and it omits nothing essential to the achievement of its purpose... A work is considered coherent when the sequence of its parts... is controlled by some principle which is meaningful to the reader. Unity is the quality attributed to writing which has all its necessary and sufficient parts. Coherence is the quality attributed to the presentation of material in a sequence which is intelligible to its reader.[2]

Contrarily, the English paragraph may use just the reverse procedure; that is, it may state a whole series of examples and then relate those examples into a single statement at the end of the paragraph. These two types of development represent the common inductive and deductive reasoning which the English reader expects to be an integral part of any formal communication.

For example, the following paragraph written by Macaulay demonstrates normal paragraph development:

Whitehall, when [Charles the Second] dwelt there, was the focus of political intrigue and of fashionable gaiety. Half the jobbing and half the flirting of the metropolis went on under his roof. Whoever could make himself agreeable to the prince or could secure the good offices of his mistress might hope to rise in the world without rendering any service to

---

1 Cleanth Brooks and Robert Penn Warren, *Modern Rhetoric*, 2nd ed. (New York, 1958), pp. 267—268.
2 Richard E. Hughes and P. Albert Duhamel, *Rhetoric: Principles and Usage* (Engle-wood Cliffs, New Jersey, 1962), pp. 19—20.

the government, without even being known by sight to any minister of state. This courtier got a frigate and that a company, a third the pardon of a rich offender, a fourth a lease of crown-land on easy terms. If the king notified his pleasure that a brief less lawyer should be made a judge or that a libertine baronet should be made a peer, the gravest counselors, after a little murmuring, submitted. Interest, therefore, drew a constant press of suitors to the gates of the palace, and those gates always stood wide. The King kept open house every day and all day long for the good society of London, the extreme Whigs only excepted. Hardly any gentleman had any difficulty in making his way to the royal presence. The levee was exactly what the word imports. Some men of quality came every morning to stand round their master, to chat with him while his wig was combed and his cravat tied, and to accompany him in his early walk through the Park. All persons who had been properly introduced might, without any special invitation, go to see him dine, sup, dance, and play at hazard and might have the pleasure of hearing him tell stories, which indeed, he told remarkably well, about his flight from Worcester and about the misery which he had endured when he was a state prisoner in the hands of the canting meddling preachers of Scotland.[1]

The paragraph begins with a general statement of its content, and then carefully develops that statement by a long series of rather specific illustrations. While it is discursive, the paragraph is never digressive. There is nothing in this paragraph that does not belong here; nothing that does not contribute significantly to the central idea. The flow of ideas occurs in a straight line from the opening sentence to the last sentence.

Without doing too much damage to other ways of thinking, perhaps it might be possible to contrast the English paragraph development with paragraph development in other linguistic systems.

For the purposes of the following brief analysis, some seven hundred foreign student compositions were carefully analyzed. Approximately one hundred of these were discarded from the study on the basis that they represent linguistic groups too small within the present sample to be significant.[2] But approximately six hundred examples, representing three basic language groups, were examined.[3]

---

1 From *The History of England from the Accession of James the Second* (London, 1849—1861).

2 The following examples were discarded: Afghan-3, African-4, Danish-1, Finn-1, German-3, Hindi-8, Persion-46, Russian-1, Greek-1, Tagalog-10, Turk-16, Urdu-5; Total 99.

3 The papers examined may be linguistically broken down as follows: Group I-Arabic-126, Hebrew-3; Group II-Chinese (Mandarin)-110, Cambodian-40, Indochinese-7, Japanese-135, Korean-157, Laotian-3, Malasian-1, Thai-27, Vietnamese-1; Group III-(Spanish-Portuguese) Brazilian-19, Central American-10, South American-41, Cuban-4, Spanish-8, (French) French-2, African-2, (Italian) Swiss-1. Group I total-129; Group II total-381; Group III total-88; TOTAL-598. These papers were accumulated and examined over a two year period, from the beginning of the fall 1963 semester through the fall 1965 academic semester.

In the Arabic language, for example (and this generalization would be more or less true for all Semitic languages), paragraph development is based on a complex series of parallel constructions, both positive and negative. This kind of parallelism may most clearly be demonstrated in English by reference to the King James version of the Old Testament. Several types of parallelism typical of Semitic languages are apparent there because that book, of course, is a translation from an ancient Semitic language, a translation accomplished at a time when English was in a state of development suitable to the imitation of those forms.

1. Synonymous Parallelism: The balancing of the thought and phrasing of the first part of a statement or idea by the second part. In such cases, the two parts are often connected by a coordinating conjunction.

Example: His descendants will be mighty in the land

and

the generation of the upright will be blessed.

2. Synthetic Parallelism: The completion of the idea or thought of the first part in the second part. A conjunctive adverb is often stated or implied.

Example: Because he inclined his ear to me

therefore

I will call on him as long as I live.

3. Antithetic Parallelism: The idea stated in the first part is emphasized by the expression of a contrasting idea in the second part. The contrast is expressed not only in thought but often in phrasing as well.

Example: For the Lord knoweth the way of the righteous:

But the way of the wicked shall perish.

4. Climactic Parallelism: The idea of the passage is not completed until the very end of the passage. This form is similar to the modern periodic sentence in which the subject is postponed to the very end of the sentence.

Example: Give unto the Lord, O ye sons of the mighty,

Give unto the Lord glory and strength.[1]

The type of parallel construction here illustrated in single sentences also forms the core of paragraphs in some Arabic writing. Obviously, such a development in a modern English paragraph would strike the modern English reader as archaic or awkward, and more importantly it would stand in the way of clear communication. It is important to note that in English, maturity of style is often gauged by degree of subordination rather than by coordination.

The following paper was written as a class exercise by an Arabic-speaking student in an

---

1　I am indebted to Dr. Ben Siegel for this analysis.

English-as-a-second-language class at an American university:

> The contemporary Bedouins, who live in the deserts of Saudi Arabia, are the successors of the old bedouin tribes, the tribes that was fascinated with Mohammad's massage, and on their shoulders Islam built it's empire. I had lived among those contemporary Bedouins for a short period of time, and I have learned lots of things about them. I found out that they have retained most of their ancestor's characteristics, in spite of the hundreds of years that separate them.
>
> They are famous of many praiseworthy characteristics, but they are considered to be the symbol of generosity, bravery, and self-esteem. Like most of the wandering peoples, a stranger is an undesirable person among them. But, once they trust him as a friend, he will be most welcome. However, their trust is a hard thing to gain. And the heroism of many famous figures, who ventured in the Arabian deserts like T. E. Lawrence, is based on their ability to acquire this dear trust!
>
> Romance is an important part in their life. And "love" is an important subject in their verses and their tales.
>
> Nevertheless, they are criticized of many things. The worst of all is that they are extremists in all the ways of their lives. It is there extremism that changes sometimes their generosity into squandering, their bravery into brutality, and their self-esteem into haughtiness. But in any case, I have been, and will continue to be greatly interested in this old, fascinating group of people.

Disregarding for the moment the grammatical errors in this student composition, it becomes apparent that the characteristics of parallelism do occur. The next-to-last element in the first sentence, for example, is appositive to the preceding one, while the last element is an example of synonymous parallelism. The two clauses of the second sentence illustrate synonymous parallelism. In the second "paragraph" the first sentence contains both an example of antithetic parallelism and a list of parallel nouns. The next two sentences form an antithetic pair, and so on. It is perhaps not necessary to point out further examples in the selection. It is important, however, to observe that in the first sentence, for example, the grammatical complexity is caused by the attempt to achieve an intricate parallelism. While this extensive parallel construction is linguistically possible in Arabic, the English language lacks the necessary flexibility. Eight conjunctions and four sentence connectors are employed in a matter of only fourteen "sentences." In addition, there are five "lists" of units connected by commas and conjunctions.

Another paper, also written by an Arabic-speaking student under comparable circumstances, further demonstrates the same tendencies:

At that time of the year I was not studying enough to pass my courses in school. And all the time I was asking my cousin to let me ride the bicycle, but he wouldn't let me. But after two weeks, noticing that I was so much interested in the bicycle, he promised me that if I pass my courses in school for that year he would give it to me as a present. So I began to study hard. And I studying eight hours a day instead of two.

My cousin seeing me studying that much he was sure that I was going to succeed in school. So he decided to give me some lessons in riding the bicycle. After four or five weeks of teaching me and ten or twelve times hurting myself as I used to go out of balance, I finally knew how to ride it. And the finals in school came and I was very good prepared for them so I passed them. My cousin kept his promise and gave me the bicycle as a present. And till now I keep the bicycle in a safe place, and everytime I see it, it reminds me how it helped to pass my courses for that year.

In the first paragraph of this example, four of the five sentences, or 80% of the sentences, begin with a coordinating element. In the second paragraph, three of the six sentences, or 50% of the total, also begin with a coordinating element. In the whole passage, seven of the eleven sentences, or roughly 65%, conform to this pattern. In addition, the first paragraph contains one internal coordinator, and the second contains five internal coordinators; thus, the brief passage (210 words) contains a total of thirteen coordinators. It is important to notice that almost all of the ideas in the passage are coordinately linked, that there is very little subordination, and that the parallel units exemplify the types of parallelism already noted.

Some Oriental writing[1], on the other hand, is marked by what may be called an approach by indirection. In this kind of writing, the development of the paragraph may be said to be "turning and turning in a widening gyre." The circles or gyres turn around the subject and show it from a variety of tangential views, but the subject is never looked at directly. Things are developed in terms of what they are not, rather than in terms of what they are. Again, such a development in a modern English paragraph would strike the English reader as awkward and unnecessarily indirect.

The following composition was written, as a class exercise, by a native speaker of Korean, under the same circumstances which produced the two previous examples. Obviously, this student is weaker in general English proficiency than the students who produced the two prior examples.

---

1   Oriental here is intended to mean specifically Chinese and Korean but not Japanese.

Definition of college education

College is an institution of an higher learning that gives degrees. All of us needed culture and education in life, if no education to us, we should to go living hell.

One of the greatest causes that while other animals have remained as they first man along has made such rapid progress is has learned about civilization.

The improvement of the highest civilization is in order to education up-to-date.

So college education is very important thing which we don't need mention about it.

Again, disregarding the typically Oriental grammar and the misconception of the function of "parts of speech," the first sentence defines college, not college education. This may conceivably be a problem based upon the student's misunderstanding of the assignment. But the second sentence appears to shoot off in a totally different direction. It makes a general statement about culture and education, perhaps as results of a college education. The third sentence, presented as a separate "paragraph," moves still farther away from definition by expanding the topic to "man" in a generic sense, as opposed to "non-man." This unit is tied to the next, also presented as a separate paragraph, by the connecting idea of "civilization" as an aspect of education. The concluding paragraph-sentence presents, in the guise of a summary logically derived from previously posited ideas, a conclusion which is in fact partially a topic sentence and partially a statement that the whole basic concept of the assignment is so obvious that it does not need discussion. The paper arrives where it should have started, with the added statement that it really had no place to go to begin with.

The poorer proficiency of this student, however, introduces two other considerations. It is possible that this student, as an individual rather than as a representative native speaker of Korean, lacks the ability to abstract sufficiently for extended definition. In the case under discussion, however, the student was majoring in mathematics and did have the ability to abstract in mathematical terms. While the demands of mathematics are somewhat different from the demands of language in a conventional sense, it is possible to assume that a student who can handle abstraction in one area can also probably handle it at least to some extent in the other. It is also possible that the ability to abstract is absent from the Korean culture. This appears quite unlikely in view of the abundance of Korean art available and in view of the fact that other native speakers of Korean have not demonstrated that shortcoming.

(Excerpted from Kaplan, R. 1966. Cultural thought patterns in inter-cultural education. *Language Learning*, 16, 1-20. doi:10.1111/j.1467-1770. 1966.tb00804.x)

Text B Cultural Thought Patterns in Inter-cultural Education (II)

The examples cited so far have been student themes. The following example is from a professional translation. Essentially, the same variations can be observed in it. In this case, the translation is from French.

The first point to which I would like to call your attention is that nothing exists outside the boundary of what is strictly human. A landscape may be beautiful, graceful, sublime, insignificant, or ugly; it will never be ludicrous. We may laugh at an animal, but only because we have detected in it some human expression or attitude. We may laugh at a hat, but we are not laughing at the piece of felt or straw. We are laughing at the shape that men have given to it, the human whim whose mold it has assumed. *I wonder why a fact so important has not attracted the attention of philosophers to a greater degree. Some have defined man as an animal that knows how to laugh. They could equally well have defined him as an animal which provokes laughter*; for If any other animal or some lifeless object, achieves the same effect, it is always because of some similarity to man.[1]

In this paragraph, the italicized portion constitutes a digression. It is an interesting digression, but it really does not seem to contribute significant structural material to the basic thought of the paragraph. While the author of the paragraph is a philosopher, and a philosopher is often forgiven for digressions, the more important fact is that the example is a typical one for writers of French as well as for writers of philosophy. Much greater freedom to digress or to introduce extraneous material is available in French, or in Spanish, than in English.

Similar characteristics can be demonstrated in the writing of native French-speaking students in English. In the interests of keeping this report within some bounds, such illustrations will be inserted without comment. The first example was written under circumstances similar to those described for the preceding student samples. The writer is a native speaker of French.

American Traffic law as compared with Traffic law in Switzerland

At first glance the traffic law in United States appeared to me simpler than in Switzerland.

The American towns in general have the disposition of a cross, and for a driver who knows how to situate himself between the four cardinal points, there is no problem to find his way. Each street has numbers going crecendo from the center of the town to the outside.

---

1 From *Laughter, An Assay on the Meaning of the Comic*, trans. Marcel Bolomet (Paris, 1900).

There are many accidents in Switzerland, as everywhere else, and the average of mortality comparatively to the proportion of the countries is not better than in United States. We have the problem of straight streets, not enough surveillance by policemen on the national roads, and alcohol. The country of delicious wines has made too many damages.

The following illustration, drawn from the work of a native speaker of Latin American Spanish, was produced under conditions parallel to those already cited:

The American Children

In America, the American children are brought differently from the rest of the children in other countries. In their childhood, from the first day they are born, the parents give their children the love and attention they need. They teach their children the meaning of Religion among the family and to have respect and obedience for their parents.

I am Spanish, and I was brought up differently than the children in America. My parents are stricter and they taught me discipline and not to interrupt when someone was talking.

The next and last example is again not a piece of student writing, but a translation. The original was written in Russian, and the translation attempts to capture the structure of the original as much as possible, but without sacrificing meaning completely.

On the 14th of October, Kruschev left the stage of history. Was it a plot the result of which was that Kruschev was out of business remains not clear. It is very probable that even if it were anything resembling a plot it would not be for the complete removal of Kruschev from political guidance, but rather a pressure exerted to obtain some changes in his policies: for continuations of his policies of peaceful coexistence in international relations or making it as far as possible a situation to avoid formal rupture with the Chinese communist party and at any rate not to go unobstructed to such a rupture — and in the area of internal politics, especially in the section of economics, to continue efforts of a certain softening of "dogmatism", but without the hurried and not sufficiently reasoned experimentation, which became the characteristic traits of Kruschev's politics in recent years.[1]

Some of the difficulty in this paragraph is linguistic rather than rhetorical. The structure of the Russian sentence is entirely different from the structure of the English sentence. But some of the linguistic difficulty is closely related to the rhetorical difficulty. The above paragraph

---

1 From S. Schwartz, "After Kruschev," trans. E. B. Kaplan, *The Socialist Courier* (April, 1965), p.3.

is composed of three sentences. The first two are very short, while the last is extremely long, constituting about three quarters of the paragraph. It is made up of a series of presumably parallel constructions and a number of sub-ordinate structures. At least half of these are irrelevant to the central idea of the paragraph in the sense that they are parenthetical amplifications of structurally related subordinate elements.

There are, of course, other examples that might be discussed as well, but these paragraphs may suffice to show that each language and each culture has a paragraph order unique to itself, and that part of the learning of a particular language is the mastering of its logical system.

> ...One should join to any logic of the language a phenomenology of the spoken word. Moreover, this phenomenology will, in its turn, rediscover the idea of a logos immanent in the language; but it will seek the justification for this in a more general philosophy of the relations between man and the world...
>
> From one culture to another it is possible to establish communication. The Rorschach test has been successfully applied to the natives of the island of Alor.[1]

This discussion is not intended to offer any criticism of other existing paragraph developments; rather it is intended only to demonstrate that paragraph developments other than those normally regarded as desirable in English do exist. In the teaching of paragraph structure to foreign students, whether in terms of reading or in terms of composition, the teacher must be himself aware of these differences, and he must make these differences overtly apparent to his students. In short, contrastive rhetoric must be taught in the same sense that contrastive grammar is presently taught. Now not much has been done in the area of contrastive rhetoric. It is first necessary to arrive at accurate descriptions of existing paragraph orders other than those common to English. Furthermore, it is necessary to understand that these categories are in no sense meant to be mutually exclusive. Patterns may be derived for typical English paragraphs, but paragraphs like those described above as being atypical in English do exist in English. By way of obvious example, Ezra Pound writes paragraphs which are circular in their structure, and William Faulkner writes paragraphs which are wildly digressive. The paragraph being discussed here is not the "literary" paragraph, however, but the expository paragraph. The necessities of art impose structures on any language, while the requirements of communication can often be best solved by relatively close adhesion to established patterns.

Superficially, the movement of the various paragraphs discussed above may be graphically represented in the following manner:

---

1 Mikel Dufrenne, *Language and Philosophy*, trans. Henry B. Veatch (Bloomington, 1963), pp. 39—40.

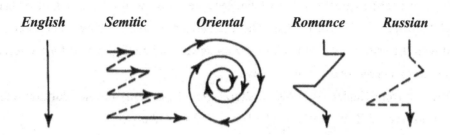

Much more detailed and more accurate descriptions are required before any meaningful contrastive system can be elaborated. Nonetheless, an important problem exists immediately. In the teaching of English as a second language, what does one do with the student who is reasonably proficient in the use of syntactic structure but who needs to learn to write themes, theses, essay examinations, and dissertations? The "advanced" student has long constituted a problem for teachers of English as a second language. This approach, the contrastive analysis of rhetoric, is offered as one possible answer to the existing need. Such an approach has the advantage that it may help the foreign student to form standards of judgment consistent with the demands made upon him by the educational system of which he has become a part. At the same time, by accounting for the cultural aspects of logic which underlie the rhetorical structure, this approach may bring the student not only to an understanding of contrastive grammar and a new vocabulary, which are parts of any reading task, but also to a grasp of idea and structure in units larger than the sentence. A sentence, after all, rarely exists outside a context. Applied linguistics teaches the student to deal with the sentence, but it is necessary to bring the student beyond that to a comprehension of the whole context. He can only understand the whole context if he recognizes the logic on which the context is based. The foreign student who has mastered the syntax of English may still write a bad paragraph or a bad paper unless he also masters the logic of English. "*In serious expository prose, the paragraph tends to be a logical, rather than a typographical, unit.*"[1] The understanding of paragraph patterns can allow the student to relate syntactic elements within a paragraph and perhaps even to relate paragraphs within a total context.

Finally, it is necessary to recognize the fact that a paragraph is an artificial thought unit employed in the written language to suggest a cohesion which commonly may not exist in oral language. "Paragraphing, like punctuation, is a feature only of the written language."[2] As an artificial unit of thought, it lends itself to patterning quite readily. In fact, since it is imposed from without, and since it is a frame for the structuring of thought into patterns, it is by its very nature patterned. The rhetorical structures of English paragraphs may be found in any good composition

---

1 Hans P. Guth, *A Short New Rhetoric* (Belmont, California, 1965), p. 205.

2 Edward P. J. Corbett, *Classical Rhetoric for the Modern Student* (New York, 1965), p. 416.

text.¹ The patterns of paragraphs in other languages are not so well established, or perhaps only not so well known to speakers of English. These patterns need to be discovered or uncovered and compared with the patterns of English in order to arrive at a practical means for the teaching of such structures to non-native users of the language.

(Excerpted from Kaplan, R. 1966. Cultural thought patterns in inter-cultural education. *Language Learning*, 16, 1-20. doi:10.1111/j.1467-1770.1966.tb00804.x)

After You Read

Knowledge Focus

1. **Pair Work: Discuss the following questions with your partner.**
   1) What is the author's general point of view in this academic paper?
   2) If a student can write an adequate essay in his native language, can he necessarily write an adequate essay in a second language? Why?
   3) What is a typical English expository paragraph like?
   4) What kind of reasoning is usually represented in the development of English paragraphs?
   5) What teaching approach is suggested by the author to tackle the problem of different thought patterns in the teaching of English as a second language?

2. **Solo Work: Decide whether the following statements are true or false.**
   1) According to the author, the language teaching in recent years has been emphasizing more on the prescriptive functions rather than the descriptive approaches.
   2) Logic and rhetoric are not universal, but vary from culture to culture and even from time to time within a given culture.
   3) If a student can write an adequate essay in his native language, it is very likely that he can write an adequate essay in a second language.
   4) Grammar has very little to do with sequence of thought.
   5) The thought patterns which speakers and readers of English demonstrate is a sequence dominantly linear in its development.
   6) The author argues that in the teaching of English as a second language, it is necessary for the teacher to be aware of differences in cultural patterns, and he should also make these differences overtly apparent to his students.

---

1 Important works in the rhetoric of the paragraph is being done by Francis Christensen, among others. See especially "A Generative Rhetoric of the Paragraph," *College Composition and Communication* (October, 1965), pp. 144—156.

7) The typical "linear" development of English paragraphs exists in all English writings.

8) The patterns of paragraphs in other languages should be discovered and compared with the patterns of English in order to arrive at a practical means for the teachings of English as a second language.

Language Focus

1. Fill in the blanks with the words or expressions you have learned in the texts.

| synonymous | tangential | amplification | adhesion |
| atypical | archaic | gauge | expedite |

1) The voice of despair may be weak and need _____.
2) The meaning of some _____ forms of writing is not always well understood today.
3) In the UK, one small Scottish village has become _____ with the act of eloping.
4) His mood can be _____ by his reaction to the most trivial of incidents.
5) They thought the whole thing was a side-show, _____ to the real world of business.
6) The economy of the province was _____ because it was particularly small.
7) The government will also _____ the implementation of the series of fire prevention measures announced recently.
8) Better driving equipment will improve track _____ in slippery conditions.

2. Fill in the blanks with the proper form of the words you have learned in the texts.

1) His book applies this model to writing outlines for _____ (exposition) articles and narrative articles.
2) Ms Stuart is the mixed-race _____ (descend) of both an African slave and an English slave owner.
3) Words and phrases are organized according to the _____ (syntax) categories they belong to.
4) Logical connectors are one of the major _____ (cohesion) devices, it can achieve coherence in discourse.
5) I could _____ (deductive) that they are a couple come from countryside from their clothes.
6) I usually become _____ (digression) when I am exhausted or bored.
7) The warming of the Earth and the consequent _____ (climate) changes affect us all.
8) I cannot _____ (conceivable) of anybody writing a play by sitting down and mapping it out.

3. Proofreading

The following passage contains TEN errors. Each line contains a maximum of ONE error. In each case, only ONE word is involved. You should proofread the passage and correct the errors in the following way:

For a wrong word, underline the wrong word and write the correct one in the blank provided at the end of the line.

For a missing word, mark the position of the missing word with a "∧" sign and write the word you believe to be missing in the blank provided at the end of the line.

For an unnecessary word, cross out the unnecessary word with a slash "/" and put the word in the blank provided at the end of the line.

The most universal of forms of language behavior are those people use in everyday life. Ordinary everyday conversation is much more broadly determined than literal composition. With limits literature may be personal and occasional for individuality of style. Everyday conversation, therefore, is communal, general, and as free from unusual features of pronunciation and usage as sociability and conformity can make. The interesting topic is that oral stories differ from written ones or oral language use from written language use for general. It is easy when studying the basic units of language so as sounds, morphemes, words, sentences, and so on to gain sight of the fact that the parts must function together smooth when one puts his/her linguistic ability to actual usage.	1. _____ 2. _____ 3. _____ 4. _____ 5. _____ 6. _____ 7. _____ 8. _____ 9. _____ 10. _____

Comprehensive Work

1. Oral Discussions: Differences between Chinese and English Rhetorical Patterns.

Robert Kaplan (1966), the forerunner of the study of contrastive rhetoric, identified thought patterns and structure specific to individual languages. These are represented visually here. Examine the pictures carefully and then discuss with your classmates with regard to the following questions.

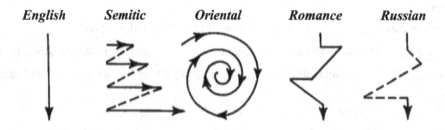

English   Semitic   Oriental   Romance   Russian

1) How do you understand the pictures and the relevant claims?
2) Comparing Chinese and English writing, do you agree with the claims?
3) What are the similarities and differences between Chinese and English rhetoric?
4) As English majors, what can we do to avoid misunderstandings in writing in English?

2. Writing Practice

Non-native speakers of English who learn how to write in English usually have already learned how to write in their native language. Their knowledge about and skills in writing in their first language affect the way they write in English. Because of this influence, students of English as a second language may use rhetorical patterns and stylistic elements characteristic of writing in their native language but alien to the Anglo-American writing tradition. This transfer impedes effective communication between the writer and the reader and also affects the assessment of the writer's performance negatively.

Write a composition of about 400 words explaining with examples how our native language, Chinese, interferes with English writing and then offer some suggestions as to reducing the negative effect of it.

3. Translation: Translate the following passage into Chinese.

Contrastive rhetoric began in 1966 as the result of a self-initiated study of international students writing in English by Kaplan, who then made the pronouncement that "each language and each culture has a paragraph order unique to itself, and that part of the learning of a particular language is the mastery of its logical system" (Kaplan, 1966, p.14). Since then, there has been a substantial number of research reports, conference proceedings, colloquia papers, and doctoral dissertations being written or published on contrastive rhetoric. As a result, contrastive rhetoric (henceforth, CR) has invariably established itself as a viable object of linguistic inquiry and secured for itself a niche in the field of applied linguistics.

Ulla Connor's book is further testimony to that fact. Connor's book presents new directions in CR. As the author puts it, the purposes of the book are "to discuss the general value of CR in the field of applied linguistics, to suggest practical implications for teachers and researchers, and most importantly, to define an emerging contrastive rhetoric discipline that draws on relevant disciplinary fields, particularly composition studies, rhetoric, text linguistics, and cultural anthropology" (p. 6). Her ultimate aim for the book is to go beyond the traditional approach of CR in its concern with investigating second language written products, in particular, university-level first-year English writing, and to argue for "a different contrastive model...for the description of cross-cultural writing in academic and professional situations... [which is] more inclusive than the concept that the early researchers in the field would have employed" (p. 9). The book is an ambitious undertaking on the part of the author in building a comprehensive theory of contrastive rhetoric encompassing theories of such divergent fields as applied linguistics, linguistic relativity, and rhetoric.

Read More

Text C An American Writing Teacher in China

Rhetoric, like ecology, is about relationships, and different cultures define and value different relationships. Examining the rhetorical practices of a culture other than our own, that is, engaging in the study known as contrastive rhetoric, can provide us with a clearer understanding of the culture we study and can make us more aware of our own rhetorical value system. Studies in contrastive rhetoric must be based upon an understanding of the hierarchy of culture, language, and rhetoric and of their inevitable symbiosis. Only by attempting to examine and analyze these relationships can we begin to perceive the real differences between rhetorical systems.

Our own rhetorical values are profoundly affected by the fact that we are post-Romantic Westerners, teaching and writing in the humanities. As such, we value originality and individuality,

what we call the "Authentic Voice." We encourage self-expression and stylistic innovation. In persuasive discourse, we subscribe to Aristotle's dictum, "State your case and prove it," and we expect to be provided with premises and conclusions connected by inductive or deductive reasoning. We call this a "logical" argument. We strongly favor Pound's dictum "Make it new," and we insist that our students use their own words in their own unique ways. We allow that original writing involves a chaotic discovery process but require that finished texts be cohesive, coherent, and explicitly unified. We expect rhetoric to help us achieve control and to be a force for change.

But Western rhetoric is only Western. As we commit ourselves to reinventing our own rhetorical tradition, we need to understand the limits as well as the virtues of that tradition. And as our world becomes a global village in which ethnocentrism is a less and less appropriate response, we need to understand and appreciate rhetorical systems that are different from our own.

This essay attempts to identify and suggest some of the differences between Chinese and Western rhetoric that confront an American writing teacher in China. It is based on the premise that a culture's rhetoric constitutes an interface where the prescriptions of the language meet the practices of the culture. That Chinese literacy, for example, requires staggering feats of memorization has profoundly affected the nature of Chinese discourse as well as the content of social interaction. In China, the hierarchy of culture, language and rhetoric has a powerful coherence or internal logic, and because this hierarchy is so different from our own, Chinese culture often appears seamless, mysterious, and impenetrable. This study tries to unravel, very tentatively, some of the strands that make up the fabric of Chinese rhetoric.

Certainly, I did not understand these different cultural assumptions while I was experiencing them during my semester at Shanxi University, a provincial university of about four thousand students in Taiyuan, the capital of Shanxi Province. Here I taught composition to fifty senior English majors for a semester. Only in retrospect and after study and discussion did I begin to understand the linguistic and  rhetorical agendas that were influencing my students' writing in English. Had I known then what I have come to know now, I am sure that my classroom presence and my social interactions might well have been less obtrusive and more effective.

Over my head as I stood at the yellow lectern with the red star were the thoughts of Chairman Mao in eight large characters: Be united, Be alert, Be earnest, Be lively. That "be united" meant "don't be different" did not occur to me when I suggested to my students that they keep journals, the favorite self-expressive mode of Western writing teachers. Not surprisingly, only some students were comfortable with this kind of writing, and as the semester progressed, "the leaders" seemed to be more and more uncomfortable with it. The number of journals turned in gradually and silently diminished. A young woman named Wu Yongping, however, took to journal writing with ease and grace, and on her small perfect pages, she used to record the events of her day:

> The moment I woke from a dream, I took out a piece of paper from under my pillow. Turning on the electric torch, I saw new words on the paper: "veterinarian," "calligraphy," "amateur." Under the billow of the paper, there was a sentence: "The veterinarian is a calligraphy amateur." As I was putting on my clothes, I repeated: "v-e-t-e-r-i-n-a-r-i-a-n; c-a-l-l-i-g-r-a-p-h-y; a-m-a-t-e-u-r." Then I began to make my bed and memorize the sentence: "The veterinarian is a calligraphy amateur." At 6:00 a.m., I rushed out to do the morning exercises. After washing my face, brushing my teeth, and combing my hair, it was time for breakfast.

While Wu Yongping was doing her morning exercises, some of her fellow students would have been out walking, reading aloud from their texts, committing the sentences to memory.

"We have learned the story," they would say, and they would in fact have memorized it. The usual Chinese response to a literary text is to repeat it, not to paraphrase, analyze, or interpret it, as another student, Wang Fen, wrote, "Learning the text by heart while walking is the habit of students from the Foreign Languages Department. They keep at it day after day, month after month, and year in and year out. In winter no matter how cold and dark outside, in summer no matter how hot and humid outside, they are always there. What a hardworking spirit it is."

Hardworking indeed. To be a literate Chinese requires feats of memorization so prodigious that we have difficulty in even understanding the nature of the task. When an American two-year-old learns—with the help of Sesame Street—our twenty-six-character alphabet, he or she gained at least entrance to the entire English language, to practically the entire Indo-European language family. But the Chinese language has no alphabet, at least not according to our sense of one; the Chinese written language consists instead of thousands of different characters. A character usually stands for a word, sometimes for a syllable, and sometimes two or three characters together constitute a word. Thus, the Chinese child who has learned twenty-six characters has learned only the tiniest fraction of what must be learned to be literate. To read a newspaper requires knowing from three to five thousand characters; to be an intellectual means knowing from ten to fifteen or twenty thousand.

Memorization as the central process of education is thus mandated by the writing system itself. For the Chinese student then, the fourth art of rhetoric, memory, the one we ignore, is and always has been more important than any other. It also informs the other arts of invention, arrangement, and style in ways that are not immediately apparent. Ultimately, the Chinese memorize not just the characters of their beautiful and difficult written language; they memorize the culture itself.

The Western writing teacher, coming upon set phrases again and again, is programmed to respond with her own ready-made remarks: "Be original," "Use new language," "Avoid clichés." And she is thus counseling the students to write like uneducated barbarians. But Chinese students are too puzzled and too polite to point this out — and they are certainly not in the habit of questioning teachers.

Chinese speakers — literate or not — also absorb a vast number of proverbs, maxims, and pieces of folklore. There is an "old Chinese say" for every situation: "When a girl marries it is like water sprinkled on the ground,"

"Fallen leaves fly to the trunk," "Under the sun all crows are black," and from Confucius himself, "By reviewing old knowledge one can acquire new." Chinese speakers and writers depend heavily upon such sayings. Thus, one of my students lamented, "The difference between composing in Chinese and composing in English is that in Chinese there are many proverbs, and in order to make my composition more vivid and beautiful, I can use many proverbs in composing in Chinese, but in English, because of the limit of our non-native speakers' vocabulary, it's very hard to write a real beautiful and vivid essay." Western parodies of the Chinese propensity for maxims in the form of "Confucius say" jokes indicate our failure to understand or to respect this rhetorical practice. On the other hand, the Chinese are surprised to discover that even the most fluent American speakers of Chinese usually cannot write a simple letter that seems at all literate to a native speaker. The Chinese rightly conclude that the Americans have not learned the fundamentals of the Chinese language by heart; that is, they may have learned the words and the grammar, but they have not mastered the phrases.

It is, any literate Chinese will insist, "an absolute fact" that to be a good writer requires wide reading in the Chinese classics. Only through such reading in classical Chinese can a writer become equipped with the phrases, sayings, and literary allusions necessary to "ornament and enliven" discourse.

Certainly, all language users rely upon idioms, clichés, and set phrases, but the Chinese seem always to rely upon them. Visitors to China eventually notice the endless repetition of exactly the same courteous phrases. But visitors also notice that the Chinese always seem to know how to behave; they have memorized the fixed and traditional forms of Chinese culture — the way — along with the set phrases and the characters of the Chinese language. Their responses to any common topic are, therefore, likely to be collective and standardized. For example, my students' first essays on the topic of learning English almost all contained the same rationale: they wanted "to learn English as a tool, to adopt the advanced technology, to support the Four Modernizations, to make a contribution to the Motherland." And, according to the traditional method of Chinese instruction, almost all offered me similar instructions as to how I should proceed: "You must be a very strict teacher," "You must give us good models and make us follow them." I was often struck by the poetry in their writing: "For three times the flowers in our school have bloomed and fallen and for three years I have studied here." "As time passed, the desire of learning the language grew in my heart like a tree, bigger and bigger, so beautiful that I decided to be with her all my life." (To begin by referring to the passing of time is common; letters from my students often start, "Time flies like an arrow.")

But more often the fixed phrases seemed to predominate. And as they accumulated in the papers and in my brain, it seemed to me that just as Li Ssu, China's great unifier under the Emperor Qin Shi Huang (259—210 B.C.), had standardized axle lengths, thereby making the ruts in the roads of China traversable by all vehicles, so had the ruts of Chinese rhetoric been worn deep and predictable through the centuries. They have, after all, been used effectively for over two thousand years. Thus, for the Chinese writer, style means manipulating one's memory bank of phrases, arrangement means filling the forms, and invention means doing it the way it has been done. Each of these three arts of rhetoric depends profoundly on the fourth, memory.

As Western writing teachers, when we admit the ethnocentricity of our notion of the "Authentic Voice," we can begin to appreciate the sound of other voices, voices nurtured on linguistic formulas, drilled in memorization, rehearsed in collective responses. We can begin to hear the poetry that sometimes seems built into the Chinese soul. Here is the final paragraph of Wu Yongping's diary entry about her day:

One day passed away, and I was one day older, one day nearer to my death. Life was hard, but anyhow it was tolerable. I am used to such life and will go on living this way.

Here is Chen's Christmas card to me:

On every Christmas Eve, when Santa puts flowers in your vase, you may go to your window, and you can see us in the morning waving to you from a remote land, or in the white snow which carried our best wishes to you and your friends.

Those who have done their years of memorizing and have mastered this tradition have done more than become literate. They have learned how to behave, what to say, and how to say it. They have gained entrance to the beauty, often the tragic beauty, of a centuries-old literary tradition and the right and the privilege to contribute to it. Our responsibility is surely to try to understand and appreciate, to admit the relativity of our own rhetoric, and to realize that logics different from our own are not necessarily illogical.

(Excerpted from Matalene, C. 1985. Contrastive rhetoric: An American writing teacher in China. *College English*, Vol. 47)

Questions for Discussion

1) What is the author's point of view in this passage?
2) What examples or evidence does the author use to support his viewpoint?
3) To what extent do you agree with the author?

Unit 9 Cultural Relativism

> One man's meat is another man's poison.
>
> — an English idiom
>
> On a group of theories one can found a school; but on a group of values one can found a culture, a civilization, a new way of living together among men.
>
> — Ignazio Silone

Unit Goals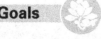

- To understand the concept of cultural relativism
- To comprehend the differences between ethnocentrism and cultural relativism
- To understand the importance of respecting different cultures
- To be aware of the devastating consequences of cultural ethnocentrism

 ### Before You Read

1. Draw a map of the world in 1—2 minutes. Answer the questions that follow.

Questions for you to think
   ✓ Where did you start drawing the world map?
   ✓ Which country is in the center? What is the meaning of this country being in the center?
   ✓ Which country is drawn in most detail? Why is this?
   ✓ Is your map similar to any map above?
   ✓ For the maps that are different from the one that you draw, why do you think they are different?

2. Find a picture of any kind and note down as much as you can about what you see. Ask someone else to look at the same picture and let him/her speak out what he/she sees and compare his/her findings with yours. Are your

findings the same or different? How do you explain the similarities and /or the differences?

3. A Case Study: Read the following case, and discuss the questions that follow.

> A British person is used to fairly strong tea, made with boiling water, and served with milk. She goes to a foreign country and asks for tea. She gets weak tea, possibly made with water which hasn't yet been boiled, and is served black. She tastes the tea and says it's bad.

Questions for reflection

1) What do you think of the British woman's response? Do you find it appropriate? Why do you think so?

   _____

2) In your opinion, what reasons are behind such a response?

   _____

3) If you were in this situation, how would you respond?

   _____

4) Do you have a similar experience before? Share with classmates about what happened and what you think about it.

   _____

Start to Read

Text A Understanding Cultural Relativism

We live in a rapidly changing world society, which is increasingly bringing people of various cultures in closer interaction with each other. This interaction can be positive or negative depending on the level of sensitivity and respect people have for other cultural groups. These two types of behaviors are related to two important concepts—ethnocentrism and cultural relativism. Negative attitudes towards other cultures and/or ethnic groups arise out of ethnocentrism, while positive attitudes are the result of a culturally relativist approach. If people are going to be successful in today's multicultural, information age, world society, they will need to develop a culturally sensitive frame of reference and mode of operation. It is the purpose of this presentation to help people move from an ethnocentric, exclusive mindset to a culturally sensitive *modus operandi*, by clarifying what is meant by ethnocentrism and cultural relativism, how each operates, and what are the steps that move a person from one perspective to the other.

One of the most controversial challenges to the study of social ethics comes from a methodological approach of the social sciences called, *cultural relativism*. Cultural relativism is in essence an approach to the question of the nature and role of values in culture. If values are shared ideals which give rise to beliefs and norms of behavior around which a people or a group organizes its collective life and goals, cultural relativism declares that these values are relative to the cultural ambiance out of which they arise.

Because of this many ethicists believe that the concept of cultural relativism threatens the discipline of ethics since, if values are relative to a given culture then this must mean that there are no universal moral absolutes by which the behavior of people can be judged. Therefore, if there is no observable control transcending all cultures, no eternal book of rules, then right and wrong are a matter of opinion and it doesn't matter what we do: anything goes! Thus, we can't go around passing judgment on what other people do. For, if all morality is relative, then what moral objection could one make to the Nazi holocaust, to the economic deprivation of a Latin American underclass, or to a militaristic nation's unleashing nuclear devastation on others? And what would be wrong with conducting painful experiments on young children, using them for case studies on the long-term psychological effects of mutilation? In a world where no moral court of appeals exists, might makes right. The only appeal can be to power.

But it is such a position that cultural relativism seeks to challenge. And the reason why cultural relativism has come under fire is because it has been subject to divergent interpretation. Anthropologist Clyde Kluckhohn declares: The concept of culture, like any other piece of knowledge, can be abused and misinterpreted. Some fear that the principle of cultural relativity will weaken morality. "If the Bugabuga do it why can't we? It's all relative anyway." But this is exactly what cultural relativity does not mean.

The principle of cultural relativity does not mean that because the members of some savage tribe are allowed to behave in a certain way that this fact gives intellectual warrant for such behavior in all groups. Cultural relativity means, on the contrary, that the appropriateness of any positive or negative custom must be evaluated with regard to how this habit fits with other group habits. Having several wives makes economic sense among herders, not among hunters. While breeding a healthy skepticism as to the eternity of any value prized by a particular people, anthropology does not as a matter of theory deny the existence of moral absolutes. Rather, the use of the comparative method provides a scientific means of discovering such absolutes. If all surviving societies have found it necessary to impose some of the same restrictions upon the behavior of their members, this makes a strong argument that these aspects of the moral code are indispensable.

Part of the problem has to do with *ethnocentrism*, the polar opposite of cultural relativism. Both concepts, ethnocentrism and cultural relativism, can be placed as polar ends of a continuum, each reflecting a different approach, either as exclusive or inclusive; a different mindset either closed or open to differences, and an attitude and behavior that is either insensitive or sensitive to another culture.

What is ethnocentrism? There are three levels of ethnocentrism: a positive one, a negative one, and an extreme negative one. The positive definition defines ethnocentrism as "the point of view that one's own way of life is to be preferred to all others." There is nothing wrong with such feelings, for it characterizes the way most individuals feel about their own cultures, whether or not they verbalize their feeling. It is ethnocentrism that gives people their sense of peoplehood, group identity, and place in history — all of which are valuable traits to possess. Ethnocentrism becomes negative when one's own group becomes the center of everything, and all others are scaled and rated with reference to it. It reaches its extreme negative form when a more powerful group not only imposes its rule on another, but actively depreciates the things they hold to be of value. Apartheid, the holocaust, and the genocide of the American Indian are all examples of this third level of ethnocentrism.

Audrey Smedley gives us the key to understanding ethnocentrism — the importance of cultural differences — when she declares: "The important point about ethnocentrism is that it is grounded in the empirical reality and perceptions of socio-cultural differences and the separateness of interests and goals that this may entail. There can be no ethnocentrism without cultural differences, no matter how trivial or insignificant these may appear to an outsider."

Vincent Ruggiero tells us that, "just as it is natural for us to read the behavior of others in terms of our own standards, so it is natural to view actions in other *cultures* from the codes of our culture. What seems fair to us we assume is fair to them; and when we see an action we regard as treacherous, we likewise assume that they have violated their code. Yet a deeper understanding of their code may reveal that they have not only not been violating it, but in fact observing it."

How can one eliminate ethnocentrism? Vincent Ruggiero suggests three important steps to take which will enable us to penetrate deception of appearance.

1. Study the cultural context in which the action occurs.

2. Determine the circumstances of time, place, and condition surrounding it.

3. Learn the reasoning that underlies it and the moral value it reflects.

At the heart of these three steps lies the importance of learning to "take the role of the other," the ability to see things, especially that with which we are not familiar, from the perspective of the other before any consideration of judgment is considered.

After You Read

Knowledge Focus

1. Solo Work: Tell whether the following statements are true or false according to the knowledge you learned.

1) Positive interaction between people often arises out of a culturally ethnocentric approach.
2) Cultural relativism constitutes one of the most controversial challenges to the study of social ethics.
3) Cultural relativism deals with the nature and role of values in culture.
4) The concept of cultural relativism threatens the discipline of ethics because there is a universal moral absolute by which the behavior of people can be judged.
5) Ethnocentrism can be defined as inclusive, a mindset open to differences, and an attitude that is sensitive to another culture.
6) The first level of ethnocentrism is justified in that it gives people a sense of group identity and place in history.
7) The negative ethnocentrism is a view of things in which one's own group is the center of everything and all others are scaled and rated in relation to this.
8) In order to eliminate ethnocentrism, we need to make a considerate judgment on people's behavior before we see things from the perspective of the other.

2. Pair Work: Discuss the following questions with your partner.

1) If people want to be successful in today's multicultural world, what will they need to develop according to the text?
2) What is the relation between values and cultural relativism?
3) Why do many ethicists believe that the concept of cultural relativism threatens the discipline of ethics?
4) What does the author mean by saying "In a world where no moral court of appeals exist, might makes right"?
5) What are the three levels of ethnocentrism?
6) Is there anything wrong with the first level of ethnocentrism? Why?
7) When will ethnocentrism become negative? Please give examples.
8) When will ethnocentrism reach its extreme negative form? Please give examples.
9) How can we eliminate ethnocentrism according to Vincent Ruggiero? Give examples.
10) In summary, how do you understand cultural relativism?

Language, Society and Culture

Language Focus

1. Fill in the blanks with the words or expressions you have learned in the text.

| mindset | devastation | come under fire | absolute (*n.*) |
| impose | transcend | unleash | with reference to |

1) The best films are those which _____ national or cultural barriers.
2) Rachel's arrival on the scene _____ passions in him that he could scarcely control.
3) It's extraordinary how hard it is to change the _____ of the public and the press.
4) James _____ in the office after he wrote a very critical article in the company magazine.
5) A huge bomb blast brought chaos and _____ to the centre of Belfast yesterday.
6) We would like to send you a sample _____ the last shipment.
7) A/An _____ is a rule or principle that is believed to be true, right, or relevant in all situations.
8) I don't want them to _____ their religious beliefs on my children.

2. Fill in the blanks with the proper form of the word in the brackets.

1) In deference to our host I decided not to challenge his _____ (controversy) remarks.
2) It's a science in that it can be measured by results and is subject to _____ (methodology) analysis.
3) _____ (collective) is a theory or political system based on the principle that all of the farms, factories and other places of work in a country should be owned by or for all the people in that country.
4) _____ (skeptical) and doubt lead to study and investigation, and investigation is the beginning of wisdom.
5) Religions gain some of their worldly power by claiming they have the key to _____ (eternal).
6) He found it hard to _____ (verbal) his feelings towards his son.
7) The police have been criticized for being _____ (sensitive) to complaints from the public.
8) This article offers a model to account for the evolution of _____ (ethnocentrism) behavior.
9) The report has spotlighted real _____ (deprive) in the inner cities.
10) I have to question the _____ (moral) of forcing poor people to pay for their medical treatment.

3. Proofreading

The following passage contains TEN errors. Each line contains a maximum of ONE error. In each case, only ONE word is involved. You should proofread the passage and correct the errors in the following way:

For a wrong word, underline the wrong word and write the correct one in the blank provided at the end of the line.

For a missing word, mark the position of the missing word with a "∧" sign and write the word you believe to be missing in the blank provided at the end of the line.

For an unnecessary word, cross out the unnecessary word with a slash "/" and put the word in the blank provided at the end of the line.

Cultural relativism is the view that no	
culture is superior to any culture when	1. _____
compared systems of morality, law, politics,	2. _____
etc. It's the philosophical notion when all	3. _____
cultural beliefs are equal valid and that	4. _____
truth itself is relative, depended on the	5. _____
cultural environment. Those when hold	6. _____
against cultural relativism hold that all	
religious, ethical, aesthetics, and political	7. _____
beliefs are completely relative with the	8. _____
individual with a cultural identity.	9. _____
Relativism often includes moral relativism,	
situation relativism, and cognitive	10. _____
relativism.	

Comprehensive Work

1. Discussions: Dog meat — East vs. West

Read the following paragraphs and discuss the questions that follow with your classmates.

Dog meat is believed to keep the body warm and improve virility. It has a sour and salty taste and comforts the digestive system. The South Korean dog meat industry in itself involved about 1 million dogs, 6,000 restaurants, and 10 percent of the population. Various parts of China also find eating dog meat socially acceptable.

The Western society, however, is outraged, calling such a practice barbaric. Not only is the consumption of dog meat in America a cultural taboo, those who do eat dog meat are criticized. Numerous animal rights activists have publicly criticized the dog meat industry and even FIFA, the

world soccer organization, has called on South Koreans to stop eating dogs.

Questions for discussion

1) What are the different attitudes in relation to dog meat in the East and the West?
2) What are the reasons behind such different attitudes in the East and the West respectively?
3) What do you think is the right attitude towards this issue? You may use what you have learned about cultural relativism in Text A to illustrate your points.

2. Writing Practice

Have you ever had an experience in relation to cultural relativism or ethnocentrism? Please write an essay of about 400 words describing your experience in detail by using descriptive and narrative skills. In the end of the essay, please write a few words about what you have learned from such an experience.

3. Translation: Translate the following passage into Chinese.

Another example illustrates how basic ethnocentrism is. If we go to a store and ask for a green coat and the sales clerk gives us a blue one, we would think the person was color blind at the best or stupid at the worst. However, "colors" are not so simple. The Inuit lump shades of what Anglo Americans call "blue" and "green" into one color category, tungortuk, which can only be translated as "bluegreen." Does this mean that they cannot see the difference? Just as we can distinguish between different shades (such as "sky blue" and "navy blue," and "kelly green" and "forest green"), so can the Inuit. If they want to refer to what we would call "green," they would say tung or tuk, which can be translated something like "that bluegreen that looks like the color of a [conifer] tree." The point is that something so "simple" as colors have very different meanings to us and to the Inuit. How could an Inuk "feel blue"? Colors, after all, are only different wavelengths of light, and the rainbow can be divided in many different ways.

When Yiaaku people gather, or a father blesses his family, the prayers uttered are full of symbolism and poetic beauty.

May the land of our fathers and

Mothers embrace you

May you grow as huge as a

Loimugo tree
May you smell as sweet as the
Songoyo tree
Be as straight as the Itarokwa tree
Be as studious as Ol Donyo
Keri mountain
And as cool as the forests of Mukogodo

When a Yiaaku person has been scorched by the hot sun beating on the plains, he faces the direction of Mukogodo forest and cries, "How I long for the forest of my father and mother!"

Since time immemorial the Yiaaku have been a part of the Mukogodo forest in the central Kenya highlands, living as cave dwellers and practicing a hunter-gatherer lifestyle. Today, however, they are settled in six villages located in a wide area around the forest where they supplement their traditional beekeeping with the raising of cattle and goats. Still, it is the Mukogodo that gives meaning to their concept of life and spirituality, and they continue to hold a deep attachment to the trees, hills, animals, and caves that comprise their natural environment and their cultural heritage.

A dwindling ethnic minority, fewer than a thousand people identify themselves as Yiaaku. They speak the Maa language, which they adopted from their populous Maasai neighbors through many years of assimilation. Maasai are of Nilotic origin while Yiaaku are Cushitic. According to UNESCO's *Red Book of Endangered Languages*, Yiaaku is officially extinct. Fewer than ten speakers remain of their original mother tongue.

Because they were initially cave dwellers and without livestock, the Maasai branded the Yiaaku as "ontorobo," meaning "poor people" — a name that stuck for centuries, deeply affecting the psyche and pride of the Yiaaku. "We were never a poor people," counters Jennifer Koinante, a Yiaaku by birth and the Director of Yiaaku Peoples Association, a recently formed organization championing Yiaaku rights. "The resources of our forest have always been abundant."

Colonialism in the nineteenth century brought unprecedented tribulations to the Yiaaku. Game hunting was banned and the colonial government attempted to settle the Yiaaku outside their forest in order to "civilize" them. Coupled with a high rate of assimilation into Maasai culture, such external onslaughts left the Yiaaku weakened and disoriented, both culturally and socially. But perhaps the worst that befell them was when in 1937 the government designated the Mukogodo a protected forest, which in turn led to their eventual relocation into villages and their transition toward a more pastoral lifestyle similar to the Maasai. Since that time the Yiaaku community has been undergoing an identity crisis amounting to a slow death. It has only been in recent years, following education and the passing of a generation, that the Yiaaku have rediscovered a deep pride in their unique ethnic and cultural identity.

Although the Mukogodo is now protected by official forest guards, the small number of remaining Yiaaku continue to have direct and unrestricted access to the forest and its resources — for the moment. However, it is known that several years ago forest guards spoke to locals about government plans of eviction. Such threats have resulted in forced evictions for other forest dwellers, such as the Ogiek group of the neighboring Nakuru District, and the warning has left the Yiaaku alarmed and unsure of their future.

"We have been the silent guardians and keepers of Mukogodo forest for centuries," explains Koinante. "When other forests across Kenya are being destroyed, ours is still intact. We protect it because it is our only heritage on this planet. How can a law passed in a far-away city decide that our forest is now public property? Does the law consider us as part of the wildlife?"

Whereas the government views the Mukogodo as a strategic national resource worthy of protection, the Yiaaku view the Mukogodo as a cultural heritage and as inseparable from Yiaaku life. Yiaaku refer to the forest as *loip* (the shade) and as *gorgola* (the armpit): The shade protects them from severe droughts, the armpit shields them from enemies and other potential harm. In the traditional Yiaaku land tenure system, different clans own the various hills of Mukogodo forest. It is within these hills that clan members hang their beehives. As Koinante explains, "When children of pastoralists inherit cattle, the sons of Yiaaku inherit trees with beehives...We know every type of tree and the flowers that yield nectar." Yiaaku also invoke their ancestral attachments to the Mukogodo forest. "Our ancestors sleep in this forest," asserts Koinante. "This is where all umbilical cords of our community life. Our attachment to this forest is maternal. To ask us to leave is to sever all our links with the past generations. We will be without history."

Indeed, Yiaaku guardianship and occupation of the forest ensures their unity and the continuity of their ancestral domains. The vital connection between the people and the forest is reflected in their language, folklore, traditions, and indigenous knowledge in such areas as beekeeping, ethno ecology, and herbal medicine. As Koinante explains:

> Our language is one of the forest. It describes our flora and fauna heritage in ways only we can understand. It's a language of trees, wild animals, bees, and caves. Without the forest, our language becomes obsolete and ceases to exist. To remove us from the forest is to ask us to develop a new language. It's unimaginable.

In short, to deny the Yiaaku their ancestral right to the forest is a form of ethnocide.

What the Yiaaku want is for the status of the Mukogodo forest to be changed from a protected forest to a Trust Forest in their name. That change of status should come with the relevant legal documentation, demarcation of boundaries, and a Title Deed. A Title Deed would legally allow the Yiaaku and Forest Department joint management of Mukogodo. The Yiaaku consider these measures the only way to herald a new beginning for their threatened ethnic and cultural identity. It would also set a precedent for other forest-dwelling ethnic minorities of Kenya. At this time when Kenya is drawing up a new constitution and a comprehensive land policy, Yiaaku people hope that the demands of forest dwellers will be taken into account and given legitimacy. To them, the new concepts of nation-state and globalization should embrace, respect, and preserve cultural diversity and not suffocate it in the quest for a homogenous society.

Koinante clearly sees the claim to the forest as a struggle for human rights. She asserts:

> Cultural rights are human rights. That is why we are articulating our claims from a human rights perspective. The Kenyan constitution guarantees the right to culture, and so does the Universal Declaration of Human Rights. We are entitled to Mukogodo forest as our cultural abode and to a full recognition as a complete and living ethnic group. We are ready to defend our claims in Kenyan and international courts of law.

Lobbying for support of their cause is in high gear. The Yiaaku Peoples Association is an active member of local and national human rights networks, and the Yiaaku are a member of the Indigenous Peoples of Africa Coordinating Committee (IPACC). Over the past years the Association has held awareness forums for elders, women, and youth aimed at mobilizing community resources and strengthening the struggle through collective decisions. To promote community management of forest resources, the Association has set up a community honey refinery and marketing center in Dol Dol Township, on the fringes of the forest. The proceeds go to joint community development activities spearheaded by the Association. The Association also intends to build a cultural center in Mukogodo forest, which will serve as a documentation and education facility; among its activities it will teach the Yiaaku dialect to young children and compile a Yiaaku-Maasai dictionary.

"We know we are going to win in the end," says Koinante. "To take the Yiaaku out of their forest is like asking fish to live out of water. Mukogodo forest is our culture and identity. We are not bargaining with anyone. This forest is ours."

Questions for Discussion

1. How does the Kenyan government view the Mukogodo forest?
2. How does Indigenous Yiaaku view the Mukogodo forest?
3. Why do the government and the Yiaaku people have such different attitudes towards the forest?
4. In your opinion, who should have access to the forest? Why?

Text C Education Abroad—Going Native or Standing Firm

It was dusk in Kerala, India, and the placard-toting American students under my watch were gathering for a demonstration. Some stood away from the trees as hundreds of crows returned to their roost. The Indian student leader in her multi-layered salwar kameez spryly said, "We are here to say that girls should be allowed to leave their hostel after 7 p.m. at night if they are sick. But we are not feminists."

The American students' shoulders slumped. Their cries of "Take Back the Night" reverted to "Take Back the Early Evening" and they began their march.

American students abroad may come to realize, to their surprise, that their home society is relatively permissive. In India at least this realization can lead to a unique set of cross-cultural challenges. In hindsight many challenges are seen as growing experiences and often described in amusing, romanticized, or heroic storytelling. Nevertheless, the "things" of culture are often easier to deal with than the attitudes.

Students quickly learn to eat thali meals with their right hand and speak enough of the local language to both fend off vendors and invite conversations with passers-by. Adaptations to "interesting" new realities such as housing and climate are expected and routine. But adaptations to relatively restrictive cultural attitudes are different.

Modest at Home, "Wild" Abroad

It is sometimes daunting for American students who see themselves as relatively modest in their demands at home to be treated as if they are wildly pushing the limits in India. For example, a woman at a Midwestern college may consider herself rather well-behaved if on a Saturday evening she and her roommate walk to a man's residence hall room where they drink one alcoholic beverage, play a game of cards, and spend a few hours in conversation with the male friend and his roommates. That same woman would not be considered conventional in India. In fact, the response to her behavior would be far from flattering.

Obviously, coming to terms with cultural relativism is easier said than done. American students may resist even the gentlest of negative sanctioning. When a suggestion is given that "this is not acceptable behavior" students may take it personally and on behalf of their entire society. One reaction is that if they conform to the local (restrictive) customs they have failed to take a stand for individual rights. Several young women with my group felt alienated when they found no feminist kindred spirits at the entire Cochin Univ. of Science and Technology.

"There's nothing to talk about," said one. "I want to encourage them to speak out, but everything they say is so superficial and trivial."

Living abroad brings special demands. It is easier to deal with the stares that come from being a tourist than with the stares of disapproval and suspicion that come when the visitor is a temporary resident and expected to know better. One temptation is to become indignant and even exaggerate the offending behavior. Anecdotes are endless, often reflecting expectations relative to age, gender, and a sexual double standard.

Compounding the Problem

Frustrated students wishing to prove that there is indeed nothing implicitly wrong with their lifestyle inadvertently compound the problem when they flagrantly, or even good-naturedly, deviate from a local social more. Imagine a student repeatedly wearing shorts to prove that there is nothing implicitly promiscuous about a bare leg, particularly when the temperature and humidity are both in the 90s. Pushing the boundaries is more likely when the behavior is thought to be communicating "who I am" instead of "what I do."

Because the U.S. is seen as permissive relative to India, students are seen by their hosts to respond in at least four ways:

First, in order to not inadvertently offend, the visitors maintain their American lifestyle in a student guesthouse ghetto, a textbook reaction to culture shock.

Second, students blatantly disregard any local customs that they find either "unjust" or just plain illogical.

Third, they make concessions by modestly adjusting their lifestyle so as to honor professors and administrators during the daytime hours, but they do not give up their nocturnal chatting, imbibing, and generally being involved in group revelry past local bedtimes.

Fourth, students resolve that for one or two semesters they will not go out past 10:30 p.m., not visit the rooms of the other gender, not drink publicly (especially if they are females), not date, and generally live as the local students live. (Spending a Friday night hand-washing clothes may not sound exciting, but it can do no harm.)

Acceptance Aids Understanding

Accepting cultural expectations as gracious guests may be difficult, especially when these customs appear to be illogical or inconsistently enforced. But acceptance will insure positive interpersonal relations and positive institutional collaboration. Furthermore, students are likely to obtain greater understanding of the host culture by becoming sensitive informal quasi-ambassadors.

As a former study center director in Southern India and as a long-term study abroad administrator, I encourage students to participate fully in the host culture. This includes honoring local customs such as keeping the same hours and showing deference to professors. Such behavior does not suggest moral compromise or passivity regarding general safety and welfare. Participating in the culture fully means just that. Despite the fact that this may initially bring the feeling that one is "selling out" to the establishment, especially as a young adult, the reality is that one barely has time to participate in the host society and not nearly enough time to become a prophetic voice for social change.

Questions for Discussion

1. What surprises the author when he observes American students learning abroad?
2. According to the author, how can one approach a different culture with the help of films and music?
3. In what way can Internet help one develop different perspectives towards diversified cultures?
4. What else, according to the author, will help one stop ethnocentrism?

Text D The Challenge of Cultural Relativism

How Different Cultures Have Different Moral Codes

Darius, a king of ancient Persia, was intrigued by the variety of cultures he encountered in his travels. He had found, for example, that the Callatians (a tribe of Indians) customarily ate the bodies of their dead fathers. The Greeks, of course, did not do that—the Greeks practiced cremation and regarded the funeral pyre as the natural and fitting way to dispose of the dead. Darius thought that a sophisticated understanding of the world must include an appreciation of such differences between cultures. One day, to teach this lesson, he summoned some Greeks who happened to be present at his court and asked them what they would take to eat the bodies of their dead fathers. They were shocked, as Darius knew they would be, and replied that no amount of money could persuade them to do such a thing. Then Darius called in some Callatians, and while the Greeks listened asked them what they would take to burn their dead fathers' bodies. The Callatians were horrified and told Darius not even to mention such a dreadful thing.

This story, recounted by Herodotus in his *History* illustrates a recurring theme in the literature of social science: Different cultures have different moral codes. What is thought right within one group may be utterly abhorrent to the members of another group, and vice versa. Should we eat the bodies of the dead or burn them? If you were a Greek, one answer would seem obviously correct; but if you were a Callatian, the opposite would seem equally certain.

It is easy to give additional examples of the same kind. Consider the Eskimos. They are a remote and inaccessible people. Numbering only about 25,000, they live in small, isolated settlements scattered mostly along the northern fringes of North America and Greenland. Until the beginning of the 20th century, the outside world knew little about them. Then explorers began to bring back strange tales.

Eskimos customs turned out to be very different from our own. The men often had more than one wife, and they would share their wives with guests, lending them for the night as a sign of hospitality. Moreover, within a community, a dominant male might demand and get regular sexual access to other men's wives. The women, however, were free to break these arrangements simply by leaving their husbands and taking up with new partners — free, that is, so long as their former husbands chose not to make trouble. All in all, the Eskimo practice was a volatile scheme that bore little resemblance to what we call marriage.

But it was not only their marriage and sexual practices that were different. The Eskimos also seemed to have less regard for human life. Infanticide, for example, was common. Knud Rasmussen, one of the most famous early explorers, reported that he met one woman who bad borne 20 children but had killed 10 of them at birth. Female babies, he found, were especially liable to be destroyed, and this was permitted simply at the parents' discretion, with no social stigma attached to it. Old people also, when they became too feeble to contribute to the family, were left out in the snow to die. So there seemed to be, in this society, remarkably little respect for life.

To the general public, these were disturbing revelations. Our own way of living seems so natural and right that for many of us it is hard to conceive of others living so differently. And when we do hear of such things, we tend immediately to categorize those other peoples as "backward" or "primitive." But to anthropologists and sociologists, there was nothing particularly surprising about the Eskimos. Since the time of Herodotus, enlightened observers have been accustomed to the idea that conceptions of right and wrong differ from culture to culture. If we assume that our ideas of right and wrong will be shared by all peoples at all times, we are merely naive.

Cultural Relativism

To many thinkers, this observation — "Different cultures have different moral codes" — has seemed to be the key to understanding morality. The idea of universal truth in ethics, they say, is a myth. The customs of different societies are all that exist. These customs cannot be said to be "correct" or "incorrect," for that implies we have an independent standard of right and wrong by which they may be judged. But there is no such independent standard; every standard is culture-bound. The great pioneering sociologist William Graham Sumner, writing in 1906, put the point like this:

The "right" way is the way which the ancestors used and which has been handed down. The tradition is its own warrant. It is not held subject to verification by experience. The notion of right is in the folkways. It is not outside of them, of independent origin, and brought to test them. In the folkways, whatever is, is right. This is because they are traditional, and therefore contain in themselves the authority of the ancestral ghosts. When we come to the folkways we are at the end of our analysis.

This line of thought has probably persuaded more people to be skeptical about ethics than any other single thing. Cultural Relativism, as it has been called, challenges our ordinary belief

in the objectivity and universality of moral truth. It says, in effect, that there is not such thing as universal truth in ethics; there are only the various cultural codes, and nothing more. Moreover, our own code has no special status; it is merely one among many.

As we shall see, this basic idea is really a compound of several different thoughts. It is important to separate the various elements of the theory because, on analysis, some parts turn out to be correct, while others seem to be mistaken. As a beginning, we may distinguish the following claims, all of which have been made by cultural relativists:

1) Different societies have different moral codes.

2) There is no objective standard that can be used to judge one societal code better than another.

3) The moral code of our own society has no special status; it is merely one among many.

4) There is no "universal truth" in ethics; that is, there are no moral truths that hold for all peoples at all times.

5) The moral code of a society determines what is right within that society; that is, if the moral code of a society says that a certain action is right, then that action is right, at least within that society.

6) It is mere arrogance for us to try to judge the conduct of other peoples. We should adopt an attitude of tolerance toward the practices of other cultures.

Although it may seem that these six propositions go naturally together, they are independent of one another, in the sense that some of them might be false even if others are true. In what follows, we will try to identify what is correct in Cultural Relativism, but we will also be concerned to expose what is mistaken about it.

The Cultural Differences Argument

Cultural Relativism is a theory about the nature of morality. At first blush it seems quite plausible. However, like all such theories, it may be evaluated by subjecting it to rational analysis; and when we analyze Cultural Relativism we find that it is not so plausible as it first appears to be.

The first thing we need to notice is that at the heart of Cultural Relativism there is a certain *form of argument*. The strategy used by cultural relativists is to argue from facts about the differences between cultural outlooks to a conclusion about the status of morality. Thus we are invited to accept this reasoning:

✓ The Greeks believed it was wrong to eat the dead, whereas the Callatians believed it was right to eat the dead.

✓ Therefore, eating the dead is neither objectively right nor objectively wrong. It is merely a matter of opinion, which varies from culture to culture.

Or, alternatively:

✓ The Eskimos see nothing wrong with infanticide, whereas Americans believe infanticide is immoral.

✓ Therefore, infanticide is neither objectively right nor objectively wrong. It is merely a matter of opinion, which varies from culture to culture.

Clearly, these arguments are variations of one fundamental idea They are both special cases of a more general argument, which says:

✓ Different cultures have different moral codes.

✓ Therefore, there is no objective "truth" in morality. Right and wrong are only matters of opinion, and opinions vary from culture to culture.

We may call this the Cultural Differences Argument. To many people, it is persuasive. But from a logical point of view, is it sound?

It is not sound. The trouble is that the conclusion does not follow from the premise — that is, even if the premise is true, the conclusion still might be false. The premise concerns what people believe. In some societies, people believe one thing; in other societies, people believe differently. The conclusion, however, concerns what really is the case. The trouble is that this sort of conclusion does not follow logically from this sort of premise.

Consider again the example of the Greeks and Callatians. The Greeks believed it was wrong to eat the dead; the Callatians believed it was right. Does it follow, *from the mere fact that they disagreed*, that there is no objective truth in the matter? No, it does not follow; for it could be that the practice was objectively right (or wrong) and that one or the other of them was simply mistaken.

To make the point clearer, consider a different matter. In some societies, people believe the earth is flat. In other societies, such as our own, people believe the earth is (roughly) spherical. Does it follow, from the mere fact that people disagree, that there is no "objective truth" in geography? Of course not; we would never draw such a conclusion because we realize that, in their beliefs about the world, the members of some societies might simply be wrong. There is no reason to think that if the world is round everyone must know it. Similarly, there is no reason to think that if there is moral truth everyone must know it. The fundamental mistake in the Cultural

Differences Argument is that it attempts to derive a substantive conclusion about a subject from the mere fact that people disagree about it.

This is a simple point of logic, and it is important not to misunderstand it. We are not saying (not yet, anyway) that the conclusion of the argument is false. It is still an open question whether the conclusion is true or false. The logical point is just that the conclusion does not *follow from* the premise. This is important, because in order to determine whether the conclusion is true, we need arguments in its support. Cultural Relativism proposes this argument, but unfortunately the argument turns out to be fallacious. So it proves nothing.

(Excerpted from J. Rachels, *The Elements of Moral Philosophy*, 1999)

Unit 10   Linguistic Relativism

> That language embodies different ways of knowing the world seems intuitive, given the number of times we reach for a word or phrase in another language that communicates that certain *je ne sais quoi* we can't find on our own.
>
> — Steve Kallaugher

Unit Goals

- To understand the concept of linguistic relativism
- To understand how our use of language influences the way we see the world
- To investigate the relationship between language and thought
- To comprehend the differences between linguistic relativism and linguistic universalism

Before You Read

1. How many color words do you know in Chinese and English? Please write down as many color words as possible.

    English color words:
    _____

    Chinese color words:
    _____

2. Compare your list of Chinese color words and the list of English color words. Do you find that some color words in one language do not have their equivalents in the other language? What differences have you found between the two languages in terms of color words?

语言、社会与文化
Language, Society and Culture

Start to Read

Text A Language and Thought Processes

Language is more than just a means of communication. It influences our culture and even our thought processes. During the first four decades of the 20th century, language was viewed by American linguists and anthropologists as being more important than it actually is in shaping our perception of reality. This was mostly due to Edward Sapir[1] and his student Benjamin Whorf[2] who said that language predetermines what we see in the world around us. In other words, language acts like a polarizing lens on a camera in filtering reality — we see the real world only in the categories of our language.

you → your language → "reality"

Cross cultural comparisons of such things as color terms were used by Sapir and Whorf as evidence of this hypothesis. When we perceive color with our eyes, we are sensing that portion of electromagnetic radiation that is visible light. In fact, the spectrum of visible light is a continuum of light waves with frequencies that increase at a continuous rate from one end to the other. In other words, there are no distinct colors like red and green in nature. Our culture, through language, guides us in seeing the spectrum in terms of the arbitrarily established categories that we call colors. Different cultures may divide up the spectrum in different ways. This can be seen in the comparison of some English language colors with their counterparts in the Tiv language of Nigeria:

English	Tiv
green	pupu
blue	(low value)
gray	ii (high value)

---

1 Edward Sapir
   Edward Sapir (1884—1939) was a German-born American anthropologist-linguist and a leader in American structural linguistics. He was one of the creators of what is now called the Sapir-Whorf hypothesis. He is arguably the most influential figure in American linguistics, influencing several generations of linguists across several schools of the discipline.

2 Benjamin Whorf
   Benjamin Lee Whorf (1897—1941) was an American linguist. Whorf is widely known for his ideas about linguistic relativity, the hypothesis that language influences thought. He has been credited as one of the fathers of this approach, often referred to as the "Sapir-Whorf hypothesis", named after him and his mentor Edward Sapir.

	(continued)
brown	
red	nyian
yellow	

Note:

Walue refers to the lightness or darkness of a color. High value is light and low value is dark.

Sapir and Whorf interpreted these data as indicating that colors are not objective, naturally determined segments of reality. In other words, the colors we see are predetermined by what our culture prepares us to see. This example used to support the Sapir-Whorf hypothesis[1] was objectively tested in the 1960's. That research indicated that they went too far. All normal humans share similar sense perceptions of color despite differences in color terminology from one language to another. The physiology of our eyes is essentially the same. People all over the world can see subtle gradations of color and can comprehend other ways of dividing up the spectrum of visible light. However, as a society's economy and technology increase in complexity, the number of color terms usually also increases. That is to say, the spectrum of visible light gets subdivided into more categories. As the environment changes, culture and language typically respond by creating new terminology to describe it.

NOTE: In 1976 Paul Kay, a University of California, Berkeley linguistics professor, led a team of researchers in collecting color terms used by 110 different languages around the world. Reexamining these data in 2006, Delwin Lindsey and Angela Brown of Ohio State University, Columbus discovered that most languages in this study do not make a distinction between green and blue. Further, the closer the homeland of a language group is to the equator the less likely they are to distinguish between green and blue. Lindsey suggests as a possible explanation that people in intensely sunny environments, such as open country near the equator, have had their ability to see color altered due to the yellowing of the eye lens caused by excessive ultraviolet radiation.

---

1   Sapir-Whorf hypothesis
    The Sapir-Whorf hypothesis is the idea that differences in the way languages encode cultural and cognitive categories affect the way people think, so that speakers of different languages think and behave differently because of it. A strong version of the hypothesis holds that language determines thought and that linguistic categories limit and determine cognitive categories. A weaker version states that linguistic categories and usage influence thought and certain kinds of non-linguistic behavior.

It is now clear that the terminology used by a culture primarily reflects that culture's interests and concerns. For instance, Indians in Canada's Northwest Territories typically have at least 13 terms for different types and conditions of snow, while most non-skiing native Southern Californians use only 2 terms — ice and snow. That does not mean that the English language only has 2 terms. Quite the contrary, there are many more English words that refer to different states of frozen water, such as blizzard, dusting, flurry, frost, hail, hardpack, powder, sleet, slush, and snowflake. The point is that these terms are rarely if ever used by people living in tropical or subtropical regions because they rarely encounter frozen water in any form other than ice cubes. The distinctions between different snow conditions are not relevant to everyday life and children may not even have the words explained to them. However, people in these warmer regions make fine distinctions about other phenomena that are important to them. For instance, coastal Southern Californians often have dozens of surfing related words that would likely be unknown to most Indians in the Northwest Territories or to people living in Britain for that matter.

The number of terms related to a particular topic also may be greater or smaller depending on such social factors as gender. For example, North American women generally make far more color distinctions than do men. This may be largely due to the fact that subtle color differences are important factors in women's clothing and makeup. Parents and peers usually encourage and train girls early to be knowledgeable about these distinctions.

The cultural environment that people grow up in can have surprising effects on how they interpret the world around them. This became apparent during a Washington D.C. murder trial in 2002. A deaf man was convicted of stabbing to death two of his classmates at Gallaudet University. At his trial, the defendant said that he was told to do it by mysterious black-gloved hands. His delusions did not come in the form of spoken language. He was told to commit these brutal murders through sign language — his mode of communication. Another example is provided by Guugu Timithirr language speakers of the Cape York Peninsula in northeastern Australia. This group of Aborigines do not have words for left, right, front, or back. They use absolute rather than relative directions. When they refer to people or objects in their environment, they use compass directions. They would say "I am standing southwest of my sister" rather than "I am standing to the left of my sister." Critics of the Sapir-Whorf hypothesis would point out that the Aborigines who speak this language also usually learn English and can use left, right, front, and back just as we do. However, if they do not learn English during early childhood, they have difficulty in orienting themselves relatively and absolute orientation makes much more sense to them.

After You Read

Knowledge Focus

1. Solo Work: Choose the best answer that can complete each sentence.

1) Edward Sapir and Benjamin Whorf believed that _____.
a. there are distinct colors in nature like red and green
b. we see the real world only in the categories of our language
c. all normal humans share the capability of having essentially the same sense perceptions of color
d. None of the above.

2) The spectrum of visible light _____.
a. is a continuum of light waves with frequencies that increase at a continuous rate from one end to the other
b. has distinct colors such as red and green that every normal individual can perceive
c. is divided up into colors in the same way by all normal people in all cultures of the world
d. None of the above.

3) The Tiv of Nigeria _____.
a. had the same color terms as Europeans and North Americans
b. had more terms for snow conditions than did Europeans and North Americans
c. had more color words than did Europeans and North Americans
d. Neither of the above

4) Which of the following statements is true?
a. Linguistic relativism is primarily the study of relations between language use and its environment.
b. The number of terms an individual knows related to a particular topic is usually independent of his or her gender.
c. The number of color terms usually increases as a society's economy and technology become more complex.
d. How people interpret the world around them have little to do with the cultural environment that people grow up in.

5) Anthropologists today generally believe that the Whorf-Sapir hypothesis _____.
a. is correct
b. over emphasizes the importance of language in determining what people can see
c. ignores the significant roles language play in shaping one's thought
d. is entirely wrong

2. Pair Work: Discuss the following questions with your partner.

1) What did Sapir and Whorf believe about the relationship between language and human thought?
2) What example is used by Sapir and Whorf as evidence of their hypothesis?
3) Why did the author say that the research conducted to support Sapir-Whorf hypothesis went too far?
4) Why do Southern Californians have only 2 terms for different types of snow while the Indians in Canada's Northeast Territories have a dozen of them?
5) Can you think of other examples in which the terminology used by a culture primarily reflects that culture's interests and concerns?
6) What other factors influence the number of terms related to a particular topic? Give examples.
7) What can you infer from the example of a murder trial in Washington D.C. in 2002?
8) How do you understand the critics of the Sapir-Whorf hypothesis in the example of Aboriginal language speakers of the Cape York Peninsular in Australia?

Language Focus

1. Fill in the blanks with the words or expressions you have learned in the text.

| convict | spectrum | in the form of | perceive |
| hypothesis | other than | predetermine | terminology |

1) _____ is an idea or explanation for something that is based on known facts but has not yet been proved.
2) He could _____ distinctly how everyone's misfortunes but his own were expressions of God's will.
3) A wide _____ of opinion was represented at the meeting.
4) It's impossible to say how much a person's behavior is _____ by their genes.
5) "Net work" is a comparatively recent addition to the _____ of librarianship.
6) The form cannot be signed by anyone _____ yourself.
7) I have all the evidence necessary to _____ this young criminal now.
8) Social structure, especially _____ social networks, affects economic outcomes.

2. Fill in the blanks with the proper form of the word in the brackets.

1) The _____ (polar) of society into rich and poor can clearly be seen in the city centers.
2) The increasing _____ (visible) of the nation's poor and homeless has forced the government into taking action.

3) We made the decision to go to Italy quite _____ (arbitrary).

4) At the level of collecting data, all the scientists strive for _____ (objective).

5) Difficulties were caused by the _____ (complex) of the legislation.

6) Caspar had spoken _____ (knowledge) about the state of agriculture in Europe.

7) This is all very _____ (hypothesis) but supposing Jackie got the job, how would that affect you?

8) They have to come up with reasonable and _____ (defend) public policies that can be explained in terms of the public interest.

3. Cloze: Choose the word that best completes each sentence.

Human beings do not live in the objective world alone, nor alone in the world of social activity 1) _____ ordinarily understood, but are very much 2) _____ the mercy of the particular language which has become the 3) _____ of expression for their society. It is quite an illusion to imagine that one adjusts to reality essentially 4) _____ the use of language and 5) _____ language is merely an incidental means of solving specific problems of communication or reflection. The fact of the matter is that the "real world" is to a large extent 6) _____ built up on the language habits of the group. No two languages are ever 7) _____ similar to be considered as representing the same social reality. The worlds 8) _____ different societies live are distinct worlds, not merely the same world with different labels 9) _____.

In other words, the 10) _____ language you speak affects the ideas you can have: the linguistic relativity hypothesis. Benjamin Whorf, an amateur linguist and 11) _____ for Hartford Insurance Company, studied with Sapir at Yale and was deeply impressed with his mentor's view of thought and language. Whorf 12) _____ Sapir's idea and illustrated it with examples drawn from both his knowledge of American Indian languages and from his fire-investigation work experience. The stronger form of the hypothesis proposed by Whorf is known 13) _____ linguistic determinism. This hypothesis has become so closely associated with these two thinkers 14) _____ it is often "lexicalized" as either the Whorfian hypothesis 15) _____ the Sapir-Whorf hypothesis.

1) A. like   B. that   C. as   D. being
2) A. at   B. in   C. with   D. under
3) A. media   B. medium   C. means   D. middling
4) A. with   B. for   C. except   D. without
5) A. which   B. that   C. when   D. as
6) A. unconsciously B. randomly   C. arbitrarily D. deliberately
7) A. surely   B. merely   C. simply   D. sufficiently
8) A. which   B. in which   C. at which   D. that

9) A. attaching　　　B. having been attached　　C. attached　　D. attach
10) A. same　　　　B. common　　　　　　　　C. single　　　D. particular
11) A. fire inspector　　B. a fire inspector
　　C. the fire inspector　D. one fire inspector
12) A. stretched　　　B. extended　　　　　　　C. enlarged　　D. broadened
13) A. to be　　　　 B. as　　　　　　　　　　C. to being　　 D. to have been
14) A. that　　　　　B. when　　　　　　　　　C. which　　　 D. as
15) A. nor　　　　　 B. and　　　　　　　　　　C. or　　　　　D. but

Comprehensive Work

1. Research Work

Please do a survey among your fellow students or friends about their using of the terminology of a certain category, such as weather, food, etc. Collect as many terms as possible, and study how these words reflect different ways of seeing the world and different cultural environment.

When doing the research work, you can take the following steps:

1) Decide a category of language from the chart that you would like to investigate on.
- ✓ Weather
- ✓ Food
- ✓ Greeting words
- ✓ Time language
- ✓ Drinks

2) Ask your classmates/friends the terms that they know about the category you have chosen.

3) Classify your classmates/friends into different groups according to a certain principle (gender, age, educational background, etc.).

4) Find the similarities and differences between the use of language in different groups.

5) Study the similarities/differences you have found. Try to explain the reasons for these similarities/differences. Prepare a presentation reporting your research findings.

2. Writing Practice

As an English major, you may have had some experience of interacting with a foreigner who comes from a different culture. What deep impression have you got on him/her? Describe the strange or funny behaviors of the person in about 400 words.

3. Translation: Translate the following passage into English.

语言与思维的问题是一个"先有鸡还是先有蛋"的问题，究竟是语言影响了思维，还是思维影响了语言？比如我们谈到古希腊人和古希腊语，古希腊语被认为是极为明晰、精确的语言，古希腊人的逻辑思辨能力也很强。但是，是古希腊语这种明晰、精确的语言造就了古希腊人发达的逻辑思维，还是古希腊人发达的逻辑思维造就了古希腊语？

这确实是个难以说清的问题，要搞清楚这个问题，首先要弄清在人类进化的过程中，思维和语言哪个先产生。如果是思维先产生，则是思维影响语言；如果是语言先产生，则是语言影响思维。而按照传统观点，思维和语言是互为依存、不可分割的，是内容与形式的关系，语言是思维的物质外壳，思维的过程必须借助语言才能进行，思维和语言是同时产生的，在发展过程中是互相影响的。

也有人认为，思维可以不依赖语言而存在。聋哑人所用的手语就不是语言，但他们是有思维的，他们是可以通过手语表达和交流的。但是，思维可以不依赖语言而存在的说法其实是扩大了思维的内涵，按照严格的思维定义，聋哑人在学会手语之前的大脑活动不是思维活动，因为没有形成概念的形式，只是一种本能的反应。只有在聋哑人学会第一个手语语汇的那一刻，他的大脑活动才可以称得上思维。

Read More

Text B Language and Thought

The relationship between language, thought and reality has occupied philosophers, linguists, anthropologists and psychologists for centuries. Dating back to Plato and his theory of forms, in which Plato described the idea of thought and language having meaning as stemming from abstract definitions or concepts called "forms" and which all the "entities and qualities designated thereby can be subsumed." Along with the standard western thought Plato ultimately describes language as being based on reality.

Contrary to these common beliefs among philosophers concerning language, a well-known German scholar and diplomat from the 18th century, Wilhelm von Humboldt equated language and thought as inseparable, as language completely determining thought, in a hypothesis known as the Weltanschauung (world view) hypothesis. Although little attention was given to this extreme view at the time, this same idea drew much interest and criticism in the 1930's in the emergence of a hypothesis known as the Sapir-Whorf Hypothesis. This hypothesis was rooted in Sapir's study of Native American Languages, which later drew the particular attention of Sapir's student Benjamin Lee Whorf.

Whorf attempted to illustrate that language is the medium by which one views the world. Culture, reality and thought have aroused an intense desire in not only scholars but also for non-scholars to validate or disprove this hypothesis. Most researchers today currently argue one of the following three positions in relation to the Sapir-Whorf Hypothesis or Linguistic Relativity:

language heavily influences thought (strong interpretation), language does not influence thought or language partially influences thought (weak interpretation).

Language strongly influences thought.

Benjamin Whorf, like Sapir studied Native American languages. Whorf sites several examples from the Native American language, Hopi, to support his hypothesis that thought is strongly based on language. According to Whorf the Hopi language does not contain any words,

grammatical constructions or expressions that refer to the English concept of "time." Whorf goes on to explain that it is possible in the Hopi language to express the world or reality in ways other than what many languages refer to as "time." The Hopi view of reality is specific to the language and can only be best expressed if one is familiar with the language. In this example where Whorf feels language strongly influences thought, he is often criticized with circularity because he "infers cognitive differences between two speakers from an examination of their respective languages." His proof of cognitive differences is only "based on reiteration of the linguistic differences."

The Sapir-Whorf Hypothesis has remained a divisive topic for many years because many researchers feel that Whorf's examples failed to show a real relationship between language and thought while others agree with Whorf that thought is truly dependent on language. Similarly, researchers find it difficult to find a set of variables that fit a valid research and do not come under the same criticism as Whorf's alleged circularity. Although these constraints continue to make it difficult for researchers, many continue to look for ways to prove or disprove the Sapir-Whorf Hypothesis.

Language does not influence thought.

There are three main points that researchers use to dispute the Sapir-Whorf Hypothesis: translatability, differences between linguistic and non-linguistic events and universals. Translatability is a common argument scholars use against the hypothesis, for although language may differ considerably in the way they express certain details, it is still quite possible to translate those details from one language to another.

The argument made by Eric Lenneberg against the Sapir-Whorf Hypothesis is that "linguistic and non-linguistic events must be separately observed and described before they can be correlated." He argues that there is no way to define language as influencing thought when there is no distinction between these two events and that the evidence which supports language as influencing thought is based purely on linguistic differences.

The third argument that gives evidence against language influencing thought is the concept of universals. The Theory of Universals, commonly attributed to Chomsky and generative grammar is the claim that there are deep structures that are common to all languages. In examining this thought in relation to linguistic relativity all cultures would be related and have similar realities which is in deep contrast with Whorf's ideas that all cultures see the world differently because of their language.

Language partially influences thought.

The writings of Sapir and Whorf brought about a huge change in the way scholars view language and thought. Researchers scurried to find evidence that would give the hypothesis validity. Although the research is easy to formulate, the problem lies in finding a set of variables that accurately test the hypothesis. Most researchers up to this time have found it hard to conclude that language determines thought; however through examples from Whorf's studies in Hopi and other observations from researchers it is valid to suggest that language does partially determine thought. In determining linguistic relativity the question is not whether a language affects one's thoughts but to what degree.

Many examples are given to support a weak interpretation of linguistic relativity. One experiment done by Linda Rogers gives evidence to support a weak interpretation. Rogers read a story to a group of bilingual children while recording their brain-wave patterns. She first read the story in English while observing that the children's brains were active in the left hemisphere and then read the story in Navaho and observed their brain activity in the right hemisphere. This, according to Rogers, gave evidence to the fact that English as a noun-centered language was processed in the left side of the brain and the Navaho as a verb-centered language was processed in the right side of the brain. This gave evidence to the fact that although the same story was told to the same children they processed the story differently according to which language it was told in.

Another example is a study contrasting Japanese and English passive constructions done by Agnes Niyekawa-Howard in 1968. The study explains that Japanese has two types of passive constructions in which when one is combined with the other the meaning changes so that the subject of the sentence was "caused" to take the action that is found in the verb. In translating stories from Japanese to English this construction was not seen; however, in the translation from English to Japanese the Japanese translators included this construction. Similarly, when asked to interpret cartoons that dealt with interpersonal conflict, the Japanese "were found to attribute responsibility for the negative outcome to others" more than did the English. The study's purpose was to show that although not consciously seen by native Japanese, this construction of grammar contributes to a "perceptual habit or cultural outlook" in the Japanese culture.

Support for the idea that language partially influences thought can also be seen in the concept of codability. Codability can be seen as the ability to translate a word, phrase or idea from one language to another. Anyone that speaks two languages would agree that some ideas are easier said in one language over the other. Many times in language there are words that explain a thought, location, emotion etc. that in other languages could take up to a paragraph long to describe. An Eskimo tribe in Alaska called the Dena'ina Athabaskans has an entire lexicon that describes different kinds of streams and trails. In one word the Dena'ina are able to describe the following phrases: "a place of fast or slow current, covered with slush ice or overflow ice, a packed snow trail or a trail with snow drifted over, an animal trail, or a trail used for getting wood." The concept of codability, the ability to code in one language a word or phrase in another, exemplifies the idea of language partially influencing thought because in one language a speaker may be able to perceive a lexical category better than another but that in no way limits another language from being able to perceive the same category.

Linguists and Anthropologists have been concerned with the Sapir-Whorf Hypothesis and the implications that surround the claims made by Sapir in 1928 and continue to look for ways to prove or disprove the idea that language directly influences the way reality is perceived. Because the perfect research situation to completely prove or disprove this hypothesis does not exist researchers are left to examine small examples of specific registers in which language can be seen to affect thought and reality and through research in these registers most researchers agree with the weak interpretation of the Sapir-Whorf Hypothesis.

Conclusion

"Language and society are so intertwined that it is impossible to understand one without the other. There is no human society that does not depend on, is not shaped by, and does not itself shape language." This statement best defines the relationship between language, thought and reality for language not only shapes the way reality is perceived but reality can also shape language. The Sapir-Whorf Hypothesis has changed the way many people look at language. It has influenced many scholars and opened up large areas of study. While many like Sapir and Whorf support the notion that language strongly influences thought and others argue that language does not influence thought, the evidence from research indicates that language does influence thought and perception of reality but language does not govern thought or reality.

Questions for Discussion

1. What are the three positions scholars constantly argue in relation to the Sapir-Whorf Hypothesis?
2. Why do some scholars argue that language does not influence thought?
3. What is the evidence to prove that language partially influences thought?
4. How do you comment on Sapir-Whorf Hypothesis?

Text C Language May Shape Human Thought

Language may shape human thought—suggests a counting study in a Brazilian tribe whose language does not define numbers above two.

Hunter-gatherers from the Pirahã tribe, whose language only contains words for the numbers one and two, were unable to reliably tell the difference between four objects placed in a row and five in the same configuration, revealed the study.

Experts agree that the startling result provides the strongest support yet for the controversial hypothesis that the language available to humans defines our thoughts. So-called "linguistic determinism" was first proposed in 1950 but has been hotly debated ever since.

"It is a very surprising and very important result," says Lisa Feigenson, a developmental psychologist at Johns Hopkins University in Baltimore, Maryland, US, who has tested babies' abilities to distinguish between different numerical quantities. "Whether language actually allows you to have new thoughts is a very controversial issue."

Peter Gordon, the psychologist at Columbia University in New York City who carried out the experiment, does not claim that his finding holds for all kinds of thought. "There are certainly things that we can think about that we cannot talk about. But for numbers I have shown that a limitation in language affects cognition," he says.

"One, two, many"

The language, Pirahã, is known as a "one, two, many" language because it only contains words for "one" and "two" — for all other numbers, a single word for "many" is used. "There are not really occasions in their daily lives where the Pirahã need to count," explains Gordon.

In order to test if this prevented members of the tribe from perceiving higher numbers, Gordon set seven Pirahã a variety of tasks. In the simplest, he sat opposite an individual and laid out a random number of familiar objects, including batteries, sticks and nuts, in a row. The Pirahã were supposed to respond by laying out the same number of objects from their own pile.

For one, two and three objects, members of the tribe consistently matched Gordon's pile correctly. But for four and five and up to ten, they could only match it approximately, deviating more from the correct number as the row got longer.

The Pirahã also failed to remember whether a box they had been shown seconds ago had four or five fish drawn on the top. When Gordon's colleagues tapped on the floor three times, the Pirahã were able to imitate this precisely, but failed to mimic strings of four or five taps.

Babies and animals

Gordon says this is the first convincing evidence that a language lacking words for certain concepts could actually prevent speakers of the language from understanding those concepts.

Previous experiments show that while babies and intelligent animals, such as rats, pigeons and monkeys, are capable of precisely counting small quantities, they can only approximately distinguish between clusters consisting of larger numbers. However, in these studies it was unclear whether an inability to articulate numbers was the reason for this.

The Pirahã results provide a much stronger case for linguistic determinism, says Gordon, because, aside from their language, they are otherwise similar to other adult humans, whereas there are many more factors that separate babies and animals from adult humans.

However, scientists are far from a consensus. Feigenson points out that there could be other reasons, aside from pure language, why the Pirahã could not distinguish accurately for higher numbers including not being used to dealing with large numbers or set such tasks.

"The question remains highly controversial," says psychologist Randy Gallistel of Rutgers University in Piscataway, New Jersey. "But this work will spark a great deal of discussion."

(Excerpted from: http://www.newscientist.com/article/dn6303-language-may-shape-human-thought.html)

Questions for Discussion

1. How does Lisa Feigenson comment on her recent research?
2. What can you infer from the example of the Pirahã language?
3. Are scientists satisfied with their research? Please explain why.

Unit 11 Linguistic Imperialism

> In most of the European countries, France stands out in its resistance to this particular form of American cultural imperialism; the national film industries were forced onto the defensive after the war by such binding agreements.
>
> — Fredric Jameson

Unit Goals

- To understand the concept of linguistic imperialism
- To discuss different theories concerning linguistic imperialism
- To explore the relationship between linguistic imperialism and cultural imperialism

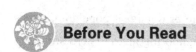 Before You Read

1. Why Learn English?

English is the mother tongue of some 400 million people, and the second language of an equally large number of speakers. There are also an estimated 750 million people who learn English as a foreign language. Why do you learn English? What are the benefits of learning English? Fill in the following blanks and share what you think with your classmates.

English	Benefits of learning English

2. **One of the debating issues in the world today is Americanization, that is, the influence of the United States on popular culture, technology, business practices, political techniques or the language of other countries. Do you think the Chinese culture has been Americanized? Please prepare a presentation of 5 minutes on the topic of Americanization, sharing your ideas with your classmates.**

Start to Read

Text A   What Is Linguistic Imperialism?

Linguistic imperialism occurs when the language of a large or dominant population or the language of power transfers to other people in the same or neighboring areas. There are many types of linguistic imperialism and many causes of it. Causes include immigration, conquest, trade and cultural superiority. The spread of religions that transcend local cultures and languages can also cause linguistic imperialism. Such changes in language can be forced or can take place through natural changes.

Acts of linguistic imperialism have taken place throughout the world's history. Not all of these cases have been successful. After 1066, the Franco-Normans attempted to make French, or rather the Norman dialect of French, the national language. After 300 years, they eventually gave up trying and learned English. The Hungarians resisted centuries of attempts by Ottoman Turks and later Habsburg Austrians to make Hungarian illegal.

Immigration is a large cause of linguistic imperialism. This is most often seen as the act of an invading or migrating people making others learn their language. At the end of the Roman Empire in the 4th and 5th centuries AD, a number of Germanic peoples moved westward into the Empire's territories. Of those invading powers, many took control of the area, but their responses to the indigenous language varied. The Angles, Saxons and Jutes managed to eradicate the language of the native Romano-British. On the other hand, the Franks who invaded Gaul and the

Ostragoths, who invaded Iberia, both adopted the language of the native population.

Large-scale linguistic imperialism occurred during the colonial era. It first began with the Portuguese in Brazil, the Spanish in Mesoamerica and the English in North America, but widened to large parts of the world. In most cases, new countries and new territories covered a wide patchwork of linguistic groups. In these cases, the dominant colonial power imposed its language on the native population for the system of government. In some countries, like those of the Spanish empire, the colonial language became the majority language.

In other countries, as seen in India, it became a language used to unite disparate linguistic groups. In these cases, an imposed language, while often resented for its imposition, works as a unifying force and a means of preventing the imposition of the language group on the rest of the country. The imposed language becomes a second language to many people.

The rise of nationalism across Europe and in other countries has caused linguistic imperialism on a more local or national level. Political leaders and members of the dominant ethnic or linguistic group within the country wanted to develop a sense of nationhood, collectivity and singleness by downgrading minority languages. This has seen the many small languages of regions from Cornish and Breton to Dalmatian and Yaeyama-go reduced to historic fossils and dialects.

A dominance of culture can cause another kind of linguistic imperialism. The idea of imperialism is the imposition of power by one group over another. The dominance of a dialect or language can be spread by arts and culture in the form of music, television shows and music. The power and wealth of American popular culture has had a great linguistic impact on countries and peoples around the world, including those countries that already speak English.

Text B Global English

I like to think of British and Americans moving about freely over each other's wide estates with hardly a sense of being foreigners to one another. But I do not see why we should not try to spread our common language even more widely throughout the globe and, without seeking selfish advantage over any, possess ourselves of this invaluable amenity and birthright.

— *Winston Churchill*

In 1943 the British Empire was seriously weakened, British success in the Second World War was dependent on the American war machine, and massive financial loans from the USA. Transatlantic partnership builds on the cultural origins of millions of Europeans who emigrated to the USA, Britain as the dominant colonizing power, supplanting the Dutch, Spanish and French, and English as a link language. Churchill's first major point in his talk at Harvard is support for

USA global dominance, camouflaged as "world responsibility."

Secondly, Churchill sees the UK and USA as linked by 'blood and history'. Links between the two countries remained close even after the US Declaration of Independence. Churchill sees the two nations as united by "law, language, and literature," exemplified by morality, justice, fair play, and support for the weak — norms that both countries are better at articulating than implementing.

Thirdly, he stresses that in the war effort, American, British and Canadian forces have a joint command. He proposes that this should continue after the war, and only cease once a global system for peace maintenance has been established. The United Nations was soon established for this purpose, in a form that maintained the principle of the permanent members of the Security Council, including the USA and UK, playing a decisive role, which they still do.

Fourth, a key issue in Churchill's speech is his articulation of a plan for English as a globally dominant language worldwide, this task pretentiously claimed to be the "birthright" of the British and Americans.

These four dimensions-globalization, consanguinity, military unification, and linguistic expansion form a complete package. The aims of global American dominance, with the UK in full support, included the integration of the economies of Europe—a condition for Marshall Aid—and the establishment of English as the dominant international language.

Churchill also articulates a vision of potential UK and USA "common citizenship."

Here he echoes Cecil Rhodes, who envisaged the USA rejoining the United Kingdom that it broke away from in 1776. He bequeathed the vast fortune made in the gold mines of South Africa to fund activities to cement links between the USA and UK and to promote Anglo-American dominance worldwide. His legacy funds the Rhodes scholarships at Oxford University, with Bill Clinton as a typical beneficiary.

Churchill's total faith in the USA has been shared by all subsequent British Prime Ministers. The Margaret Thatcher Center for Freedom at the Heritage Foundation in Washington DC has as its goal the promotion of US/UK dominance worldwide, as does its British counterpart. The ubiquitous activities of Tony Blair are in the same spirit, while enabling him to accumulate prodigious personal wealth.

Churchill's plan to spread the English language throughout the world is packaged as being disinterested, which all evidence of British and American colonization worldwide contradicts. Plans for English to function as a "world language" under UK and US leadership had already emerged in the 1930s, with funding from the Carnegie Foundation. They were intensively pursued from the 1950s. The promotion of English became a key dimension of the policies of the UK and the USA. The English language industry has expanded massively and is of major importance for the British economy. Its key constituents are publishers, university departments of applied linguistics and English teaching, language schools, BBC multi-media English teaching, and educational consultancies worldwide.

"The English language teaching sector directly earns nearly £1.3 billion for the UK in invisible exports and our other education related exports earn up to £10 billion a year more," writes Lord Neil Kinnock in a Foreword to *English next*, a report commissioned by the British Council, "the United Kingdom's international organization for educational opportunities and cultural relations," a central conduit for British cultural and economic diplomacy. It is committed to expanding the learning and use of English worldwide. The teaching and examining of English are a major source of this parastate's revenue. A country that is notoriously monolingual intriguingly markets itself as having an infinite supply of "experts" who are capable of solving the language learning problems of educational systems in multilingual countries worldwide.

The British Council ought, according to a policy survey conducted by a pro-government NGO to be more energetic: the students it teaches and "the 800,000 people who take exams administered by the Council every year would make good targets for public diplomacy activity," as part of "Diplomacy by Stealth: Working with others to achieve our goals. The general lesson is ... make sure it appears to be coming from a foreign government as little as possible. Increasingly it must work through organizations and networks that are separate from, independent of, and even culturally suspicious toward government itself." Thus the activities of English teachers, some of whom may disapprove of their own government, can stealthily serve whatever the government sees as a national cause — local English for the global purposes of Britain, and indirectly for American empire within the emerging European empire, in which English linguistic capital is accumulating.

In Europe the use of English has expanded rapidly in recent decades. Its extensive visibility serves to make the learning of English more attractive than learning other languages. The UK has a vested interest in promoting this trend, and the increased influence that follows with it, as well as economic benefits. Other European countries are subsidizing this process, to the detriment of the learning of languages such as French, German and Russian. A report prepared for a French language education policy body has calculated the effects on the economy of the UK and Ireland of the investment in the market for English learning. Favoring English results in five types of quantifiable effect: a privileged market, communication savings, language learning savings, alternative human capital investment, and legitimacy and rhetorical effects. Grin concludes that a conservative estimate is that continental European countries are transferring to the UK and Ireland at least €10 bn per year, more probably about €16 to 17 bn a year. This figure substantially exceeds the British budget rebate of €5bn annually.

English is at the summit of a linguistic hierarchy. English linguistic hegemony is reinforced structurally (material investment) and ideologically. The practice of learning English in ways that marginalize other languages and hinder or prevent their learning — through linguistic policies that amount to linguistic imperialism — was established in colonizing contexts in the British Isles (the imposition of English in Wales, Ireland and Scotland) and the Americas (the destruction of local languages, gradual elimination of other immigrant languages). Linguistic capital was invested in the dominant language (time in schools, university departments, publications etc.) and not in other languages. In colonial empires European languages were invariably the languages of power. The system has largely been maintained in former colonies, the term "postcolonial" occluding a linguistic hegemony that has remained in place.

Empirical study of the factors determining language policies can elucidate in any given context whether linguistic imperialism is in force. With the learning and use of English expanding in continental Europe, the issue of whether or not it impacts negatively on other languages is of increasing concern. Perception of English as a threat to the continued vitality of national languages has been analyzed in Germany, the four Scandinavian countries and Finland, and higher education in continental Europe. A Nordic inter-governmental Declaration on Language Policy aims at maintaining the vitality of national languages while also ensuring that international languages, mainly English, are learned. The position is dynamically evolving, and unpredictable: linguistic capital accumulation may be exclusively beneficial, through the addition of English to linguistic repertoires, with national languages remaining as the unifying language in all areas of life. By contrast if the linguistic capital is accumulated by processes of dispossession, as in classic colonialism, and a national language is no longer used in key societal functions — in higher education, government business, major commercial enterprises, the media — then there is evidence of linguistic imperialism.

After You Read

Knowledge Focus

1. **Solo Work: Tell whether the following statements are true or false according to the knowledge you learned.**
    1) Linguistic imperialism occurs when the language of a large or dominant population or the language of power transfers to other people in the same or neighboring areas.
    2) All acts of linguistic imperialism have taken place throughout the world's history successfully.
    3) Invading powers respond to the indigenous language in the same manner.
    4) A dominance of culture can cause another kind of linguistic imperialism.
    5) The author sees the UK and USA as united by "law, language, and literature," exemplified by morality, justice, fair play, and support for the weak.
    6) The promotion of English became a key dimension of the policies of the UK and the USA.
    7) English linguistic hegemony is reinforced structurally (material investment) and

ideologically.

8) The learning and use of English expanding in continental Europe, has made the issue of whether or not it impacts positively on other languages of increasing concern.

2. Pair Work: Discuss the following questions with your partner.
1) What is linguistic imperialism? Please give examples to support your definition.
2) What are the causes for linguistic imperialism? Explain the causes with your own examples.
3) What is the historical background for the global expansion of English?
4) What are key constituents in English language industry?
5) What does the global expansion of English mean both to the UK and USA? Support your idea with examples.
6) What is the role played by the British Council in the global expansion of English?
7) How can we elucidate in any given context whether linguistic imperialism is in force?
8) Is English the only language to be criticized for linguistic imperialism?

Language Focus
1. Fill in the blanks with the idioms/expressions you have learned in the text.

| transcend | indigenous | eradicate | disparate |
| supplant | consanguinity | envisage | conduit |

1) The transplanted nerves will act as a _____ to allow the baby's undamaged right-hand nerves to grow over to his left side.
2) The government is making efforts to _____ racial discriminating.
3) Each country must tailor its energy plan to its _____ endowment of replenishable energy resources.
4) We can't _____ the limitations of the ego.
5) Once again, the system of _____ in force in Hawaii did not correspond to the actual form of the Hawaiian family.
6) Products that are poorly designed, or not designed at all, often look and feel like they are cobbled together from _____ pieces haphazardly knit together.
7) And how do you _____ China's foreign affairs in the Year 2030 under the present circumstances?
8) TV and computers shouldn't _____ time with others and cyberchats don't develop social skills.

语言、社会与文化
Language, Society and Culture

2. Cloze: Choose the word that best completes each sentence.

What's faster than a speeding bullet, more powerful than a locomotive, and able to leap over hostile elitists in a single bound? Well, it's 1) _____ the all-American duo of Mickey Mouse and Ronald McDonald.

It may come as a surprise to most Americans 2) _____ overseas these beloved symbols are sometimes about 3) _____ welcome as typhoid or leprosy. The cries of cultural imperialism are a 4) _____ recent phenomenon. 5) _____ the withering away of Western colonial empires, nationalists in the newly independent countries often became outraged 6) _____ the staying power of colonial cultures. These nationalists came to 7) _____ the presence and domination of Western culture as "cultural imperialism." Paul Harrison's description in his book *Inside the Third World* is typical: "And so there grew up, 8) _____ political and economic imperialism, that more insidious form of control — cultural imperialism. It conquered not just the bodies, but the souls of its victims …"

9) _____, the strength and attraction of Western popular culture became even more 10) _____ by that of the United States. This development allowed the 11) _____ of cultural imperialism to become just as common in European intellectual circles 12) _____ in the Third World.

Because the French have traditionally been very proud of their culture, the emergence of American popular culture has been an especially bitter pill for them to 13) _____. The fear of encroaching Americana has often been 14) ____ the mind of France's Minister of Culture, Jack Lang. Shortly after the Socialist Party's election Lang called "for a real crusade against... this financial and intellectual imperialism that no longer grabs territory... but grabs consciousness, ways of thinking, ways of living."

One of the people 15) _____ cultural imperialism most closely is the exiled Chilean author Ariel Dorfman. Dorfman has published two books on the subject: *How to Read Donald Duck: Imperialist Ideology in the Disney Comics* and *The Empire's Old Clothes: What the Lone Ranger, Babar, and Other Innocent Heroes Do to Our Minds*.

1) A. no other than   B. none other than
   C. no more than   D. no less than

2) A. that   B. who   C. which   D. whom
3) A. as   B. so   C. too   D. far
4) A. logically   B. moderately   C. relatively   D. reasonably
5) A. By   B. For   C. As   D. With
6) A. over   B. with   C. for   D. to
7) A. call   B. term   C. name   D. phrase
8) A. apart   B. along   C. next to   D. alongside
9) A. Over time   B. With time   C. In time   D. On time

10) A. conquered	B. dominated	C. subjugated	D. occupied
11) A. allegations	B. charges	C. claims	D. accusations
12) A. for	B. as	C. that	D. like
13) A. swallow	B. eat	C. bite	D. digest
14) A. in	B. on	C. over	D. with
15) A. who has examined		B. who have examined	
C. who has been examined		D. who have been examined	

Comprehensive Work

1. Discussion: Linguistic Imperialism

Read the following article and discuss the questions that follow.

A Chinese Perspective of Linguistic Imperialism

One of the biggest job markets for students nowadays involves ESL teaching in foreign countries. The idea is quite appealing: free travel, cash and a chance to educate the rest of the world. In reality, the bigger picture shows they are participating in a global conquest for perfecting Standard English.

Indeed, in many countries, the more English you know, the better off you'll be. It's a pity many kids don't even respect their mother tongue anymore and only aim to learn the more "useful" English.

Having spent most of my life in China, I know the advantages that come with knowing English. I recall many times when my father, who obtained his degree in Canada, would put his co-workers in their places simply by speaking to them in English. Furthermore, his ability to manipulate slang usage and technical terms always gained him an advantage in the world of commerce. Even American business partners give way when they listen to him, openly applauding his linguistic abilities.

"Wow, you're really good at English!" they say, following the logic that "if he can speak English then he must be smart."

My parents know damn well that language is power, so they shuffled me between as many schools teaching in as many different languages as they could since the day I could babble. Try French preschool, Cantonese elementary, English junior high and Mandarin senior high. Instead of feeling "powerful," I went from struggling with Chinese characters to wiggling through English as a Second Language classes.

Right now, I'm thankful for it, but the lesson I learned was that if you knew English, you can screw all other languages.

When I was in Shanghai, I had many English-speaking friends. Everywhere we went, there was this superior air around us. From the two international schools I attended, I knew over 2,000 people of non-Chinese descent and less than one per cent of them ever attempted to learn any

Chinese. There was a Belgian kid in my grade six class who lived in China for more than eight years and couldn't speak a word of Chinese — but his English was better than most Americans.

The funny thing was all the Polish, Korean, Finnish and other non-Americans I knew came to China with little knowledge of English or Chinese but within half a year they had already picked up English. They didn't need to know Chinese, they got by just fine — more than fine, to be accurate.

Soon, I also learned to speak only English in certain settings to get what I want. Every time I got into trouble or wanted to buy alcohol, I would burst out my English words. It didn't matter that I was skateboarding inside a mall, drinking gin at MacDonald's or throwing empty bottles at apartment buildings, the moment I spoke the magic words, authorities would disappear or simply become more lenient. Sometimes they would even attempt to learn a couple of English words from me. I felt the imperial powers of English and I'm not even white!

I came back to Canada in 1999 thinking that if I showed off my English the moment I landed, no one would see me as "inferior." In reality, Canada was more tolerant of other cultures than any international school I ever attended. People here actually want to learn from foreigners.

The whole overseas ESL deal is attractive to Canadians because they want to experience different cultures. Little do they know their future students on the other side of the ocean simply want a piece of that English power-speak. These worldwide ESL teachers are promoting linguistic imperialism in the name of multiculturalism.

Where I come from, a person's non-English language skills are, at times, something to be ashamed of. Even with the best of intentions, ESL teachers to-be should reevaluate some of the social implications behind these language programs.

Questions for Discussion

1) According to the text, what are the advantages of speaking English? Do you know other advantages of learning English in China?

   _____

2) What is the author's attitude towards English linguistic imperialism? Do you agree with him/her or not? And why?

   _____

3) What suggestions does the author give at the end of the article? Do you agree with him/her? Do you have other suggestions?

   _____

2. Writing Practice

To what extent do you think the Chinese culture has been Americanized? What suggestions will you offer to preserve the traditional Chinese culture? Please write a composition in the following steps:

1) For the first part, write about whether you think Chinese culture has been Americanized or not. Give reasons or examples to illustrate your idea.
2) For the second part, please give some suggestions for the preservation of traditional Chinese culture. You may also give examples in this part.
3) For the last part, please give a natural conclusion to your composition.

3. Translation: Translate the following passage into Chinese.

The world's literati will be happy to know that America itself is not immune to the fear of cultural imperialism. Americans living between Los Angeles and New York often bemoan the cultural products of these two foreign capitals. More serious is the risk posed by what anthropologists term "the law of cultural dominance." This theory states that whichever culture is technologically superior will eventually dominate its inferiors.

Until World War II, this position of dominance was shared by Great Britain and France and was ceded to the United States in the wake of the war. If this theory holds true, perhaps the next dominant culture will be Japan's. As it is, Japanese food, fashion, and art are more popular than ever both in America and worldwide; Japanese technology and management techniques are in even greater demand. While this idea might seem a little far-fetched to some, it would surprise no one in the rest-belt cities of Detroit or Pittsburgh. Auto and steel executives speak openly of their hatred for their Oriental competitors, taking the phrase "trade war" literally. "This time," one auto executive told me, "the Japs won't lose."

At the moment, however, American culture is — if nothing else — technology, and it is in this realm that the fewest complaints abroad are heard about cultural imperialism. But vaccines, telephones, and airplanes are as symbolic of America as Mickey Mouse and Ronald McDonald. Once American technology is introduced — even though technology is generally considered non-imperialistic—a closer mirroring of America is likely to follow. For example, once cars become important to a society, road systems and cities designed to accommodate the vehicles will result. Thus, a more American-looking city is created. As a faster lifestyle comes about, fast-food restaurants such as McDonald's and Kentucky Fried Chicken become more acceptable and necessary.

语言、社会与文化
Language, Society and Culture

Read More

Text C Quebec: A Case of Cultural and Linguistic Imperialism?

Gaetan Tremblay's essay poses the question — "Is Quebec culture doomed to become American?" He answers that there is a real threat of cultural invasion. But, the situation is not that bad, he writes, at least in the early 1990s when the article came out.

Tremblay uses certain data concerning television supply and demand. He begins his thesis by citing the Broadcasting Act, and then reviews those elements which highlight broadcasting as a service to preserving Canadian culture. The Quebec government's effort to defend and develop Quebecois culture is also examined. He contrasts this notion with the American one to see cultural products as commodities like any other, subject to free market rules. In the essay, Tremblay presents his research and makes observations. He notes that two-thirds of all programs broadcast by Quebecois networks are of Canadian origin. The remaining third of programming is foreign. Public television has slight higher quotas than private television. The situation in programming is in the area of entertainment, particularly drama programming, which includes series, "teleromans," films, and cartoons. Films make up the bulk of these programs, and more of these films are of American origin.

Tremblay observes that there is a strong presence of American products. However, he says the 50 percent proportion is not out of control. The reason it is not out of control is because of the language barrier, CRTC regulations, and view preferences. The BBM reports that Quebecois programming make up the majority of the 20 most watch programs. Tremblay asserts that the Quebecois want to keep their protective policies and regulations for fear that the problem will deteriorate. This fear stems from four things: the proximity of America, the limited internal market, Quebec's status as a linguistic minority in North America, and market rules favouring American products.

Though Tremblay accomplishes much in his essay, it does have some shortcomings. For instance, Tremblay asserts that the Quebecois want to keep protective policies and regulations on Quebecois culture, but he does not support this claim with any data or evidence. Since throughout the essay he supports his ideas with data and his own research, it seems odd that his claim in the essay has none. In the data that Tremblay uses, it would have been interesting to have an age breakdown. To know what younger people are watching would give some sense of the future of Quebeocois television viewing habits.

Another shortcoming of Tremblay's article is that he sets out to answer a question about

Quebecois culture by only looking at television. What the Quebecois watch on TV is only a portion of what the culture is. If Tremblay really wants an accurate answer to the question and title of his essay, his research will have to include more than just television.

Throughout the essay on television and Quebecois culture, many questions arise: should cultural products be commodities like any other and thus be subject to market rules? What happens to a cultural form when you change the language? Does it become part of the culture, is it recreated? What is Quebecois culture? Should there continue to be laws protecting Quebecois culture? Tremblay's essay was written in 1992. The most recent part of his data is from 1990. Tremblay's article raises some very important issues that are still relevant today. In order to update the information in his article an informal survey was conducted and recent reports of the BBM were consulted.

BBM conducts surveys for its members, who include media organizations across Canada, both Francophone and Anglophone. It selects a sample of the population to see what they are watching on TV, and listening to on the radio. For the purpose of this analysis, only the share for the television market in the extended Montreal area was consulted. Particularly, the Francophone stations were compared with the American stations in terms of viewing habits in primetime, from 6:00 p.m. to 11:00 p.m., Monday to Friday. Ratings and the share were taken from the summer of 1996, which includes surveys from the weeks of June 20 to June 26 and July 4 to 10. BBM monitors individual viewing habits in one-week windows. The results of this survey include 3,368 respondents from the extended Montreal area. The share is the percentage of the total number of hours watched of television in a time slot. For example, in a 6:00 p.m. to 6:30 p.m. slot, CFTM's TVA edition got a 32 per cent share of the total number of people watching in that time. Yves Robert, account executive at BBM, says one should look at the share when figuring out how a TV station is doing compared to others. An example of the survey used for the following analysis is enclosed at the end of this paper.

The report reveals that at the supper hour most people are watching the news on the Francophone stations, but there are a significant number, between 16 to 22 percent of the share, who watch ABC News. Moving further into primetime, from 8:00 p.m. to 9:00 p.m., the most watched shows on Monday night are American programs, such as Beverly Hills 90210. On a Friday night, however, the most watched show is Cine-Columbo on CFTM, Télé-Metropole and second is Family Matters, an American show. Overall, from looking at primetime viewing habits, the audiences of Francophone TV slightly outnumber the American programs. Tremblay's research still holds true, but he never mentions the American sitcom, whose influence becomes apparent when looking at the BBM report.

To update the information in Tremblay's article even more than give voice to his ideas, an informal survey was conducted on Saturday, November 8, 1997 in the Eaton Centre, Montreal Trust Place and the streets of downtown Montreal. The survey is in no way as representative as

BBM's. It was conducted with 30 respondents, but it still gives a sense of what the Quebecois (in this case Francophone) are thinking and feeling about issues that stem from Tremblay's essay. Thirty Francophone respondents were chosen randomly in an effort to be divers in terms of gender and age. The respondents were asked three questions.

1) What kind of television do you watch the most, Quebecois or American? Why?
2) Do you think that Quebecois culture will become American? Why?
3) Do you think there should continue to be laws to protect Quebecois culture? Why?

Overall, the results were in keeping with Tremblay's findings.

Table 1: Quebecois versus American Television Viewing Habits
Quebecois TV — 12; American TV — 10; Both — 8; Total respondents — 30

Similar to Tremblay's findings, overall Francophones are watching more Quebecois television than American television. A significant number are watching both. Not everyone gave reasons for their viewing habits. Here are some of the reasons for those who did answer the question:

Jean, 18:	watches more American programming. He finds it funnier, watches American TV for movies.
Sara, 29:	watches more American television. "It's what everybody watches at work and this way I can talk about it too."
Sophie, 38:	watches more American TV. "I watch with my child and all he likes are the English sitcoms and cartoons."
Denis, 43:	watches more American TV. He watches the movies and the comedy shows. Denis watches French TV at the supper hour.
Constance, 32:	watches both. "They both have good things to offer. I like the news on French TV and movies on American TV."

So, just as Tremblay found, the Quebecois are watching American programs for the movies and cartoons, or basically the entertainment programming. It is also interesting to note from this survey that it is mainly those people who watch more American programming who explained the reasons for their viewing choice. Even seven years later, (from the original date of this publication in 1997), Tremblay's findings are still relevant.

Francophones surveyed also seemed to agree with Tremblay in terms of the major question he raises in his essay, according to Table 2.

Table 2: Is Quebecois Culture Becoming American?
Yes — 8; No — 14; Already is — 7; Maybe — 1; Total Respondents — 30

According to Table 2, the majority of Francophones do not think Quebecois culture will become American; that's 14 out of 30 respondents, almost half or 47 percent. However, a significant number thought there is a threat of cultural invasion, 8 out of 30 respondents, or 27 percent. What is also interesting is that almost as many people thought that Quebecois culture already is American, 7 out of 30, or 23 percent. If the respondents who thought Quebecois culture would become American and those who thought it already is American are combined, then that makes 50 percent, more than those who answered "no."

A variety of reasons were given as to whether or not Quebecois culture would become American. A few people cited Quebec laws preserving the culture as the reason why Americans would not take over. Several people saw the power of the Americans winning out, and a few people noted the similarity of the cultures.

What greatly distinguishes this survey from Tremblay's research is how responses can be categorized corresponding to age (Table 3).

Table 3: Respondent Choices by Age

Question 1: What kind of television do you watch the most, Quebecois or American? Why?

Age	Under 25	25—64	65
French TV	4	8	0
American TV	4	6	0
Both	0	6	2

Question 2: Do you think that Quebecois culture will become American? Why?

Age	Under 25	25—64	65
Yes	4	4	0
No	1	11	2
Already is	3	4	0
Maybe	0	1	0

There were definite differences in responses by age. For the purpose of this paper, the answers from the age group that is under 25, the future leaders, will be highlighted. An equal amount of people watched Quebecois TV and American TV, while no one watched both. Perhaps 38-year-old Sophie was "half-right" according to the survey. This number for the under 25-age group is less than those of the 26 to 64 age group. On the question of whether Quebecois culture will become American, only one respondent under 25 answered "no" compared to 11 from ages 26 to 64 and all the respondents over 65. According to this survey, those under 25 tended to be more pessimistic about the future of Quebecois culture than other age groups.

This paper has critically analyzed the article by Gaetan Tremblay, "Is Quebec Culture Doomed to Become American." A BBM report from the summer of 1996 was used to update the material in Tremblay's essay. According to the report, the material from Tremblay is still relevant. Also, an informal survey of 30 respondents in the downtown Montreal area was conducted. The responses corresponded with the findings of Tremblay and also shed some light on issues he never raises, such as the sentiments of the future leaders of Quebec society.

Questions for Discussion

1. Please summarize the key points of Gaetan Tremblay's essay.
2. How is the survey conducted by the author of this article? Are the findings in agreement with those in Tremblay's essay?
3. According to the survey, are Francophones watching more Quebecois television than American television?
4. What is the biggest difference between the author's survey and Tremblay's research?

Text D Lingua Franca Discourse

Some people imagine that English is likely to become the lingua franca of India. That seems to me a fantastic conception, except in respect of a handful of upper-class intelligentsia. It has no relation to the problem of mass education and culture even the most rabid of our nationalists hardly realize how much they are cribbed and confined by the British outlook in relation to India.

— Jawaharlal Nehru

Is it possible that the future Prime Minister of India's worry can bear comparison with what we are currently experiencing in Europe? Could the European upper echelon of decision-makers (I hesitate to refer to them as an intelligentsia) be so cribbed (confined to a small space) and confined by their admiration for things American that incorporation into a 21st century American empire is already well established? American ambitions have for centuries been explicitly imperial: "The whole world should adopt the American system. The American system can survive in America only if it becomes a world system." Any such world system or empire will have English as the dominant language, to the dismay of French presidents and to many European intellectuals as well as nationalists.

How could adoption of English as an imperial European language be justified or legitimated?

English is often described as a lingua franca. This generally seems to imply that the language is a neutral instrument for "international" communication between speakers who do not share a mother tongue. This understanding of the term may mislead one into believing that lingua franca English is disconnected from the many purposes it serves in key societal domains. English might be more accurately related to distinct contexts of use. It can and does function as a pre-eminent international lingua economica (in business and advertising, the main language of corporate neoliberalism), a lingua emotiva (the imaginary of Hollywood, popular music, consumerism and hedonism), a lingua academica (in research publications, at international conferences, and as a medium for content learning in higher education), and a lingua cultura (rooted in the literary texts of English-speaking nations that school foreign language education traditionally aims at, and integrates with language learning as one element of general education). English is a major lingua bellica (the USA with 350 bases and 800 military facilities in 130 countries, NATO not only active in Europe but worldwide, "US armed forces are now involved in 49 out of 54 African states, along with the former colonial powers of France and Britain, in what's becoming a new carve-up of the continent," the fabrication of a "war on terror," etc). English is also a major lingua politica in international organizations such as the United Nations and the European Union. The worldwide presence of English as a lingua americana is due to the massive economic, cultural and military impact of the USA, English functioning in each of the categories adumbrated here.

In the EU system, English, French and German are described as procedural languages for select purposes in the Commission. This term is used because these languages, now mainly English, serve as a lingua executiva for very specific functions in EU administration, and in political negotiations for reaching consensus on policies. Effectiveness in such interaction requires an extremely high level of linguistic proficiency.

There is an ironic historical continuity in the use of a term lingua franca to refer to contemporary English since it was first used to describe the language of Christian crusaders from western Europe in the Middle Ages (1095—1300), who travelled to drive out Islam from Jerusalem and Palestine. The crusaders were understood as speaking lingua franca, the term deriving from the Arabic *lisan alfiranj*, when crusading Europeans of various origins were seen by Arabs as Franks. These were a tribe from Germany who settled in France, hence the name of the country France. The continent that bears the name Europe now was then generally referred to as Christendom.

The term lingua franca became established in later centuries in the eastern Mediterranean to describe the simplified language that was used between people from different linguistic backgrounds for commercial trading purposes. It was a restricted form of language, mixing elements from several European languages that had evolved from Latin (French, Italian, Catalan), Greek, and Arabic. A lingua franca in this sense of the term is limited, shrunken, incomplete language. It is comparable to pidgin languages used for commercial transactions in other regions of the world. There is therefore a logical inconsistency in applying it to a rich national language that also has international functions.

Among the many orchestrating a rhetoric that uncritically promotes global English, Churchill's descendants, are uninformed and uncritical native speakers. Advocacy of global English is at its most aggressive when the Director of the British Council in Germany claims that "English should be the sole official language of the European Union." Glyn Morgan, a Welshman now in the USA, in *The Idea of a European Super-state: Public Justification and European Integration*, (2005) writes that

> *The spread of English as the European lingua franca, the emergence of a common transnational youth culture, the convergence of business practices, and — most important of all — widespread adoption of European constitutional practices (and perhaps even a Constitution) can be seen as steps along the road to a European nation-state.*

He may be right about such steps, but he seems unaware that his possible scenario builds on biased presuppositions:

- it assumes that English is a neutral lingua franca, serving all equally well, whereas high-level proficiency in English is rare in much of Europe, and in any case, many languages serve lingua franca purposes in Europe,
- it fails to reveal that "a common transnational youth culture" is essentially American, promoting a Hollywood consumerist ideology,
- it ignores the fact that "business practices" derive from the US corporate world, and the conceptual universe it embodies, and that is taught at business schools, in asymmetrical symbiosis with national traditions,
- EU constitutional practices and legislation have hybrid origins, and equal force in 24 languages, so that a possible European nation-state could never be monolingual.

Morgan exemplifies the tendency of many native speakers of English to consider Anglo-American linguistic norms and practices as universally valid and archetypically human. I would add that he also takes Americanization as a universal norm.

The Belgian political scientist Philippe van Parijs states in an EU publication: "English will gradually replace multilingualism not only in the huge posters that hang from the Berlaymont building, but also in highly sensitive contexts such as directly-applicable legislation or plenary session interventions by members of the European Parliament." This was in a study of lingua francas, written by staff of the European Commission, and published by it anonymously, which gives it a semblance of representing the institution's position on the role of English. On fallacies in a book by van Parijs that argues for English becoming universal, scholars who focus exclusively on the instrumental use of a language ignore its connection to power, class, and the interests behind use of the language. By advocating English for everyone, their work unintentionally "becomes a crucial element of an international business class structure. It facilitates the growth and spread of multinational corporations and trade." This of course is a primary goal of the EU. This strengthens the global 1%, the transnational capitalist class.

 The EU lingua franca study fits squarely into the mold of biased special pleading for English. It covers some historical and contemporary ground, but selectively, and without ever clarifying in what way the term lingua franca is understood or used in EU contexts. The study fails to address the issue of the actual use made of English in the EU system, which was a prime goal of the study. It assumes English functions in a neutral egalitarian way, and while noting that there can be an element of hierarchy involved, it ignores the political and economic factors that account for the way English has expanded worldwide and in continental Europe. The study includes transcripts of interviews with three individuals, without their status or role being described. Two of those interviewed are passionately committed to promoting a greater use of English. It is disturbing that an institution that works to maintain multilingualism can publish such an unscholarly text, one that simply equates lingua franca with English.

 Labelling English as a lingua franca, if this is understood as a culturally neutral medium that puts everyone on an equal footing, is simply incorrect. It is a pernicious term if the communicative interaction in question relates to what is a first language for some, but for others a foreign language. It is a false term for a language that is taught as a subject in general education, which presupposes study of the cultural contexts in which the language has evolved and is used.

Questions for Discussion

1. What does Jawaharlal Nehru think of English to be a lingua franca in India?
2. What is lingua franca? List major historical lingua francas.
3. What is implied by lingua franca English?
4. Which biased presuppositions does Glyn Morgan's comment on English as a European lingua franca build on?
5. What is the author's attitude towards English as a lingua franca in Europe?

Unit 12   Language in an Online Global World

> Several technological and political forces have converged, and that has produced a global, Web-enabled playing field that allows for multiple forms of collaboration without regard to geography or distance — or soon, even language.
>
> — Thomas Fredman

Unit Goals

- To describe the issues concerning language changes in a digital world
- To discuss how current digital communication and language affect each other
- To examine the cultural and sociological factors behind language changes in the global world
- To identify problems with regard to the language issues in the online global world and offer possible solutions

Before You Read

Emojis and Human Communication

Is chatting on the mobile phone boring without colorful emojis? Those happy, sad and laughing faces help us talk. Emojis, invented by the Japanese originally, have become an indispensable part of human communication today.

1) Look at the following emojis. What is the meaning of each? In what situations will you use such emojis?

2) Do a research in the class about "My Favorite Emoji." Which emoji do you use most often? When and how will you use it? Do boys and girls report differently in this research? Compare your findings with your classmates.

Start to Read

Text A Always on: New Literacy and Language in an Online Global World

It is likely that if you are a typical student reading this book, you will probably have some other task going on at the moment. Maybe you are watching television or checking your Facebook page. Maybe you are also instant messaging. Maybe you are checking some fact you have just read on your iPad. Perhaps you are listening to music. Undoubtedly your smart phone is charged, sitting on your desk. And when you use that cell phone, it is just as likely that you will send a text message as press the dial button. An obvious question is, "What are we, as speakers and writers, doing to our language by virtue of our new communication technologies, and how, in turn, do our linguistic practices impact the way we think and the way we relate to other people?" (Baron 2008:x). In other words, what is our linguistic life like now that we are "always on"?

Sociolinguistic Changes from *Being Always On*

As we have already said, the use of language is perhaps the most important reflection of one's personal and social identity. Simply put, language is who you are. Some fifty years ago, the well-known sociologist Erving Goffman (1959) introduced the theoretical construct of the "presentation of self in everyday life": although anticipated by Shakespeare four centuries earlier (all the world is a stage, after all), Goffman argued that much of social life—our face time—is spent managing how we want others to see us. And because we are in many

ways what we pretend to be, as novelist Kurt Vonnegut said, this has important psychological implications as well.

In non-digital environments, our speech and dress are the most conspicuous presentations of ourselves. However, in day-to-day, face-to-face real life we are constrained in many ways. No matter how cool he talks and how baggy his pants are, a fifty-year-old male college professor still remains *that*, even if his ball cap is on backward. But on the Internet, these restrictions are diluted or nonexistent. On the Web, not only can we be anonymous, we can be anybody. All bets are off. Where previously the implicit rules of social politeness may have kept my language judicious, in a comment to a blog or an online news story, I can literally say whatever I please without fear of social consequences.

Likewise, in face-to-face communication, I am compelled to interact with people and conversations as they come up. You have to deal with meeting that old boyfriend on the quad; I have to deal with that problem student who comes to the office for hand-holding every day. We cannot avoid these encounters. But in the world of digital communications, we are all "language Czars," as Naomi Baron argues (2008). That is, we control whom we want to talk to and when, and on what terms. Although in the past, letters and telephones allowed some degree of management of whom we would communicate with, this complete control of accessibility we now have in the twenty-first century is unprecedented.

The types of communications have also radically changed. To take just one example, the anthropologist Bronislaw Malinowski (1923) proposed that some speech is phatic communication, small talk for its own sake rather than for conveying information. All people do it, everywhere, because it is both a bonding ritual and a way of regulating discourse. For instance, two negotiators may "get down to business" after they exchange pleasantries for a while, even though each may care little about the other's family or last night's ball game. But how these pleasantries are exchanged may set the stage for how the rest of the meeting will go. Digital communication offers both faster and more distant phatic communication. As any professor can tell you, the moment class ends, out come the cell phones. If it is a spoken conversation, invariably, it is brief and very phatic: "It's me. How you doing? I'm fine. Just got out of class. Yeah. Catch you later. Bye." Texting does the equivalent thing, with probably a similar message. Although these alternatives, such as Twitter and texting, offer another way of sending phatic signals, these are "away-messages" (Baron 2008:73) waiting to be read at the receiver's convenience. The 140-character limit makes Twitter almost intentionally designed for phatic communication.

Combined with social network sites, we are never at a loss to know what our friends had for lunch or the latest cute thing Grandma's cat did.

Changes in Orthography

Converting spoken language into writing has never been easy, even though the school system tries to give us prescriptive rules and teach that they are absolute and unalterable. But even today there is not complete agreement about "correct" spelling and punctuation. Writing changes over time as fashions and opinions change. For example, what do you call that small permeable container that holds tea leaves (Baron 2008:177)? The *Oxford English Dictionary* cites *tea bag* in 1898, *tea-bag* in 1936, and *teabag* in 1977. And Shakespeare, the icon of all English courses, spelled his name a half-dozen different ways. That orthographic conventions are flexible is particularly true regarding digital communication. Is it *on-line* or *online*, or *e-mail* or *email*? Is the *Internet* supposed to be capitalized? What do we do about all those -s's that are now -z's, as in *Dawgz*, pirated soft *warez*, and shared *filez*? Is it *OK* or *okay*? Is it acceptable to use *btw* for "by the way" in an e-mail message—to anyone (even a professor)?

And does *lol* really even mean "laugh out loud" anymore? The *Atlantic's* Megan Garber (2016) examined what several linguists had to say about this after seeing a picture of a disrobed Kim Kardashian that she posted on Instagram with the caption, "When you're like I have nothing to wear LOL." Garber says that Kim is doing many things in this picture, but laughing is not one of them. Indeed. Linguist Gretchen McCulloch argues "that LOL (commonly without caps) barely indicates an internal chuckle, never mind an uproarious audible guffaw." John McWhorter simply says, "LOL isn't funny anymore... LOL no longer 'means' anything. Rather, it 'does something'—conveying an attitude—just as the 'ed' doesn't 'mean' anything but conveys past tense. LOL is, of all things, grammar." So Kim's LOL—as are many of the LOL's of the rest of us mere mortals—is acting as a punctuation mark. As Garber says, "It is expressing the kind of meta-emotion that is very easy to make clear in in-person conversations and very difficult to make clear in other kinds." We will return to this shortly when we meet the next step on this linguistic evolutionary chain, the emoji.

Another question is, should we encourage or stifle creativity in digital communication orthography and style? Constance Hale and Jesse Scanlon in *Wired Style* (1999) argue that "no one reads email with red pen in hand" so we should "celebrate subjectivity" and "write the way people talk" (Baron 2008:172). Others feel that allowing such digital anarchy is a recipe for social and linguistic disaster. As Baron (2008:171) says, "Modern linguistic theory eschews passing judgment on any linguistic variant, and I am not about to do so now. Rather, I'm suggesting that should linguistic entropy snowball, we may discover that personally expressive, culturally accommodating, and clock-driven language users will find it increasingly difficult to understand one another's nuances." Crystal argues that so far, at least, the pedagogical and "moral panic" surrounding e-mail and texting is overblown. The belief that the "highly deviant character" of digital communication is fostering poor literacy results has been shown by psychologists and educators to be largely an "urban myth" (2010:417).

The Language of the Internet

If you ask most people what the language of the Internet is, they would probably say it is English. Even in places where English is not natively spoken, tweets and twitters are often sent out in English. English appears to be the default language of almost any site you hit. Even though operating systems now come in different language interfaces, many people still use an English version of Windows or a Mac operating system to more easily interact with the English-using computer sites.

The Dominance of English?

In his book *Language and the Internet* (2001), the noted linguist David Crystal wondered whether the English-dominated Internet would contribute to the demise of other languages, at least on the Web. Perhaps he was being pessimistic. It appears that the use of English has gone down significantly, from 82 percent in 1997 to less than 57 percent in 2002 (Stanlaw 2005). German, French, and Japanese each now make up between 5 and 8 percent of all Web pages. If we look at PDF (portable document format) pages, these differences are even more pronounced. Chinese, Korean, Russian, and Dutch all went from almost nothing in 1997 to a noticeable presence ten years later. A similar trend appears if we look at the languages used to access the Google search engine. English went down 10 percent from June 2001 to May 2004.

However, we should not predict the waning of English as the dominant language on the Web yet because statistical data suggest that the drop in English is leveling off. For example, language access on Google since September 2003 has remained essentially the same for all languages. Also, if we look at the "penetration" levels—the percentage of the speakers of a given language that have access to the Web—we see that a great majority of speakers of many European languages (such as German, French, and Dutch) already use the Internet, so the number of these speakers going online might not be expected to grow very much. In contrast, only 59 percent of English speakers use the Web, so these numbers could increase (Stanlaw 2005).

But there is another, perhaps more significant, reason that English will still be a dominant presence in the digital world for some time to come. Political unrest and international and economic affairs will likely continue to be highly contentious in the near future, and digital communications will no doubt play an important role. For example, few could forget the vivid pictures and messages being sent out of Iran during the "Green Revolution" election protests in the summer of 2009. Because the Iranian government strictly monitors and censors such conventional media as radio, television, and newspapers, social networking sites, blogs, Twitter, and YouTube became the primary source of information for the outside world (which even news organizations such as CNN, the BBC, and the major print news agencies used when their personnel on the ground were quarantined). Not only were Western governments getting word of unrest taking place that they were not getting by the usual diplomatic means; the whole world's attention was drawn to these dramatic events. Reuters reported that these channels were so important that the Obama administration asked Twitter to postpone a scheduled network upgrade because it would have taken the service offline temporarily. According to Twitter's own blog, the company agreed to the State Department's request "because events in Iran were tied directly to the growing significance of Twitter as an important communication and information network."

The Hegemony of English?

At first glance, it may appear a good thing that one language, English, is the world's de facto lingua franca, not only online but also in spoken and written communication. Everything from international air traffic control to publishing scholarly academic journals now becomes easier, using only one language. But we have to ask, is having English as the international language a good thing or not? Is there such a thing as *the* hegemony of English? The nature of hegemony implies an asymmetric relationship between two individuals, groups, or classes, with one being more powerful or in control, the other being more subordinate. This seems to be a shoe that fits the English foot.

Linguist Yukio Tsuda (2013: 453) concurs, believing that both native-English speakers and non-native speakers suffer:

> One of the most influential factors that justify the use of English in international communication is the taken-for-granted assumption that English should be used. The English speaking people unconsciously believe English to be used by all people; namely, they unconsciously hold linguistic imperialist consciousness, while the non-English-speaking people assume the use of English as the inevitable, indicating the colonization of the mind on their part.

Phillipson (1992:47) says that a "working definition of English linguistic imperialism is that the dominance of English is asserted and maintained by the establishment and continuous reconstruction of structural and cultural inequalities between English and other languages." By the very nature of Western/English-speaking countries' economic clout, English will be privileged. And in the  United States, each political season finds new calls and attempts to eliminate bilingual education or to make English the only official language in some state or county. And having not all languages being created equal has important social and cultural consequences. For example, if an American — especially a "white" American — can speak more than one language, it is usually considered a good — though rather unusual — thing. This would be advantageous unless the person speaking the languages is a subordinate speaker (like an immigrant), in which case this would often be considered an impairment or handicap to learning English (Macedo et al., 2003:9). These issues are extremely divisive and political, and they cannot be solved here. But anyone with even a passing interest in linguistic anthropology needs to at least be aware of them.

(Excerpted from J. Stanlaw, N. Adachi, & Z. Salzmann , *Language, Culture and Society: An Introduction to Linguistic Anthropology*, 2018: 255—259)

After You Read

Knowledge Focus

1. Pair Work: Discuss the following questions with your partner.

1) How do you understand the authors' claim that "language is who you are"? Do you agree with their?
2) How does digital environment affect the way we communicate with each other?
3) How do you interpret Naomi Baron (2008)'s saying that we are all "language Czars" in the age of digital communication?
4) How do you understand the term "phatic communication"? Can you give some examples?
5) What did *lol* mean in a picture that Kim Kardashian posted in her Instagram? Was she laughing when she used this word?
6) What is the question debated with regard to the orthography and style of email-writing? What do you think about it?
7) Do the authors believe that English will still be a dominant presence in the digital world for some time to come? What are their reasons?
8) Is having English as the international language a good thing or not? Please give your reasons.

2. Solo Work: Decide whether the following statements are true or false.

1) Fifty years ago, the well-known sociologist Erving Goffman argued that human life is about what we pretend to be and how we want others to see.
2) On the Internet, there is no restriction on how we want to present ourselves.
3) According to Malinowski, phatic communication is everywhere because it is a bonding ritual and it regulates discourse.
4) The written language is absolute and unalterable.
5) Many psychologists and educators are worried about emails and texting, believing that digital communication is fostering poor literacy results.
6) David Crystal argued in his book that the English-dominated Internet would contribute to the demise of other languages.
7) From the statistics given by some scholars, the warning of English language as the

dominant language on the Web would be predicted.

8) Social networking sites are now playing an increasing role in the report of political unrest and international and economic affairs.

9) If an American can speak more than one language, it is usually considered a good thing.

10) English today is still a privileged language, and the hegemony of English truly exists.

Language Focus

1. Fill in the blanks with the words or expressions you have learned in the texts.

| dilute | pleasantry | uproarious | level off |
| eschew | hegemony | contentious | anticipate |

1) After an exchange of _____, I proceeded to outline a plan.
2) Although he appeared to enjoy a jet-setting life, he _____ publicity and avoided nightclubs.
3) A good speaker is able to _____ an audience's needs and concerns.
4) When I suggested that free trade might _____ Canadian culture, he raised strong objections.
5) The ancient Saxons celebrated the return of spring with an _____ festival commemorating their goddess of offspring and of springtime, Eastre.
6) The question of divorce and remarriage in church remains highly _____.
7) Britain, France, the United States and Japan all aspired to _____ after the end of World War I.
8) After the government had taken some effective measures, prices began to _____.

2. Fill in the blanks with the proper form of the words you have learned in the text.

1) Security is so poor as to be almost _____ (existent).
2) Seminar topics are chosen for their _____ (accessible) to a general audience.
3) The team was penalized for intentionally _____ (intention) wasting time.
4) The general trend of history is _____ (alter).
5) This study focuses on the role of the phonological code and _____ (orthography) code in reading Chinese character by foreign learners.
6) In some countries and regions, _____ (equality) worsened, as poor people did not reap the fruits of economic expansion, because of a lack of job opportunities, limited education or bad health.
7) Animals are able to hear high-pitched sounds that are _____ (audible) to humans.

8) The _____ (advantage) vast but closed geographic environments of China nurtured the then advanced farming culture.

3. Proofreading

The following passage contains TEN errors. Each line contains a maximum of ONE error. In each case, only ONE word is involved. You should proofread the passage and correct the errors in the following way:

For a wrong word, underline the wrong word and write the correct one in the blank provided at the end of the line.

For a missing word, mark the position of the missing word with a "∧" sign and write the word you believe to be missing in the blank provided at the end of the line.

For an unnecessary word, cross out the unnecessary word with a slash "/" and put the word in the blank provided at the end of the line.

There are more than 7,100 languages in use around the world, with Chinese, Spanish and English being the most widely spoken. Despite the highly placing of English, around 75% of the world's population doesn't speak a word of the language, so it might seem surprised that, like illustrated in this infographic (and based on this data), more than half of all content on the internet are in English. One reason for English being so dominate online is that it is considered a "universal language," often chosen by people of different nationalities with a common way to communicate. Unlike Chinese, which until relative recently was little spoken in its homeland, English has long been a common international language in areas such as business and science research. This gives it a natural advantage online and helps accounting for its widespread use.	1. _____ 2. _____ 3. _____ 4. _____ 5. _____ 6. _____ 7. _____ 8. _____ 9. _____ 10. _____

Comprehensive Work

1. Pair Work: A Discussion

Consider the following exchange of e-mail between two college instructors, Dr. Jane Doe and Dr. Ann Throwpologist at X University.

What do you notice about style, tone, and orthography in these messages? What kind of conversation was taking place? Who wanted to do, or not do, what? How could you tell? Was a successful exchange taking place? What cues are missing? What cues are here? How might the conversation have been different had it taken place in person?

(First e-mail message) Quoting jdoe@x.edu:

dear dr. throwpologist,

    i am jane doe and i teach commercial art at the school of business. i am teaching a special topics course on cultural identity in advertising this semester where students learn new research methodologies in advertising so they can create designs that are more meaningful for a multicultural audience.

    i am inviting guest speakers to talk about culture and identity. i would appreciate if you would be interested to be a guest speaker in my class. the class is held at Smith Hall 14 on M. and W. from 8 to 10. please let me know if this is possible. thanks for your time.

    sincerely, jane doe

(Second e-mail message) Quoting annthrowpologist@x.edu:

Dear Dr. Doe,

    Thank you very much for your invitation. I am very interested in culture and identity, as that is one of my linguistic specialties. However, I am also teaching on Mondays and Wednesdays this semester all day, so I am afraid I will not be able to be a guest speaker this Spring. Sorry. But again, thank you for your invitation.

    Ann

(Third e-mail message) Quoting jdoe@x.edu:

dear dr. throwpologist,

    thank you for responding. i do teach on fridays as well. please let me know if feb. 10th or 17th or 24th will work for you.

    thank you, jane

(Fourth e-mail message) annthrowpoogist@x.edu:

Dear Dr. Doe,

    Thank you for your offer again, but I am very sorry. This semester I need to finish a project so I will not be able to come to campus on Fridays. Perhaps I might be able to visit your class some other time. But thank you again.

    Best,

    Ann

(Fifth e-mail message) Quoting jdoe@x.edu:

dear dr. throwpologist,

    i am teaching this class again in fall please let know when you can come then. thank you

    jane

2. Writing Practice

Almost daily, some commentators or media critics decry the corruption of English and predict the collapse of the world due to the widespread use of social media, digital communication, video games, and the like. What do you think? Have these things caused a breakdown in human communication? Has English become degraded? Has literacy declined, and if so, is it because of new means of electronic communication? Have, indeed, critical thinking skills waned?

Write a composition of about 400 words on the above topic.

3. Translation: Translate the following passage into Chinese.

Some researchers also wonder how new digital communication literacy is changing human cognition and patterns of thought — and not just in ways of learning or how people relate socially to one another.

The rise of book culture, of course, inexorably altered the way people conceived of the world and their place in it. The collective pool of human knowledge exponentially multiplied, and people could travel vicariously to the far ends of the earth and time in travelogues or history books. However, as with anything, there were costs. Scholars at the start of the Renaissance lamented, for example, the decline of the power of human memory, and the reluctance of younger people to engage in daunting tasks of memorization. They were probably right, just as the spread of the hand calculator has impacted our ability to do even simple arithmetic in our heads. Already, for example, we see university libraries becoming places to network or centers for collaborative learning. Few go there to consult a journal article because often these are available in students' dorm rooms on computers.

What kind of world will it be in the (very near) future when all the world's knowledge, music, and art are instantly accessible to everyone? With remarkable improvements in Web translations taking place daily, even problems in cross-cultural communication that result from people speaking different languages might gradually become less important.

Read More

Text B Emojis, a New Writing System, a New Language, or Nothing New under the Sun?

Chances are, if you are reading this and you are under thirty, you use some kind of emoji to add visual spice to your written text, like the "grinning face" emoji here: 😀. Emojis have become so ubiquitous now that they appear across platforms, from cell phones to tablets and even to desktop computers (for those who still use them). They cover a wide range of — well! — emotions, and allow great digital orthographic creativity. We often spend a lot of time and energy thinking about them. What is the exact emoji I should use to ask a favor, but not appear I am begging? Does the 😊 emoji come off as too forward romantically? I want to appear interested but not desperate. Does the 😠 emoji show just the right amount of anger I am feeling now?

The Arrival of the Emoji

Emojis were invented by Shigetaka Kurita in 1999 while working as an engineer for NTT DoCoMo, Japan's largest mobile telephone network. He was said to be inspired by the kanji characters of the Japanese writing system and the stylized symbolic representations of emotions found in Japanese manga comic books. For example, Thomas Wallestad (2013:5) argues that "Japanese manga have a large diversity of metaphorical figure symbols called keiyu that are not considered as words or representational pictures, but act as symbolic adjectives or adverbs to events depicted. *Keiyu* consist of manga symbols (*manpu*)" — for instance, like the stylized drawing of a person — "and effect symbols (kōka)" — for example, some stylized detail being drawn on that person. "*Manpu* tend to retain their meaning independent of a subject, whereas *kōka* need to be applied to a subject to be understood. In Japan's manga these symbols are applied to characters or subjects as representational indicators denoting their 'physical' states and/or as metaphorical indicators connoting their 'psychological' states."

Emojis often act as punctuation or sentence-final particles attached to word-based sentences. For example, one can add emotional flavor after making a verbal statement. "Taking the GRE's tomorrow 😖," indicating the tremendous pressure the writer is feeling. After finishing the tests and getting the results back, she might write, "Got the scores back 😊," indicating not only the joy of having finished the process, but perhaps also feeling relief from the pressure and maybe satisfaction with the scores. Or all these feelings.

Just What Are Emojis? Their Linguistic Features

Corpus linguistics (Dimson 2015:4–5) show that the top three universal emojis — and their names, and some of their meanings — are

😂 (tears of joy): laughing out loud, too funny, hahaha, …
😍 (heart-shaped eyes): beautiful, gorgeous, hot, …
♡ (heart): love, xoxo, love you, …

It is clear that these symbols, then, are not really words in the sense that Sino-Japanese *kanji* characters are words — logograms — which stand exactly for one lexeme in a language. Nor are *kanji* polysemous in the way emojis are, standing for so many ideas. Likewise, they are not really pictograms, either (for example, ♡stands for the metaphor "broken heart," not an actual physiological condition). It seems that emojis are something we might call "semantigrams," symbols that carry meanings, probably multiple meanings, but cannot convey these meanings by themselves. The emoji's meaning only exists in connection to, or with, a lexical item or another emoji. And sometimes they have no real meaning at all, functioning only to provide phatic communication—as we saw, Malinowski's term for language that establishes and maintains social connections rather than exchanging actual information — as in "Sunny skies yesterday☺" or "Lunch was good☺".

But there is another interesting trend that is fascinating to linguists. Although expanding by the day, the number of emojis is finite, limiting the things that can be expressed with them. But users are expressing new thoughts by putting emojis together into sentence-like phrases. And the way this is done is remarkably similar, even though no one is taught the "correct" usage of emoji "grammar." For example, probably even the least facile emoji newbie can "interpret" this "sentence," which has appeared on the Internet in many places: 😊👦👧♡💔😞🍺 It is the same old love story: boy meets girl, falls head-over-heels in love, gets rejected, is sad, becomes depressed, and turns to drink. The order of these emojis is not random. For example, these same emojis might tell a different story if presented differently: 😞🍺👦♡💔👧😊😊. Here a guy is depressed, drinks too much and hits rock bottom, meets a girl who falls in love with him in spite of his drinking, gets him to stop, so he recovers and becomes normal again, and gratefully falls in love, too.

One reason for this consistency of word order is because emoji-use tends to respect linear time and action. For example, if you want to point a gun at a something, that something has to go to the left of the barrel (Steinmetz 2014:2): that is, 😊🔫 and not 🔫😊. Another rule is that the "agent" (the doer of the action) has to precede the action, and go to its left (Cohn 2015:6), hence

the sad guy drinking in 😞🍺. Another convention might be the "stance first" rule (i.e., stance or attitude emojis come before actions or signals). For example, people weep and then — afterward — have a broken heart: 😢😭♡ and not the other way around: ♡😢😭 The stance-first rule may come from the more potent power of emojis to convey emotions that are easily expressed in spoken language — through such things as tone of voice, body language, gestures, or inflection — that are largely silent in text (Steinmetz 2014:2).

Another interesting linguistic feature of emojis is the tremendous creativity and productivity by their users. Our contributor Su Yin Khor claims her favorite emoji collocation is putting the "pizza" slice emoji together with the "turd" emoji, as in 🍕💩. To interpret the — spoken vernacular! — intention of this pair, remember the first symbol is used for its phonetic value "pizza" and the second for its semantic value, feces.

These properties we have just mentioned — productivity, rules, grammaticality, and the ability to make an infinite number of messages with a limited number of units — all bring to mind the design features that were discussed in Chapter 6. So, should we consider this new use of emojis as a new kind of language, as several observers have suggested (Dimson 2015; Stockton 2015; Cohn 2015)? A first reaction says no. No less an authority than Leonard Bloomfield, one of the founders of American structuralist linguistics, still speaks for many in the discipline when he unequivocally says that "[w]riting is not language, but merely a way of recording language by means of visible marks" (1933:21). Thus, for many linguists, any writing system, with emojis or not, simply does not qualify as language.

But does this privilege the spoken word too much? Perhaps. Emojis and their users can be quite resourceful. For example, Matt Haughey (2015), a self-described "internet nerd writing about internet nerdery, mostly," posted a summary of the cult film *The Big Lebowski*, named fittingly enough "The Big Lebowskemoji." In conversation with blogger Samantha Lee (2016:1, 3–4, 8), Indiana University linguist Susan Herring claimed emojis have brought us into a "new phase of language development. More and more graphical representations, such as emojis, gifs, stickers, and memes are being incorporated into language use online." In many ways these act as incipient pidgins. "Pidgin basically comprises nouns and verbs strung together. That's what happens when you use emoji." But that said, "Text is never going away." Even "The Big Lebowskemoji" needed annotations as not every emoji sequence was transparent to the uninitiated. And retrieving the right emoji from the hundreds that are available on a device is still a problem. However, technology has solved so many other technical problems in the digital age, it is likely this will be solved as well.

(Excerpted from J. Stanlaw, N. Adachi, & Z. Salzmann, *Language, Culture and Society: An Introduction to Linguistic Anthropology*, 2018: 259—262)

Questions for Discussion

1. What are emojis? How was it invented?
2. What linguistic features do emojis have? Can you offer more examples to illustrate these features?
3. Can we consider the use of emojis as a new language? What are your reasons?

Text C The Age of Twitter

There is no doubt that Twitter has changed the way human beings communicate, at least for the immediate future. In spite of messages having a 140-character limit, taken in aggregate they add up to something with a significant communicative impact. For example, several political commentators have said that one reason for Donald Trump's victory in the 2016 presidential election was because he won the Twitter wars — not just against Hillary Clinton, but against anyone who would engage him. Besides allowing friends to easily stay in contact with each other, teachers now use Twitter to communicate with students, and celebrities and the common folk get to talk and mingle with an intensity and immediacy never possible before in everyday face face-to-face speech.

Hashtags

The development of the hashtag label — that is, placing a "pound" (#) sign before a particular word or phrase — was also a game-changer, making it easier for users to now find messages with a specific theme or with a specific subject, or allowing them to follow others with similar interests. The hashtag label also "intensifies a call to affiliate with the values expressed in the tweet by making it more searchable" (Dickinson 2013:11) for others with similar political or religious beliefs, or even prejudices.

But besides tagging messages, hashtags now can also be used to simply act as a contextualizing mechanism or self-reflexive meta-commentary on what is being written. In that sense hashtags can act much like paralanguage in spoken language, that is, written versions of facial expressions, gestures, or body language that accompany speech. And as everyone knows, in spoken language, the paralanguage and the speech do not always agree, allowing for mixed or self-contradictory messages to be sent simultaneously. These hashtag expressions, often self-mocking or satirical, have spread from Twitter to Facebook to spoken language (where ironically now, saying the word "hashtag" allows the speaker to slip in some kind of aside remark or comment to what he or she has just said).

Regardless, the use of the hashtag is "indicative of a shift in computer-mediated discourse from online conversation to 'searchable talk'" (Dickinson 2013:11). This, combined with re-tweeting posts (and additional subsequent re-re-tweetings) make for a different kind of communication. Before, digitally, we may have

been "always on", waiting for contact from some outside source. When that happened, we were free to either respond immediately or put that person or message on hold to be answered at our convenience. With Twitter, we no longer have to — only — wait. We can initiate communication about subjects on our own terms at a time of our own choosing.

Have Twitter and Social Media Improved Human Communication or Hindered It?

The world's most famous linguist, Noam Chomsky, comes down on the latter position. When asked about his feelings concerning digital communication in an interview, he said, "Text messaging, Twitter, that sort of thing ... I think it erodes normal human relations. It makes them more superficial, shallow, evanescent. One other effect is there's much less reading" (Jetton 2011:18). In an earlier interview (Ralon and Eljatib 2010) he was even more adamant: "Well, let's take, say, Twitter. It requires a very brief, concise form of thought and so on that tends toward superficiality and draws people away from real serious communication." These comments are typical of much of the criticism that has been leveled against Twitter.

However, many disagree, including Salon's Nathan Jurgenson (2011), who posted a provocative piece, "Why Chomsky Is Wrong About Twitter." He argues that Chomsky doesn't realize that texting and tweeting is not just done by "wealthy kids and knowledge workers." Instead, he cites evidence (p. 4) that "nonwhites are much more likely to connect to the Web, communicate and create content on mobile phones than whites ... [and] these so-called shallow ways of communicating are precisely the ways those in the Third World are connecting to and interacting" with the global world. And Chomsky shouldn't be submissive about the role social media plays in many current progressive social movements, from Arab Spring to Occupy Wall Street to Black Lives Matter. "When he defends his form of communicating (printed books and periodical essays) with claims that tweeting/texting lacks depth, he is implicitly suggesting that nonwhites and those in the Third World are inherently communicating less deeply." And even if we grant that social media is less deep and more instantaneous, "the important questions then become: is instant, digital communication less true? Less worthy? Less valuable? Less linguistically creative? Less politically efficacious? Chomsky, a political progressive linguist, should know better" (Jurgenson 2011:5).

The Language on Twitter

The language used on Twitter is in many ways similar to spoken language but in many ways is also quite different. For example, Dickinson (2013) argues that much of Twitter language is "formulaic." By this he means there are an extraordinarily high number of pat phrases or "morpheme equivalent units" (MEUs) found in most tweets. An MEU is a term used in psycholinguistics to describe lexical items — that is, a word or a string of words — that are processed together singly. Most idioms, for example, are MEUs. For instance, the meaning of *kick the bucket* makes no sense if one just looks at the meaning of the individual items; the meaning only makes sense when seen together as a whole morpheme-like indivisible unit.

In a concordance analysis of random Twitter posts, Dickinson found four main functions of these kinds of formulaic language: to manipulate the situation to the user's benefit, to convey individual identity, to convey group identity, and to connect meaning and structure the discourse. Each of these functions can be broken down into several types.

When messages are limited to 140 typed characters, acronyms save both space and time, so it is no surprise that they abound in tweets. Dickinson (2013:25), following others, suggests that at least two acronyms — *lol* and *btw* — have identity-marking function and have become "conventionalized to serve as group membership markers among internet users." In fact, as we saw earlier in the chapter, *lol* has become lexicalized as something different from its "laugh out loud" origin and acts as a kind of uninflected discourse marker, appearing before or after clauses. If used at the beginning of a response, *lol* appears to indicate affiliation with the tweet being responded to. After a sentence or clause, *lol* is often used as a hedge, where writers indicate that their preceding statement should not be taken too seriously.

Internet-specific abbreviations also have a group-identifying — as well as space-saving — function: separating those in-the-know from those who are not in-the-know, and thus, don't belong. Such general abbreviations include *u* or *ur* or *yr* ("you"), 4 ("for"), 2 ("to" or "too"), *tho* ("though"), and *pls* ("please"). However, surprisingly, in all cases, the abbreviations were actually used much less frequently than their equivalent full forms (Dickinson 2013:27). However, if you think about it, this is not necessarily that unintuitive. A text with unusual abbreviations, too many abbreviations in total, would be hard to decipher, and thus take longer to read as well as write in the first place.

(Excerpted from J. Stanlaw, N. Adachi, & Z. Salzmann , *Language, Culture and Society: An Introduction to Linguistic Anthropology*, 2018)

Questions for Discussion

1. What is Twitter? How has it changed the way human beings communicate?
2. What role do you think Twitter and other social media have played in human communication today? Has it improved human communication or hindered it?
3. What linguistic features does Twitter language have?
4. Compare the Twitter language with Weibo language in China. Do you find any similarities between the two?